The twenty-first century will be spiritual, Malraux said, or it will not be at all. *Spirit Matters* is a blueprint for the return of spiritual meaning to contemporary life, which may well save us. That is why the importance this book's message cannot be overestimated. In a sweeping and compelling vision, Michael Lerner shows how spirituality can be not only felt but lived, transforming us and our world in the process. In areas such as healing, law, and education, Lerner takes us step by step to show how spiritual meaning can actually be woven into the fabric of our society.

This book is a cure for the curse of our age—the tendency to fragment our lives by divorcing intellect and spirit, reason and intuition. We cannot long survive the destructive force of this split, and *Spirit Matters* shows a way out.

—Larry Dossey, M.D., author of *Reinventing Medicine* and
editor of *Alternative Therapies in Health and Medicine*

I believe that successful political action to end corporate rule and achieve a human balance with the planet must be built on the kind of profound and widely shared spiritual awakening that Michael Lerner describes in *Spirit Matters*. When our political actions flow from a sense of spiritual connection to the whole of life we become relatively immune to the self-defeating frustration, disillusionment, and power struggles that otherwise undermine our commitment and blind us to opportunity. Lerner shows us how by living fully in the spirit we can achieve both personal fulfillment and political effectiveness. *Spirit Matters* is an essential spiritual guide for the mindful progressive activist.

—David C. Korten, author of *When Corporations Rule the World* and
The Post-Corporate World, and board chair of The Positive Futures Network,
publishers of *YES! A Journal of Positive Futures*

Michael Lerner challenges us to let down our cynical guard and contemplate radical new ways of educating our children, providing health care for all, reorienting our legal system and promoting corporate responsibility. But Lerner breaks out of the narrow economic vision, insisting that a commitment to social justice be grounded in spiritual consciousness. *Spirit Matters* is certainly a provocative and visionary call to replace corporate globalization with globalization of the spirit.

—Medea Benjamin, founding director, Global Exchange

This book is a rare synthesis of contemplative practices and social activism, a compassionate yet provocative vision of how we can work both on the inner and the outer, uniting personal transformation and societal healing.

—Sharon Salzberg, author of *Lovingkindness* and *A Heart As Wide As the World*; a founder of the Insight Meditation Center at Barre, MA

In a time when spirituality is all too often no more than an empty slogan or even an incitement to hate and violence, *Spirit Matters* offers a solid alternative informed by a keen sense of justice and a call to put spirit into action. The visionary mind that provided an inspiring new perspective on politics is again at work doing the same for spirituality, and it works!"

—Riane Eisler, author of *The Chalice and the Blade, Sacred Pleasure,*
and *Tomorrow's Children*

Spirit Matters offers the clearest, most helpful, and most passionate statement on the new spirituality that I know. Michael Lerner's genuine compassion and his active engagement in our communal life shine through and give this important book its power. There are hundreds of books on spirituality you can safely avoid. Don't overlook this one.

—Thomas Moore, author of *Care of the Soul and Original Self*

Michael Lerner's newest book is an exuberant and revolutionary examination of the uprising of spirit in our culture today. Introducing his idea of an "Emancipatory Spirituality," one that unites all aspects of the self, society, and world, as opposed to a "reactionary spirituality" that excludes, denies, and dominates, Lerner is at once a probing historical thinker, a hard-hitting critic of corporate culture, and a hopeful, wise, and delightful spiritual teacher. There's a sense of joy pervading a book that dares to dig into some of the darker aspects of life in the modern world. It's this balance between a tough assessment of life in the real world and a liberating cosmic worldview that makes *Spirit Matters* a breath of fresh air in spiritual literature.

—Elizabeth Lesser, co-founder, Omega Institute
and author of *The New American Spirituality*

Many of us know Michael Lerner for his passionate and honest political commitments, but what makes him a unique figure in contemporary life is his insistence that the political and the spiritual are deeply married, are deeply one. His insight grows out of Jewish theology but has implications for us all. I recommend this book to anyone who wants to reconnect with spirit and how spirit matters in how we live, how we work and how we love.

—Rodger Kamenetz, author of *Stalking Elijah* and *The Jew in the Lotus*

Spirit Matters transcends the old left-right distinctions and takes us to a different plane where the quest for social justice converges with a biblical admonition that we shall be judged by what we do for the least among us. Michael Lerner is particularly compelling when he challenges the narcissism of spiritual searching that begins and ends with one's self. *Spirit Matters* calls on us to transform ourselves and at the same time become engaged in the painstaking work of social transformation.

—Arianna Huffington, syndicated columnist
and author of *How to Overthrow the Government*

Michael Lerner brilliantly and beautifully defines how spirituality can infuse our efforts to create a world marked by social justice and personal ecstasy. For those of us who have experienced "burnout" in our striving for social change, this book is great medicine.

—Tony Campolo, Eastern College, St. Davids, PA

This book is a miracle and a treasure. Please read it! It's a miracle because it can open the heart of the most cynical person who denies spirit and thinks it's all new-agey flakiness. And at the same time it deepens the understanding and spiritual depth of those of us who have thought we already read all the books on spirituality we need and have already been involved in our own spiritual practice.

It's a treasure because you will not only grow personally by reading this book, you will also be given a unique gift: a detailed vision of the world that we can create together as we deepen our trust, our joy and our hope. Powerfully unveiling how the deprivation of Spirit is the root of our deepest personal, societal and ecological problems, Lerner points the way for an Emancipatory Spirituality capable of making real our highest ideas. He provides powerful descriptions of what a spiritually-oriented school system, medical system, and legal system could be like, and a path for how we could change our work world and our personal relationships. Lerner gives us the nits-and-grits of a world based on love and caring, awe and wonder.

—Marianne Williamson, author of *The Healing of America*

SPIRIT MATTERS

BOOKS BY MICHAEL LERNER

Surplus Powerlessness:
The Psychodynamics of Everyday Life and
The Psychology of Individual and Social Transformation

Jewish Renewal:
A Path to Healing and Transformation

The Politics of Meaning:
Restoring Hope and Possibility in an Age of Cynicism

The Socialism of Fools:
Anti-Semitism on the Left.

Tikkun: To Heal, Repair, and Transform the World:
An Anthology.

With Cornel West:
Jews and Blacks:
A Dialogue on Race, Religion and Culture in America

SPIRIT
MATTERS

MICHAEL
LERNER

WALSCH
W
BOOKS

an imprint of
HAMPTON ROADS
PUBLISHING COMPANY, INC.
www.hrpub.com

Cover design by Marjoram Productions
Cover art
Once In A Blue Moon, 1998
An oil painting by Samuel Bak
Courtesy of Pucker Gallery, Boston, MA
Copyright © 2000

For information write:

Hampton Roads Publishing Company, Inc.
1125 Stoney Ridge Road
Charlottesville, VA 22902

Or call: 434-296-2772
FAX:434-296-5096
e-mail: hrpc@hrpub.com
Web site:www.hrpub.com

If you are unable to order this book from your local
bookseller, you may order directly from the publisher.
Quantity discounts for organizations are available.
Call 1-800-766-8009, toll-free.

Library of Congress Catalog Card Number: 00-100176
ISBN 1-57174-360-X
10 9 8 7 6 5 4 3 2 1

Printed on acid-free paper in Canada

TO DEBORA KOHN

You nurtured me back from a moment near death, and your love and your wisdom, your playfulness and joy have sustained me and brought me the love I always sought. Together, we are building a beautiful life based on our connection to God. You continually give me the opportunity to experience Spirit manifesting through you in my life. I love you.

TABLE OF CONTENTS

preface

Thank you so much for opening this book!

This book has arrived in your life at exactly the right moment. By the time you finish reading it, you'll see why. The fact that you opened it at all is an indication that some part of you wants to connect to Spirit in a deeper way, wants to understand why others are doing so, wants to get beyond all the cynicism and discounting of Spirit that surrounds us and is the common sense of daily life.

Perhaps you have a sense that the growing interest in spirituality is a major reality of the new millennium. Even if you are not personally interested in getting involved, you'd like to know what it is all about and where all this spiritual stuff might lead. You might even be thinking that it's all very dangerous and potentially destructive, but a part of you wants to check it out rather than just ignore or dismiss it.

You'll find that there is more to Spirit than you might have thought. Sure, some flaky ideas, and some dangerously reactionary ideas get justified under the name of Spirit. But there's also a lot of very serious thinking, extraordinary experience, and liberating possibilities in the world of Spirit.

Spirit Matters. It is going to be the most important reality of the next period in human history. So, it's wonderful that you have chosen this moment to learn more about it.

I have been blessed with a series of teachers who made it possible for me to listen to the voice of Spirit. At age twelve I encountered a spiritual master named Abraham Joshua Heschel, whose extraordinary book *God in Search of Man*, opened me to the mystical path within Judaism. After years of learning from him at the Jewish Theological Seminary, I became involved in the social change movements of the 1960s and had the honor to work with Dr. Martin Luther King Jr., Daniel Berrigan, and many other inspiring spiritual leaders. I was particularly inspired by the teachings and spiritual direction of Zalman Schachter-Shalomi, a great seer and visionary, whose roots as a Hasidic rebbe gave him a deep understanding of Kabbalah, the book of Jewish mysticism. It was under his tutelage that I completed my rabbinical training.

In the past years, I've been inspired by the works of two very different spiritual teachers. Ken Wilber is one of the most creative intellectual synthesizers of our time. His integration of spiritual wisdom with the most significant work in science, psychology, social theory, and social science is a masterpiece of creativity and insight. I have been blessed to know him personally as well as to learn from his work.

Neale Donald Walsch's *Conversations with God* is an act of remarkable spiritual courage. God speaks to all of us all the time, but Walsch allowed himself to listen and to record what he heard. Every time I open the pages of these three extraordinary volumes, I get excited by the insights and the prophetic energy that pour through its pages. Walsch understands that each of us will hear God's voice differently.

There are points in his trilogy (as there are moments in the works of Wilber, Heschel, and all my other teachers) where I want to say: "This is not how *I* hear God's voice." But there are so many places where Walsch seems to hear God's voice more clearly than most, and dares to report it, even when it will predictably turn off or anger some sector of the populace that might otherwise go along with a blander vision of God. For example, Walsch hears God telling him, "I have placed more than sufficient resources on your planet to ensure adequate supplies for all. If your well-off say they do not want to help the starving and the homeless because they do not want to disempower them, then your well-off are hypocrites. For no one is truly 'well-off' if they are well-off while others are dying. The evolution of a society is measured by how well it treats the least among its members." Or God tells Walsch: "You have barely evolved at all. You still operate in a primitive 'every man for himself' mentality. You plunder the Earth, rape her of her resources, exploit her people, and systematically disenfranchise those who disagree with you for doing all of this, calling them the 'radicals.' You do this for your own selfish purpose, because you've developed a lifestyle that you cannot maintain any other way."

In short, Walsch is a courageous spiritual voice.

How exciting for me, then, to have the opportunity to publish this book as part of a new imprint of books that Neale Donald Walsch has started within Hampton Roads Publishing. I am grateful for this opportunity.

I also want to acknowledge the helpful suggestions and insights I received from Michael Bader and Rebecca Adams. I am very grateful for the editing and advice I received from David Kolodney, who has been a friend and ally since our days studying philosophy together in graduate school at the University of California. At the last moment, Miranda Outman made significant contributions to reshaping and carefully editing the manuscript, and I am greatly in debt to her. Finally, none of this would have been possible without the assistance of Jo Ellen Green Kaiser, managing editor of TIKKUN magazine, who kept the TIKKUN operation running smoothly at moments when I was absorbed in writing this book, and the loving and supportive energies and insightful suggestions of my wife, Debora Kohn Lerner.

I'm very aware that most of the ideas in this book have come to me from God as revealed through hundreds of generations of spiritual seekers, writers, teachers, and practitioners. I feel humbled by the opportunity I have to stand on their shoulders and tell you a little bit of what I'm able to see from there. I accept this gift from the universe as one manifestation of the outpouring of God's love to us, and it is only with that awareness that I have overcome my fear that talking about matters of Spirit would be an act of chutzpah and spiritual arrogance coming from someone like me who knows himself to be flawed and limited.

Many of the ideas in this book were developed jointly with Peter Gabel. So close has been our collaboration over the course of the past twenty-five years that it's often hard to say whether a particular insight or formulation came from him or from me. Our connection is so deep that he speaks through me and I speak through him. My thoughts should be read in conjunction with his important thinking, particularly in his book, *The Bank Teller*.

My "take" on Spirit necessarily reflects my own personal limitations—like you, I'm just one person with a particular set of experiences and understandings. I know that my perspective isn't "the truth" but "a truth." It is just one way of seeing the world. I believe that there are many correct paths, and though at times in this book I argue strongly for mine, I am also aware that I could be mistaken in ways that others will be able to see. I approach this with the humility appropriate to someone attempting to discuss something that surpasses the capacity of our minds. So don't be surprised if I make mistakes or don't say things in ways that fully capture what you know.

I am grateful to have this opportunity to share what I've learned from many fabulous teachers and students. I'm also grateful to be alive at this incredible moment in human history. What a joy to be able to look out at the world and to see the return and renewal of spiritual consciousness and to recognize the incredibly wonderful possibilities that lie ahead. My family was decimated in the Holocaust, and I know the pain and cruelty that are possible in human life. My sense of what is possible does not come from a naive faith that everything always turns out okay, nor from a rosy-colored perspective on what human history has been. I know about cruelty and I know about the unnecessary infliction of suffering that continues to be a central fact of the world in which we live. But I also know that this is not all that is. I know that the world can be healed and transformed. That process has already begun. I want to tell you how it is happening and what role you and I can play. It is through that discussion that we can get a deeper sense of how very much Spirit Matters.

SPIRIT MATTERS

introduction

Spirit Matters.

Not just to people who call themselves spiritual.

Even the most cynical people you know—the ones who claim not to understand what the hunger for meaning and higher purpose is all about, the ones who claim not to know what the word Spirit is all about—will have their lives shaped by the growing spiritual transformation of the world that has already begun.

Understanding the spiritual reality of human needs, and how the world gets distorted when our spiritual needs are thwarted, can provide us with a much deeper understanding of what's going on in this world and in our personal lives as well.

In fact, we are in the midst of a dramatic upsurge of interest in spiritual issues, which, as I will argue in this book, will reshape the entire globe, providing a powerful and liberating alternative to the globalization of capital, and will ultimately remake every aspect of our lives.

Tens of millions of people are already involved in some form of spiritual practice. Many of these people welcome the spiritual transformation of the world, seeing in it the vindication of their private efforts and energies. Others know of their own small spiritual communities but cannot imagine that they are part of a much larger spiritual movement that will decisively shape our world. The whole notion of changing the big picture seems too overwhelming, too big—and what they get out of spiritual life is something very personal, something they don't want to see ruined by getting involved in large groups and social transformations.

And there are still others who feel scared by the spiritual movements they see around them or hear about. The media presents us with images of the most distorted elements in the spiritual world, almost always identifying it with some form of repression. Who can blame people for being fearful if they've been taught to identify spirituality with religious extremism, even violence?

Many of us have had very negative experiences with intolerant, rigid, or hyperjudgmental people who claimed to be representing some spiritual truth or other. If you grew up in such a religious community, or know others who have, you may be thinking something like, "I personally know how intolerant, self-righteous, or unpleasant people can get when they are part of a religious or spiritual community." No wonder the word "spirit" has negative connotations for many people.

But even those of us who have not had that personal negative experience have grown up in a world that demeans or marginalizes spiritual consciousness and represents the advance of rationality and science as the moment in history when spiritual forces from the Dark Ages were finally replaced by the "Enlightenment." The same story has been taught in Western societies and in Communist societies: spirituality represents the forces of the past. If it has a momentary revival, it is only because people are too scared to face the challenges of the contemporary world and seek to escape from it in various forms of mystical folly.

Capitalist and Communist ideologies share the notion that the highest good is to produce as many goods as possible and to allow technologies to develop at the fastest possible rate. They both see the world as a "resource" that can be endlessly exploited to satisfy our needs. To be "progressive," we were taught, was to make sure that as we did so, we included the greatest possible number of people in the benefits of material consumption.

The spiritual people, we were told, came from an older and more primitive period when people didn't understand how important these goals were. In those old days, before the Enlightenment, people were scared of all that they didn't understand, so they sought protection in a big father figure who would make everything okay—some god or set of gods.

Today, this story goes, those who remain involved in the world of Spirit are those who never grew up, never really faced the modern world, and hence are necessarily "reactionary" because they seem not to "get" how wonderful the advance of modernity really is and how far we've progressed from those old and outmoded ways of looking at the world. Now, with the Internet and new technologies linking us all in an ever-progressing march toward new heights of material well-being and scientific sophistication, these old religious and spiritual forms can only constrain the possibilities for future growth.

Most of us learned some variant of this story when we were growing up. So it's no wonder that many people feel scared or cynical when they hear about growing interest in spiritual concerns.

I've written this book to speak to both—those who look on spiritual transformation as a threat to rationality and humanism, and those who see it as a hopeful development for the human family.

And I also want to speak to all the rest of us who don't quite fit in either camp.

What I've discovered is that most of us have both of these voices within ourselves—we have moments in which we are spiritually attuned, and other moments in which we are deeply skeptical and doubt our spiritual insights. So, this book isn't just for the spiritual people and the cynics, but also for all the rest of us who are somewhere in between.

It's true, there really are some flaky and reactionary people who use the language of spirituality. But what the skeptics do not notice is that there are many very smart, sophisticated, and psychologically mature people who find that the realm of Spirit has led them to profound and transformative truths, to a beautiful way of understanding and living.

Many people have turned to the realm of Spirit to try to make sense of the pain and suffering they've experienced. Others have sensed that there is something deeply missing in their lives and have found that the rewards of the marketplace don't satisfy their hunger for some framework of meaning and purpose to their lives. Still others turn to Spirit because they are overwhelmed by a sense of awe and wonder at the glory of the universe.

My guess is that if you are reading this book, you already know that something very important is missing from the world we live in, and that it's something deeper than just social justice (though we need that too). You've had some experience that somehow doesn't fit the categories or value structure of the society in which you've been living.

What you may *not* know is that the suspicion that there is a deeper reality to things is shared by most people on the planet.

Most people have spiritual needs that have too long been denied or repressed in our society. The wonderful news is that more and more of us are gaining the courage to take this need seriously. Instead of hiding who we are, we are coming out of the closet as spiritual people whose deepest needs are not being adequately met. I hope this book will help you take one very important step: to listen to the voice of your own heart, a voice that is often drowned out by our own fears.

I want to show you what the world could look like through the lens of an Emancipatory Spirituality, a spirituality that could actually heal our planet and bring us to the kind of trusting, sharing world that so many want but don't believe is possible. I'll do that if you join me on this adventure.

It may seem difficult to talk about growing spirituality at a moment when television is once again filled with popular game shows in which people compete to become millionaires. The depth of the mainstream culture's spiritual depravity was revealed in the television spectacle "Who Wants to Marry a Multimillionaire," in which fifty women competed to marry a man about whom they knew nothing more than that he was rich. As tens of millions of Americans watched, the millionaire emerged from the shadows, picked one of the women, and they were immediately married before the television audience. Here was a striking example of the ethos of selfishness and materialism that have become the "bottom line" in American society. And yet, as the marriage began to unravel immediately, widespread disgust at the way love had been reduced to money pointed to another reality: most Americans may be fascinated at the level of depravity surrounding them, but simultaneously feel outraged or even sickened by it, and know that they would prefer to live in a very different kind of world were that possible.

And the message of *Spirit Matters* is that it is possible.

Spirituality and Religion Are Not the Same

Spirituality is a lived experience, a set of practices and a consciousness that aligns us with a sense of the sanctity of All Being. It usually involves:

a. an experience of love and connection to the world and to others

b. a recognition of the ultimate Unity of All Being, and through that, of the preciousness of the Earth and the sanctity of every human being on the planet

c. a conviction that the universe is not negative or neutral but tilts toward goodness and love

d. awe, wonder, and radical amazement in response to the universe and a consequent unwillingness to view the world merely in instrumental terms

e. a joyous and compassionate attitude toward oneself and others

f. a deep trust that there is enough for all and that every human being deserves to share equally in the planet's abundance and is equally responsible for shaping our future

g. a sense that the world is filled with a conscious spiritual energy that transcends the categories and concepts that govern material reality and inclines the world toward freedom, creativity, goodness, connectedness, love, and generosity

h. a deep inner knowing that our lives have meaning through our innermost being as manifestations of the ultimate goodness of the universe (or, in theistic terms, through our connection to, and service of God)

This is what spirituality is about.
Religions, on the other hand, are the various historical attempts

to organize a set of doctrines, rituals, and specific behaviors that are supposed to be "the right way to live."

Some religions may embody spirituality. Many have encompassed spiritual moments or spiritual practices at one time or another. But many religions have little to offer today in the way of spirituality, except in isolated corners of their traditions. As a rabbi, I'm part of a Jewish renewal movement to reclaim some of the spiritual practices and insights of my religion. In TIKKUN magazine I am doing my best to give space to people from Christianity, Islam, Buddhism, Hinduism, and other religious traditions who are trying to renew their own spiritual roots. But many practitioners of Western religions have only occasional encounters with spirituality in their religious communities.

Religion may exist without spirituality. Spirituality may emerge without or divorced from religious communities. Many people who have been persecuted by religious institutions have been those who embodied a spiritual worldview. Many religious leaders speak the language of spirituality but feel threatened by those who have a genuinely spiritual outlook. Embedded in systems of power and control, they have no use for those who talk about sharing and who embody generosity toward all other human beings, not just those who are part of "our" group.

Some people reject religion entirely because of this hypocrisy. But another option is to think of spirituality as a higher developmental stage—a stage in which the fears and hurts of the past are overcome and we can open ourselves up to the goodness of the universe and respond to it with awe and wonder and love.

Those who are not able to reach this level of consciousness are not "evil" or voluntarily choosing to be stuck. True, the official doctrines of their religion call for loving behavior. But all too often they've lived in a world in which the political and religious institutions of the society ridiculed, suppressed, and punished those who let love and awe shape their public actions. Though religions have often been part of the problem, they are not its only source.

The spirituality that many people are rediscovering today sometimes takes the form of a renewal of existing religious communities—seeking to bring spirituality back into religions that have lost their original compass. Even religions with very compromised pasts can have a more liberating and spiritually wholesome future.

Others are discovering spirituality in ways that are totally independent of any religious community.

What Is Spirit?

Spirit is the aspect of reality that cannot be quantified or subjected to repeated observations. It is, rather, the realm of ultimate freedom.

To speak in the language of scientists, we can say the following: if you knew all the laws of science that could ever be discovered, plus all of the initial conditions that needed to be factored into the relevant scientific formulas, you would still never be able to determine what any living creature will do in the next moment. The reason for this is not some quantum indeterminacy or randomness, but the fact that there is an aspect of the universe that is fundamentally free and self-determining. In its widest form, we call that reality God. In its narrowest form, we call that reality the essence of being human (or, in religious language, this is what we mean by saying that humans are "created in the image of God").

To take this a step further, as I've done in my book, *Jewish Renewal: A Path to Healing and Transformation*, God is the Force of healing and transformation. God is the Force that is the ultimate freedom of the universe, that which constantly allows us to transcend all that is and move toward that which can and should be. God or Spirit or Highest Reality is the Force in the universe that makes it possible for us to break the cycle of necessity, to act in ways that are not governed by scientific law. Spirit or God or Highest Reality is the phenomenon that allows us to transcend the human tendency to act out on others the pain that has been acted upon us and thus to break the "repetition compulsion." To speak of that capacity to transcend and break the repetition compulsion and become embodiments of generosity and love and goodness is to talk about Spirit. Our meaning in life comes from being embodiments of that Spirit, elements of the transcendent consciousness of the universe as it moves to actualize goodness and beauty.

Though many spiritual people (myself included) believe in God, and though I sometimes talk of "Spirit or God," there are many spiritual people who do not believe in God in the sense of some Being responsible for Creation, with a set of intentions for the universe and a capacity to reward and punish. If you've thought you are not interested in understanding Spirit because you can't accept the existence of such a God, then please note that there are many other people on the spiritual path who do not believe in God understood in that way either.

For many, the very word God is so tinged with imagery of a patriarchal authority they feel uncomfortable using it. They have been taught about some mean or judgmental big man in heaven who sits above them and judges their actions, someone who needs to be placated with prayers and rituals, someone who is demanding and scary, but occasionally, if you play your cards right, friendly and supportive. Well, lots of people have trouble believing in that image of God, and they imagine that Spirit is just a tricky way to get you back into the belief that offends them.

As a rabbi, I often tell people who come to my synagogue: If the word "God" is the problem, if it automatically brings you into an inner conflict in which you find yourself arguing against the god you were taught about when you were a child, a god you couldn't believe in, then forget the word "God" and leave that behind.

Allow yourself, as you are reading this book, to leave behind all the visions of God or Spirit as patriarchal, authoritarian, judgmental, coercive, angry, spiteful, or anything of the sort.

Why waste your time trying to argue against a "god" that doesn't exist? Let's stipulate from the start that the God you don't believe in doesn't exist and isn't worth any more attention.

Similarly, all the mushy and silly things you've heard said in the name of Spirit—forget all that too. Let's stipulate that it was all silliness, so why bother with that foolishness? Don't waste your time with all the versions of Spirit that you know to be empty, one-dimensional, hurtful, or misleading.

Instead, as you read this book, please take the time to connect to whatever spiritual reality *does* seem real to you. Use this book as a spur to that kind of spiritual/intellectual/emotional encounter. Use the word Spirit to refer to this aspect of your experience, and think about "having a soul" as meaning that you have this capacity to be in touch with the spiritual as you experience it.

In the addendum to this introduction, I go into a further discussion of ways to understand Spirit—and the reasons why it's not easy to come up with a simple definition. Feel free to skip that if you are comfortable with the concept of Spirit, but delve in if you want a fuller picture of some of the ways people have come to think about Spirit.

What Is Soul?

Most of us know that we are not simply the sum of our accomplishments. We can look at anything we've done and say, "I see that I am partly the sum of my choices, but I am also more than all those choices, I am the person who can make other choices." We can tell ourselves, "I know that I tend to act in a particular way under certain circumstances, but I am not just those particular traits and dispositions. I am more than that."

In fact, this is often what people mean when they say they have a soul: they mean that they cannot be reduced to all that they've been and done, that there is something more, a capacity for freedom and transcendence, something that goes beyond the agenda set by parents, teachers, and economic and social pressures.

However you describe yourself, whatever terminology you use, there will always be *something more* that cannot be put into words. And that something more enables us to transcend all that we've been encouraged to do and be—and become higher embodiments of our deepest values and beliefs. This transcendence has a particular trajectory: it pulls us toward love and a sense of Unity with All Being, toward goodness and a desire to make things right as best we can understand, and toward purpose and a sense that our lives can have some meaning deeper than the accumulation of power and wealth. To have this capacity is to have a soul. Soul is the personal manifestation of Spirit in our own being.

Like Spirit, soul is one of those words that people never seem to want to define. And for good reason: soul is not a thing, not even an especially ghostly thing inside of you. Rather, it's a capacity—but a capacity that cannot be explained in scientific terms. In religious terms, the soul is what makes repentance and atonement possible. No past mistake will ever be bad enough to keep us from starting over and fundamentally transforming ourselves. The capacity for self-transformation and inner healing is part of what we mean by having a soul—the soul is the part of us that energizes us to go for our highest ethical and spiritual vision of who we can be.

The Realm of Spirit Is Not Flaky New Age Mush

The hunger for meaning and purpose is as strong and central to human life as the hunger for food or for sex.

Just as some social and religious orders demean or repress our desires for sex, so today we live in a world whose institutions and social practices implicitly demean or repress our hunger for meaning. This repression has led to a wide range of pathologies in daily life, and to an attitude toward nature that has brought us to the brink of ecological disaster.

And yet, though the dominant culture of our society celebrates itself because of its material success, though it imagines that anyone who has "made it" in the competitive marketplace must be a fount of wisdom and encourages people to "look out for number one," though it does its best to ridicule or expose as self-interested anyone who claims to be motivated by some higher purpose, people are increasingly insisting on some form of spiritual nourishment and grabbing on to whatever form of spirituality they can find that provides an alternative to the dominant culture.

Hungry for some community in which their need for meaning can be explored, some are attracted to a reactionary spirituality that is used to justify right-wing political agendas. It is frequently not the right-wing politics, but rather the safety to explore spiritual issues, that attracts them to these communities—which, for many people, are the only places they've ever encountered a community of people that cares about others and doesn't evaluate others by how wealthy, physically attractive, smart-talking, or powerful they are. Later in this book, I'll explain how the reactionary spirituality in these communities differs from the Emancipatory Spirituality I advocate. But for the moment, what I want to emphasize is that people who choose a reactionary spirituality sometimes make this choice for a good reason: because they are fed up with the one-dimensional and technocratic realities of daily life. Most of the people in these right-wing religious communities are not stupid or evil—in spite of the ways they are caricatured in the media. On the contrary, they have made a choice, that, in their context, was the most noble and principled commitment available.

On the other end of the spectrum we get another distortion. Sometimes the hunger for meaning leads people to glom on to flaky and narcissistic forms of spirituality.

I've sometimes lost patience with spiritual talk I hear emanating from "New Agey" sources, because it seems as if "spiritual" is being used as permission to abandon serious thinking and open the door to every imaginable spiritual commodity. Writers in *New Age* magazine, *Utne Reader*, and other serious spiritual journals sometimes bemoan this appropriation of the term "New Age" by charlatans, opportunists, and flakes.

I have witnessed the sloppiest and silliest thinking justified under the banner of "spirit"—but so what? In my years in prestigious universities obtaining two PhDs and in my subsequent years as a university professor, I've also witnessed incredible silliness and stupidity parading as academic philosophy or empirical psychology. In fact, I've seen academics use science to justify arguments that black people are less intelligent than whites, that students who have trouble "succeeding" in schools must have some kind of genetic or physiological dysfunction (because everyone knows our schools are perfect), and that people who rebel against our current social system suffer from various forms of psychological or physiological defects (because everyone knows our current social system is perfect). It's pure hypocrisy to focus on distortions justified in the name of spirituality without recognizing the same tendency within the supposedly more respectable intellectual arenas. The fact that the academy claims to uphold rigorous criteria of verification does not necessarily produce better thinking than the verification in personal experience that is often used in spiritual circles.

I've also watched some very important spiritual ideas get presented in ways that made me feel embarrassed to be associated with them. The media is able to reduce everything to the same cheap level. Advertisers and commercial marketeers see a growing "market" in our search for spiritual meaning. Look at the ads for a nail polish called "Spiritual," that claims to "aid in the connection to the higher self." Or witness the Hollywoodization of Kabbalah (a profound and deeply mystical medieval Jewish text, which is being marketed to spiritual seekers in distorted forms). Or watch how the media manages to create various spiritual gurus who compete with movie stars and politicians for our attention. But, duh! That's what the market does . . . to everything! Don't blame Spirit for capitalism.

In fact, on several occasions I've been interviewed for television, only to see my ideas edited in ways that made them seem stupid and empty to me. Who can blame viewers for thinking that spirituality is a set of vacuous clichés and fuzzy ideas, when that's how it's presented in much of the mass media?

People who embrace dumbed-down versions of spirituality are often embracing the only spirituality they have ever encountered. At some level, these people get the idea that there is something inherently unsatisfying about the mainstream materialism and selfishness of the dominant culture. So I want to honor the part of them that wants to take Spirit seriously, even if I find some of the ways they do so unappealing to me. Rather than thinking that there is a slippery slope from an openness to Spirit to spiritual silliness or a politics that demeans others, I believe that the slope can slip the other way toward greater complexity and deeper spiritual insights.

But to take the steps toward deepening spiritual sophistication, we have to ensure that opening to Spirit is not confused with an empty cheeriness and a refusal to see the painful problems facing our world. I've seen versions of spirituality that seemed to me to be thin veneers on top of a mountain of narcissism and self-indulgence. Even very valuable spiritual practices like meditation have sometimes functioned as a way for people to move inward without ever going outward. Yet I also know many others whose spiritual and meditative practices form the foundation for a strong involvement in healing and social transformation. Having been involved in social change movements over the past thirty-five years, I personally witnessed that a far higher percentage of those who remain committed when social change was no longer socially sanctioned as "cool" were people who had a strong spiritual base. As you'll see in this book, a spiritual understanding can bring you both a deeper fulfillment in your life and, at the same time, a deeper connection to the central challenges facing our planet.

The Plan of the Book

I want to show you that an Emancipatory Spirituality is emerging, a spirituality that can bring tremendous healing to our planet.

So, here's what I'm going to do: I'm going to try to demonstrate how deeply spirituality matters in our daily lives—and how deeply we suffer because our spiritual needs are constantly denied. To do that, I'm going to tell you about some of the people I've gotten to know from a wide variety of different circumstances, so you can see how the frustration of meaning shapes our lives.

After that, I'm going to turn to the ways spiritual distortion leads us to treat the planet with ecological callousness. In particular, I'm going to show you why the only serious alternative to the globalization of selfishness (which leads us to our ecological crisis) is the globalization of Spirit.

Next, I'm going to describe the difference between a reactionary and an Emancipatory Spirituality and show how, as Emancipatory Spirituality begins to reshape our planet, every aspect of our lives will change.

I've chosen medicine, law, and education as arenas in which to explore what the world might look like were we to fully embody an Emancipatory Spirituality.

I'm hoping that you'll continue this project by taking the method I use in chapters seven, eight and nine and applying it to your own field of work so that you can help us imagine more fully what a spiritually oriented world could be. I invite you to continue the process of visioning that I begin in these pages.

Finally, I'm going to discuss a few of the things that we can do in our personal lives, and in political action to help facilitate and perhaps even accelerate the evolution of consciousness that will make the triumph of Emancipatory Spirituality possible. In chapter ten, I present an amendment to the U.S. Constitution that could counter the most destructive aspects of the globalization of capital. I offer a vision of a society that stops production every seventh year and devotes its energies to slowing down and reflecting on where it wants to go in the next seven years. But I try to be clear that these specific policy suggestions would be counterproductive unless they were part of a much larger spiritual transformation on the internal level, not just transformations in external economic and social structures.

I don't blame you if you are a bit skeptical at this point. In fact, throughout the book I want to honor the part of us that reacts skeptically, because that is also part of us, and we need to acknowledge and honor the strength of our own doubts.

I promise that, if you read through this book, you will never think of spirituality as merely a bunch of nonsense again. You'll see how it is possible for people who are deeply committed to healing and transforming this world, liberating it from all forms of oppression, and creating a world of peace, justice, and love to find the key to getting there in the realm of Spirit. And I hope you'll see that we could have much more fulfilling lives if we lived in a world where Spirit held its rightful place.

Of course, in some ways you already know that Spirit Matters.

You know that there's some indefinable something that makes us recognize someone's inner beauty and say that her "spirit is shining through." When a group of people accomplish something that seemed impossible, you say those people "have spirit." You may speak of the "good spirit" that flows between people at certain moments. And you probably already know that if you were to define all that and try to tie it down in a scientific way, you would not succeed. You probably know that much of what happens between human beings can't fully be described in material terms. You may have been tempted to call that Spirit too.

In fact, there are countless moments in our lives that we can only describe in the language of Spirit because we already know that Spirit Matters.

In this book, I invite you to take the next step: imagine a world that fully reflected our shared intuitive knowledge that Spirit Matters. I hope to show you a picture of the incredible transformation that can happen as more and more people allow themselves to take their spiritual yearnings seriously and seek a world that is more consistent with their deepest spiritual truths.

Spirit can matter in the sense that it can become the central force shaping our lives. And to do this, Spirit will no longer be seen as something split off from the "real world" of daily life and "material reality," but will be understood as the ultimate shaping force of matter (yet another meaning of Spirit Matters).

For this book to work, I invite you to suspend the part of you that has been taught to respond to every new idea with the attitude of: "Let's see what's wrong with this." Instead, allow yourself to try the framework of thinking I describe below as "Emancipatory Spirituality." Try thinking about ecology, social movements, law, medicine, and education from within the framework I present. You may even want to try out some of the spiritual practices outlined in my final chapter. Allow yourself to experience this perspective as fully as you can. Particularly if you are a person who is very skeptical about spiritual paths, see if you can allow yourself to actually experience the world from within this perspective before you make a judgment against it.

If you agree to open yourself to experiencing the world from the perspective articulated below, you will not lose your capacity for autonomous judgment. Don't worry. Once you've read this, there will be no one imprisoning you, locking you in, restricting your freedom to reject the whole thing, or in any other way limiting your ability to choose for yourself what parts of this might fit your life and what parts not.

If you want to reach a point where you can make a real choice about spirituality, allow yourself to overcome the tendency we all have to look for the weak spots (I'm sure there are plenty) and instead find what *does* speak to you, what seems to make sense, and apply it to your life in ways that provide illumination. Take what rings true for you and leave the rest. If you allow that, you'll find that reading this book can be useful whether or not you end up wanting to continue on a spiritual path.

I suspect that if you've gotten this far in your reading, some part of you recognizes that there is something not quite right in your life and in the life of our society, and that it's not likely to be fixed by the outcome of the next presidential election, the next fluctuation in the stock market, the next great television miniseries, the next great pop musician or even by seeing your home team win a Super Bowl or World Series.

You still may be wondering if there are any answers in the world of Spirit—and feel a bit skeptical.

So I invite you to explore the ideas in this book while keeping your doubts intact. The great spiritual thinkers have often been those who honored their doubts and felt no need to smash them out of existence. The great mystics have insisted that having spiritual experiences and having doubts about their meaning are hallmarks of spiritual seriousness. Human beings are multilayered, and we are able to hold different perspectives on the same reality at the same time. So, if you allow yourself to look at the world through the lens of Spirit, you need not lose your critical perspective or suspend your intellect.

In the second half of this book I describe a view of how an Emancipatory Spirituality might transform the actual way we organize our daily lives. This is another meaning of Spirit Matters—spirituality isn't just about an inner experience, but also can be embodied in material reality. To communicate how that reality might take shape, I take the risk of giving my own particular vision of what a society based on the principles of Emancipatory Spirituality might be like.

Though I argue for a particular vision, I want to remind you that each individual experiences spirituality in a unique way. The language I use may not be the best approximation to capture your spirituality. There are many approaches, and I offer mine not because I want you to think of it as the only right way, but because I hope it will stimulate you to seek your own spiritual experience. Though I vigorously present my own take, I am the first to acknowledge my own limitations and to rejoice in the fact that spiritual experience differs from person to person and hence that each attempt to put it into words is likely to miss some important aspects of your own spiritual world. Please do not let my formulations be used as a basis to discount yours or others' experience!

The Divided Self

Many people I know are caught in a special kind of split personality. In their private lives, they put lots of energy into finding some kind of meaning. They go to church, synagogue, mosque, or ashram. They put the search for love at the top of their private agendas. They try to impart spiritual values to their children. They do their best to be giving and sharing to others.

And yet, when it comes to their public lives, these same people are deeply cynical about the possibility of building a world of love and caring. They doubt that spiritual issues connect with "the real world." So, when they talk about the larger world outside of their own personal lives, they don't believe that Spirit matters in the slightest. "It's a purely personal, individual thing," they tell themselves, "and it's best dealt with on a private basis."

The result is that many people are deeply skeptical about the society, economy, and social world in which we live. They will tell you that nothing much can be different. More than that, they will tell you that you are being foolish and naive to think that anyone "out there" really cares about anyone else or that a world could be constructed on the assumption that we could take care of each other in a deep and real way.

I call these *pathogenic beliefs* (adopting a usage from psychologists Hal Sampson and Joseph Weiss), because when we hold these ideas, we tend to create a world that has the very pathologies or self-defeating ways of thinking and feeling we feared.

Pathogenic beliefs encourage us to act on the premise that we can't count on others, that we are stuck in a society that cannot be changed. These beliefs become increasingly accurate descriptions of our lives the longer we cling to them.

It would be comforting to believe that the cynics are other people, that you and I are free from these beliefs.

Yet, what I've discovered in my years as a psychotherapist and then as a rabbi is that most of us have inner voices that are cynical in exactly the same way.

In fact, most of us are continually engaged in an ongoing internal dialogue on just this point. There is a part of each of us that wants to live in a world based on love, caring, ethical sensitivity, and spiritual connection to the universe. But there's another voice, for many a much louder voice, that tells us that is really not possible.

Many of the people you know who are the most cynical about the realm of Spirit have felt this split inside themselves. At some point, they decided they didn't want to suffer with that tension anymore. So they became loud champions of the view that there is no room for spirituality in public discourse. But before criticizing the cynics, we need to acknowledge that they are only a more extreme and more wounded example of the split we face within ourselves.

That split is rooted in the way most of us were brought up and educated. Most children see the world through a much richer spiritual frame than that of adults. A lot of what our society considers "growing up" is actually "coming down" from that higher level of awareness. Children do not have the language or conceptual tools to clearly articulate their spiritual perceptions. So they have no way of validating to themselves or to the outside world the radiant spiritual reality they see. We are taught not to pay attention to the aspects of our experience that cannot be captured and validated through language or "proven" by demonstrating its existence to others.

Children soon find that the parts of their experience that do not fit into what the adults around them want to hear are dismissed as "fantasy" or as "private experience" that they should know better than to discuss in the public arena.

Teachers, under increasing pressure to produce students who will do well on "objective tests," have learned to redirect children's attention away from "fantasies" and toward "reality," namely those skills and qualities that are likely to make them "successful" in a competitive marketplace.

Children quickly learn that they can't expect others to see them as being fundamentally worthwhile. They learn that they will be given recognition and love only as long as they fill someone else's needs and expectations (starting, all too often, with parents' expectations, and followed all too soon with the expectations of teachers and friends).

The natural and almost automatic instinct to see the world in a spiritually rich and nuanced way—to experience reality as bathed in love and filled with joy, and to respond to that with wonder, amazement, and spontaneous love and caring for others—is quickly shattered on the rocks of "reality," as others respond to us according to their own agendas and their conviction that the world depends on everyone being "pragmatic"—that is, looking at everything from the standpoint of how it can be "of use."

Our "real" needs, we are taught, are those that can be measured and observed by others. So the needs for food, clothing, and shelter are "real," because we can measure changes in the body that occur when they are not met. Material needs seem to be shared by everyone and in roughly the same way, so they can be seen by everyone and validated as legitimate. The more this dominant pragmatic religion is drummed into our heads, the more our inner spiritual and emotional lives begin to wither.

Of course, this doesn't happen to everyone in exactly the same way, at the same time, or with the same intensity. But most of us, by the time we enter junior high school, have had massive lessons in "adjusting to reality." We've learned that "to be mature" we must give up our hopes of being truly recognized and loved by others.

Most of us have come to accept the central pathogenic (crazy-making) belief of the contemporary period: that if we continue to see the world in the fullness of its spiritual depth and intensity, its aliveness and beauty, its pulsating love and warmth, we will be judged crazy or otherwise marginalized and ridiculed by everyone around us.

We've learned to hide, from others and from ourselves, the spiritual knowledge and experience we had as children. But hiding this spiritual understanding ends up hurting us. A lot. We lose an important part of our selves.

Almost everyone on the planet has experienced this loss. Almost everyone recognizes the senses of emptiness, hollowness, sadness, or depression that are reflected in literature and philosophy from the earliest recorded epics to the novels of the present day.

For some, these experiences were so powerful in infancy and early childhood that the memories or language needed to express this absence were repressed. For others, the process of loss was more gradual and culminated when the child had gone through more advanced developmental stages, so that the resulting depression or despair were more tangible and accessible to language and memory.

In our innocence and beauty, we expected others to respond to us with the same kind of joyful loving and giving. It was very hard for us.

when, instead of returning love for love and awe for awe, people acted as though something were wrong with us for feeling loving or for being in touch with the awesome reality of the universe.

Those who were most hurt in this process become the most cynical. The cynicism functions as a protection. We imagine that we can protect ourselves from the painful experiences we had when we were younger and were ridiculed or made to feel bad because we still dared to hope, because we were still in touch with our spirituality, and because we were still filled to the brim with loving energy.

Throughout our lives, we've been hurt by these cynical responses to our goodness. But when we look at the people who are perpetrating this cynicism, we find that the most cynical were those who were most hurt by the cynicism around them.

The people who become most cynical have not only been disappointed, but they also have been actively humiliated and made to feel ridiculous for their awe and wonder, their aliveness, and their love. It's not uncommon to find that they were told some variant of the following message: "How could you be stupid and naive and unsophisticated enough to think that love and wonder will ever be repaid with love and wonder? Don't you know that the world is based on self-interest, that the only way to see people is in terms of what they can do for you or how you can use them? If you are really into spiritual stuff, you are either naive or dangerous."

After hearing various forms of that kind of message, most people shut down the parts of themselves that were once alive to spiritual experience. To prove themselves okay, many people who were hurt or humiliated at an early age grow up dismissive, angry, or scared of anyone who takes spiritual life seriously.

The cynics among us have been humiliated for allowing themselves to hope. They've decided to never let themselves feel that humiliation again.

I may be making it sound as though I think anyone who raises skeptical questions must be suffering from bad childhood experiences. That's partially true, but it's not the whole story.

People have plenty of good reasons for skepticism, given the many ways that the language of Spirit has been used in harmful ways—for example, as a fig leaf to cover a right-wing political agenda or patriarchal, authoritarian, ultranationalist, homophobic, or racist sentiments. Moreover, spiritual language has been used to assault science, to discredit the very enterprise of rational thinking, and to legitimate hurtful treatment of people who are not part of a given spiritual community.

It's easy to get angry at all the crimes and abuse committed in the name of religion and Spirit. But before we get carried away, it's important to remember that almost any set of ideas can be turned into the opposite of what it was intended to be. In our own time, it's not religion but the explicitly antispiritual language of technical rationality that has been most effectively used to organize the massive wars of the twentieth century and the systematic murders in the Nazi concentration camps.

It has more often been the scientists and engineers than the religious leaders who have created the weapons of mass destruction. Scientific rationality and technology were central to creating the mechanisms of production and consumption as well as the mind-set that sees the world as a resource for endless consumption and that has contributed mightily to the world's ecological crisis.

Scientifically oriented economists and technical business managers have created organizations of exploitation that concentrate wealth and impoverish significant sections of the world's population.

Finally, social scientists and rational intellectuals in the universities, government, and media have developed the rationales and intellectual blindfolds that help us "not notice" the ways that this system has been destructive or harmful to others.

My point is *not* that science or technology is bad, but that we have a double standard.

When science and rationality get appropriated for terrible purposes and tens of millions of people die, this is explained away as a misuse, whereas when spirituality gets misused, it is seen as a reason to discredit the entire enterprise. Talk about a double standard! Consider the possibility that there may be an inherent legitimacy to both the enterprise of science and the development of Spirit, though each has been misused, abused, and twisted to serve destructive ends by people with hurtful agendas.

Littleton: When Spirit Is Stunted

It's much easier to have public discussions about sex on television or in the movies than to discuss spirituality or religion. There are a few areas of disagreement about sex (what age to start, whether it's appropriate with members of the same gender) but generally these issues can be debated in the public sphere.

But when it comes to spirituality and religion, there's hardly any public discourse at all. More people say that they participated in a religious practice in the past week than report that they had sex, but hardly anyone is willing to talk about spirituality in the public sphere.

The result of the unofficial ban on spirit in public discourse was startlingly visible during the media coverage of a terrible American tragedy in Littleton, Colorado, in the spring of 1999—the murder of sixteen young high school students by two of their classmates who opened fire on them with semiautomatic weapons. The media spent weeks exploring every aspect of this tragedy except one—what was it in the lives of these two students that might possibly explain the anger and alienation that led them to this terrible act.

Consider the social context facing most teenagers today. They live in a society in which people are taught to "look out for number one" and to view everyone else as a potential competitor. Most have learned from the media to be highly suspicious of anyone who talks about love and caring (they are probably out to manipulate us) and to recognize that idealists are dangerous (they either are likely to lead the society to disaster because they are so impractical, or they are not really idealists but merely using ideals to mask and advance their own interests).

Schools reflect and teach the larger competitive ethos of the society. Students learn that they must "succeed" by some set of objective criteria or else they will be discarded by this society. Ideas are valued to the extent that they are "useful" to achieve some purpose, and very quickly students learn that they themselves are only valuable if they can prove themselves useful to some societal institution. To be a human being in touch with Spirit or capable of loving and caring for others may be very nice, but it has nothing to do with what "counts" in this world:

to "make it" in the competitive marketplace. Internalizing that vision, parents demand that schools prepare children to compete effectively and focus attention on teaching those "basics" that are most relevant to future market success. Recent efforts to reward teachers according to how well their students do on objective tests extend this success orientation to every fourth-grade classroom.

Most teenagers experience high school as a jungle of yardsticks. They are tested by their teachers in the classroom, "checked out" by their peers in the hallways, and forced to compete at sports whether they want to or not. No matter how beautiful, brilliant, talented, or "cool" they are, most kids feel like they are failing in nine ways out of ten. And almost everyone intuitively feels the looming pressure of the economic and sexual marketplaces with their potential to translate what teenagers perceive to be their inadequacies into a long life of failure.

Some kids respond to these pressures by throwing themselves into the struggle for recognition and success. They find some arena (academics, sports, dancing, computers) in which they imagine that they can "succeed" and put huge amounts of energy into it. Sticking together with a clique of others who share the same interest or skill, they covertly reassure each other that they are really okay, even if, underneath the bravado, they actually suspect that they will never be attractive enough to find a soul mate and will never be skilled enough to be able to make it at the top of the economic pecking order. But even a peer group is not sufficient to ward off feelings of inauthenticity and fears that one is inadequate and unlikely to have the qualities that will make future success possible, so many teens feel an underlying desperation and growing depression about "Who They Really Are." These feelings are often even more intense among those who never quite secure even this minimal recognition from their peers.

Even kids who feel relatively confident that their skills, class background, and connections will help them "make it" are depressed or angry for another reason. They can already feel that the reasons they might "make it" are so external, so far from the core of their being, that the recognition they might possibly achieve will be a kind of misrecognition. Their alienation comes from knowing that at best they might be lucky enough to be valued for something external rather than something they see as connected to Who They Really Are.

The Loss of Soul in High School

From the standpoint of Spirit, what's valuable about you is that you already are an embodiment of Spirit and you already deserve to be loved, cared for, and respected. You don't have to jump through someone else's hoops to be worthwhile. We may often make mistakes, treat each other inappropriately, or act in destructive and insensitive ways toward the earth. But to have a soul is to always have the capacity to start afresh, to transcend this past, to start down a path of goodness, gratitude, and love.

But from the standpoint of the dominant paradigm of the competitive marketplace, what's good about you is the degree to which you might succeed in amassing power, fame, or money. If you show signs of having those capacities, you'll learn to feel good about yourself. But only to the extent that you actually follow through and succeed.

Your soul has no value on this calculation. On the contrary, everything in society works to convince us to stop paying attention to our souls and start paying attention to our prospects.

But the downside is this: the more we lose touch with our souls, the more we get depressed. As we move into our early teenage years, many of us can almost feel this hole in the center of our being, though few of us know how to explain what it is or how it got there.

As young people enter their teenage years, they begin to get a strong sense that something is deeply wrong. They can seldom articulate what it is. Often they suspect that it's something wrong with them. "I just wasn't made for this world," many complain. They have begun to sense the strong disparity between how the world is and who they are.

Teenagers often face this reality with far less protection and far greater immediacy than the adults around them. The sudden burst of adolescent sexual energy stands in sharp contrast to the authoritarian and sex-denying institution of high school. Just as they are beginning to worry about whether they will ever "make it" in the economic marketplace, many teens also start to worry about whether they can "make it" in the world of human relationships. Sometimes this leads to sexual acting out on the part of teenagers desperate for any form of affection or recognition. For girls, this is often compounded by the fact that our culture teaches them that their real worth lies in their ability to satisfy male desires.

The market consciousness fostered by the economy shapes the way many teenagers perceive themselves and others in the world of loving relationships. How attractive am I? Will I ever find an appropriate partner? Will I have to settle for someone far less attractive, loving, gentle, intelligent, funny, or playful than I would have wanted, given the fact that I don't have the qualities everyone values in this world? As the doubts deepen, many of us begin to feel a depressive certainty that we will never really enjoy our lives, and we'd better get used to that and accept it as "reality."

In spite of all this, most of us survive high school. We emerge spiritually battered, and scarred for life, with a sense of certainty that we don't really deserve and should not expect a joyously fulfilling life. No wonder spirituality seems suspect, and hope, gratitude, and celebration of the universe strike many of us as naive, childlike, or just plain ridiculous. Spiritual notions just seem so "uncool" and out of sync with the rhythms of reality as we've experienced them.

Many teenagers will ultimately come to believe that not much fulfillment is possible. They will learn to live most of their lives with a low-level emotional depression. Still others will struggle frantically to "succeed" and will learn to live with a continuing anxiety about the possibility that everything will soon collapse. Others will sit in front of a computer screen playing games, while their parents lament that they are "wasting their time." Still others will throw themselves into some "cause" or project, or some sport or hobby, hoping to escape their growing sense of pain and confusion. Some will use drugs, alcohol, sex, frenetic exercise, dieting, or music to help them focus attention away from the underlying fears and depression that are engendered by their internalization of the competitive market and its many yardsticks. Because our media, schools, and dominant societal discourse is pervaded with cynicism and pressure to "make it," very few teenagers will find a framework of meaning and purpose that could transcend the competitive marketplace consciousness that seeps into their lives and makes them feel inadequate and wounded.

Some, like the murderous kids at Littleton, will explode with anger. Some will commit suicide.

Most won't.

But very few teenagers interviewed in the wake of Littleton expressed much surprise at the anger and alienation that underlay this particular tragedy.

What was shocking was the particular form their anger took, the particular way it was expressed. The alienation itself was as familiar to most kids as breathing.

This alienation is one manifestation of the spiritual crisis in American society: the deprivation of meaning and purpose in every aspect of daily life. So deep is the crisis that we are no longer able to recognize it—it seems to be just built in to the structure of "reality," a basic fact about the way things are.

Much of what we call "pathology" in our society is a response to that deprivation, from crime to drugs and alcohol—from hooliganism at sports events and rock concerts to reactionary nationalism, from racism to xenophobia to homophobia, to all the hostility directed at people who are different. We may reject the response as unacceptable. We may find at times that we need to punish those who act hurtfully in these ways. But we should not deny the reality that a great deal of what the dominant society considers inexplicable behavior is often an irrational response to a quite real desperation people feel in their lives, rooted in a desire to overcome the terrible feeling that their own lives are meaningless and empty and that the world feels lonely and point-less. Some of the most destructive behaviors we see around us are actually attempts to make some point, create some meaning, give some direction to life.

People will try anything to find a way to recreate meaning that has been lost. If we could immerse ourselves in others' reality, we could often find the reasons that led them to feel that their path was the best way they could find to give some point to their lives.

The deprivation of meaning is so pervasive that it is almost invisible. But when a big blowup occurs, like the murders in Littleton, it almost hits you in the face.

Almost . . . but not quite. The media, the pundits, and the political leadership scrambled to provide answers, but they lacked the vocabulary to describe the crisis of meaning. In fact, their role in making the hunger for meaning invisible was an important element in causing the crisis the media sought to explain. If people could understand the source of their own inner feelings of desperation and depression, if they could see that this hunger for meaning was really a reflection of what was *good* about them, a manifestation of Spirit in their lives, they'd be far less likely to get trapped in self-destructive activity and more likely to understand events like Littleton.

But the crisis of meaning is invisible. Society self-confidently presents itself to us as the highest manifestation of rationality and goodness and assumes that anyone who can't find his or her place must be incompetent, irrational, or deranged.

This is not an issue of Left or Right—both tend to miss the boat. Both deny the crisis of meaning and focus instead on trying to develop new strategies to control the bad people who are doing something wrong. Control the people attracted to liquor or drugs. Control the people who turn to crime. Control the people who act out in irresponsible ways. Pathologize the people who get involved in nationalism or fundamentalism. Medicate the ones who find it difficult to pay attention in school. After the Littleton murders, liberals jumped on this same "control the bad guys" bandwagon and successfully used this moment to enact some gun control legislation and to focus on violence in movies, videos, and the World Wide Web.

I do not doubt that the easy accessibility of guns or a media that glorifies violence may make it easier for young people to imagine violent solutions to their anger and outrage. What I do question is the assumption of cause and effect. A violent outlet for anger doesn't cause anger, not all by itself. There are too many people who see the movies and play the video games without getting hooked into violence, or who have access to weapons, but don't kill half their classmates, to think that these are root causes.

Sometimes it makes sense to control the mechanisms through which the outrage or anger gets expressed. Fine, let's do that. But let's not fool ourselves into thinking that we've dealt with the problem when we've dealt with a few of the myriad ways the problem gets expressed.

The fundamental problem underlying much of what is crazy, hurtful, and anger-producing in our society is what I call the deprivation of meaning. I doubt that the Littleton tragedy could have occurred if the culture of American high schools had encouraged students to be loving and caring, ethically and spiritually sensitive, ecologically concerned, and committed to healing the social and economic woes of our society. I doubt if the pain that the most troubled students were in would have been ignored had the school system rewarded students for how well they took care of each other, helped each other to learn and to feel good about themselves, and encouraged each other to be in touch with their inner selves and their loving capacities. In chapter nine, I'll talk more about what such an educational system might be. For the moment, it's enough to say that understanding the focus away from spiritual values and toward the dominant materialism, selfishness, and cynicism that permeates most high schools provides the necessary link to understanding why we face so much violence and hurtfulness in this society.

The first step in curing ourselves and our planet is to recognize that Spirit Matters!

There are two important caveats. First, although I sometimes talk in this book as though self-interest is bad, please understand all such instances as referring to a narrow, short-term materialistic self-interest. In fact, our long-term self-interest is in living in a world in which spiritual concerns predominate. We would be safer, happier, and more fulfilled if our world were filled with love, mutual recognition, and an ability to see Spirit and our place within it. Much of the argument of this book is to show you how much pain it causes us when our spiritual needs are denied and repressed. So, please don't think that I'm suggesting that there is something wrong with people who worry about their self-interest. I am only suggesting that if we understood ourselves as part of the Totality of All, saw our place as part of the Unity of All Being, and recognized our intrinsic need for each other, we'd realize that our own individual well-being and self-interest absolutely requires the well-being of every other person and of the planet itself.

Nor is there anything wrong with going for individual pleasure. The Emancipatory Spirituality affirmed in this book is in favor of maximizing pleasure as an important dimension of life. To be spiritual need not mean a life of asceticism and denial. Here, as in every part of spiritual life, what is needed is balance, in this case a balance between our own immediate pleasures and the equally powerful pleasure we get at being able to satisfy the needs of others and at being needed by others and by the universe itself. A spiritual life can be the source of great pleasure, fun, and play!

A second caveat: in this book I sometimes use "the market" as a summary of what's wrong, because the dominant ethos of the marketplace is to value money and power over all else. It's that "bottom line" that needs to be changed. But though contemporary market societies are the latest and most sophisticated expression of this distorted consciousness, those same distortions exist in premarket, socialist, and communist societies as well. One reason why Spirit Matters is because it provides the foundation for a critique of a technocratic and manipulative consciousness that can be found in a wide variety of social systems.

A basic insight of the spiritual consciousness can be summed up in this way: The world and other people are not here to be used and manipulated by us for our own narrow purposes, but to be responded to with awe and wonder and radical amazement. The world is permeated with love and goodness, and the meaning of our lives is to embody that love and goodness and to heal the world so that it is a deeper reflection of this underlying goodness and love. In chapter one, I'll discuss how these spiritual concerns disappeared from societies that were officially spiritual, and how this led to the triumph of market and postmarket societies that are also spiritually challenged. We live in a world where we are encouraged to see other people in terms of how we can use them, the resources of the planet as little more than objects to be consumed, and goodness and love as purely personal and subjective states that have nothing to do with how to organize a society. Whether it's capitalism or socialism or communism or any other ism, as long as this kind of consciousness is prevalent, we are talking about a world that needs spiritual healing (and that includes those parts of the world that call themselves spiritual as well).

The good news is this: Most people have a sense of an inner life that does not fit the manipulative and technocratic consciousness of the dominant ethos in our society. Though many still are fearful that to say this will make them subject to ridicule by others, and many of us still believe that we can't trust others because "everyone" is motivated by material needs and narrow self-interest and is fearful too that we will be humiliated if we begin to talk about spiritual reality as though it is important to us, more and more people are coming out of the closet and claiming their right to know what they know: that Spirit Matters. And more and more will join them in the years to come.

Coming Out of the Closet
as Spiritual Beings

The first few decades of the twenty-first century may see the deniers of Spirit retaining cultural hegemony—they will continue to deny and ridicule those who champion Spirit, to define them as the enemy, even as the harbingers of a new Dark Age.

The forces of cynicism will continue to insist that spirituality is fine "in its place," but that it has no relevance to "the real world," that it is not a fit subject for the evening news, for the world of public policy, for the corporate boardrooms, or for the shaping of our culture. But all that can change.

In fact, it has already begun to change. There are growing signs of a spiritual renaissance in Western societies as more and more people seek some way to understand their world and find moorings that are not provided by the one-dimensional media, the technocratic politicians, or the frenetic religion of marketplace competition and the consumption of material goods. No matter how often people hear that salvation is at hand if only they get a better car, a newer computer, faster access to the World Wide Web, a more splendid cell phone that can read their e-mail and even put them into television contact with people around the world, the emptiness at the center of being and the nagging questions about what all this frantic life is really about push more and more people to seek some form of spiritual life.

One reason this spiritual turn is taking place right now is the growing awareness of impending ecological catastrophe in the twenty-first century. By viewing the planet as a resource to be exploited, by denying that we could possibly have a collective responsibility to treat the earth as sacred ground, the champions of ever-expanding growth have created a worldwide ecological crisis. The facts of this crisis have been available to us for at least the past thirty years. Yet the economic and political and media forces that control basic decision making have been unable to come to grips with the way their thinking has contributed to this massive danger to our planet.

The very people who claim to be the embodiment of rationality are unable to provide us with the intellectual categories we need to reorganize the way we misuse the planet's resources or to stop the way we are destroying its air and water. The logic of narrow self-interest mitigates against ecological consciousness. For the person who has learned the logic of the marketplace, why not maximize one's own pleasures without regard to the consequences for the future? After all, we will be dead before the worst of the ecological crisis hits, and when it does, it will hit poor people and people living in Third World countries far more than it will the American elites. If you don't have categories that encourage a spiritual as opposed to a narrow utilitarian attitude toward the earth, if you don't have an intellectual framework that can justify social responsibility, how in the world do you imagine you are ever going to convince people growing up in a society that proclaims "he who dies with the most toys wins" to change their patterns of consumption?

You won't.

Which is one major reason lots of people who care about ecology are also opening to spirituality.

What you won't hear on the evening news is that people are increasingly turning to spirituality at least in part because they suspect that in the spiritual world there is a different way of orienting to reality, a way that is based on awe, reverence, and a deep appreciation of the *Unity of All Being*—and that these spiritual categories are necessary if we wish to produce a society that behaves in ecologically sustainable ways.

All around you, people are beginning to reject the old societal notions that were most spiritually deadening: that there isn't enough, that we are all separate from each other, that to get ahead we have to leave others behind, and that some of us are superior to others. Instead, millions of people are recognizing that there is enough, that we are not separate, that we are all One.

Spirit Matters—and more and more people are noticing.

Addendum: What Exactly Is Spirit?

I promised that for those who really want to hear some of the ways that people think about Spirit today, I'd give a fuller picture. If you think you already get what I mean by Spirit, you can skip this addendum and go to chapter one.

What makes talk about Spirit so difficult is that language is so limiting. In the earlier part of this introduction, I talked about Spirit as the Force of Healing and Transformation, that aspect of reality that makes it possible for us to transcend all that has been and shape a new reality. Yet many spiritual thinkers go beyond that and hint at other aspects of Spirit. Every such attempt has some severe problems because of the limitations of our language.

That's a problem with Spirit—we can allude to it, but every attempt to define it in itself rather than in its manifestations ends up seeming silly, empty, or vague. The deepest spiritual thinkers warn us that the realm of Spirit is the realm of the ineffable. It simply can't be adequately expressed in language. The best we can get is poetry and song, not propositional knowledge. Again Abraham Joshua Heschel: "The heart of being confronts me as enigmatic, incompatible with my categories, sheer mystery. All we have is a sense of awe and radical amazement in the face of a mystery that staggers our ability to sense it."

Those of us who feel the delight of spiritual life have a compelling desire to share the loving joy with others. So we engage in language that is inevitably inadequate. There is no one right way. Every approach to Spirit is limited, and no one who really gets what Spirit is about is going to put down other people's approach, except in one case: the case of spiritual or religious traditions that demean others and don't treat everyone as equally a manifestation of God.

It's not unreasonable to want to have some relevant words. But the words may sound confusing. They point in all different directions, and you may not feel you fully understand them until you've allowed yourself to be engaged in spiritual practice on a regular basis. It's kind of like writing about music—it doesn't capture very much until you've listened to a lot of music and have some idea of what these words might be talking about.

So, I don't mind if you skip this part. Because the best I can do is point to a few aspects of what I mean by Spirit:

1. About fifteen billion years ago a cosmic bang released all the energy and mass of the universe from a small point into billions of particles that eventually self-organized into atoms that eventually self-organized into clouds that formed

into galaxies that formed into stars that grew, died, and reorganized into new stars and planets. About four billion years ago, one of the planets gave birth to tiny life forms that began to develop in manifold forms, reproducing, experimenting, learning to share with each other, and cooperating to form unions of more and more complex multicellular organisms with capacities far beyond those of individual cells. As David Korten points out in "For the Love of Life" (TIKKUN, January/February 2000), "Our own bodies, comprised of some 30 to 70 trillion individual living cells plus an even larger number of assorted beneficial bacteria and fungi, are an extraordinary example of the complex consequences of this experimentation. Continuously experimenting, creating, building, life transformed the planet's very substance into a web of living beings of astonishing variety, beauty, awareness and capacity for intelligent choice." The energizing Force behind this process of continuing experimentation, creativity, consciousness, and cooperation is what we call Spirit.

2. Spirit is the undergirding of all that there is, the ultimate substance of the universe, in which all else is grounded. Aristotle talked about it as *nous*, Mind or Enminded Substance, but in doing so made it sound as though it were some kind of material entity, perhaps just a very ghostly material entity.

Some people think of Spirit as the membrane that connects every part of the universe and operates according to a logic of love, sympathy, and goodness rather than a material logic of hydraulic or mechanical rules. Recent controlled studies, documented by Larry Dossey in *Reinventing Medicine* and in *Meaning and Medicine*, have demonstrated that prayer can have a statistically significant impact on a group of people being prayed for from thousands of miles away (even in double blind studies, where the people praying don't know the people being prayed for and the people prayed for don't know that they are the recipients of those prayers). This and other psychic phenomena suggest a form of spiritual communication and causation in the universe that far surpasses any of our current categories. (Read Larry Dossey's important work, particularly *Meaning and Medicine*, for more information about the way medical science is struggling with this kind of spiritual information.) Some people argue that the only possible way to understand the physical impact of prayer is to imagine a universe connected by a spiritual membrane. Future generations may look at our current spiritual unknowingness with the same kind of astonishment that many people today show toward those in previous historical periods who believed the sun revolved around the earth. They will almost certainly point with a certain irony to a higher prevalence of spiritual awareness and intuitions in less "advanced" human societies.

Try thinking of Spirit as the ultimate consciousness of the universe, a consciousness that pervades, sustains, and includes All Being and yet cannot be reduced to any part of it. We are part of this ultimate consciousness in the way a particular theory or orientation might be "part" of our minds. Each of us is a particular part of spiritual consciousness and a part of the process through which Spirit is becoming self-conscious. We did not originate consciousness, but instead we tapped into a larger pool of consciousness that surrounds and grounds All Being. There are gradations of consciousness and awareness throughout the manifold of Being. Each of us participates in this consciousness, and, as Wayne Teasdale writes in *The Mystic Heart*, "We inhabit consciousness but we don't own it."

One of the great errors of human consciousness is to think of ourselves as fixed objects and to then seek to control ourselves and the world. In fact, our consciousness is part of the universal consciousness, a local manifestation of the Unity of All Being, and a stage in the development of the self-consciousness of the universe. When I talk about stages in the development of Spirit, I am actually talking about increasing levels of consciousness in which we are able to gradually comprehend the oneness and unity of all. This unity transcends all language—the ultimate fact of our being is that we are part of the Unity of All Being; it is mirrored in every cell and every pore of our selves. Unable to articulate this in language, those attuned to the realm of Spirit have turned to mysticism; to poetry, song, and dance; to ritual and meditation; and to other nonverbal activities to allude to, intuit, and experience the oneness that can never adequately be pinned down.

3. The consciousness of the universe is not separate from other aspects of Being but is that through which All Being exists and becomes manifest to us and to itself. Our desire to get hold of Spirit and to make it an object among the other objects of the world leads us into all kinds of muddles. Miguel d'Unamuno captured the problem when he talked about killing a human being and dissecting the body to find the life force. The problem, of course, is that the dissection destroys the very thing it was seeking to expose. That's the problem with all language.

4. Spirit is the Force for Freedom. But it is also the Force of Healing and Transformation.

Spirit is not a neutral force that seeks to embody freedom in any possible way (for example, by making people free to hurt each other), but a Force that pushes toward the fullest realization of consciousness, goodness, creativity, love, joy, pleasure, complexity, cooperation, beauty, and unity.

5. Spirit is the process of evolution as the universe becomes more loving and caring. Spirit is the process that brings about deeper and deeper levels of knowledge, goodness, and radiant beauty. Or, we might say, as my teacher, Zalman Schachter-Shalomi suggests, that Spirit is the voice of the future beckoning to the present. The distinctive thing about human beings is our ability to hear that voice, feel addressed by it, and find meaning in life to the extent that we respond to it. Or as Abraham Joshua Heschel put it, "I am commanded, therefore I am." That is, Spirit is the aspect of reality that needs us to be its partners in *tikkun* (the healing and transformation of the planet).

6. Spirit is, among other things, the world's permission to you to leave or temporarily suspend the focus of your attention on goal-directed mental, emotional, or physical activity and join instead in play, humor, joy, pleasure, and celebration of all that is. This is a form of love that, as Evelyn Fox Keller puts it, "allows for intimacy without annihilating difference."

Spirit is the playful, joyful, loving energy that pulsates through All Being, imminent in all, and yet fully transcendent of any given state of being and any given manifestation.

It is the invitation to dance, to song, to erotic energy, and to celebration.

Sometimes Spirit has been identified only with the realm of transcendence, as a powerful being that exists outside our bodies and beyond the Earth. The result has been patriarchal spiritual traditions that denigrate the Earth, the feminine, the body, and nature.

On the other hand, we've had matriarchal spiritual traditions that have sanctified the Earth and nature but have often allowed that to drift into a sanctification of any existing reality and lost all sense of possibility and transformation.

In my account, Spirit is both fully transformative/transcendent (or a power beyond anything we experience as tangible) and fully imminent in all that is (that is, present in nature and culture, in events and in things). The Unity of All Being is an unfolding evolutionary process, mirrored through the development of the consciousness of human beings. The Force of Healing and Transformation and the Creative Energy of the Universe are One. This Unity continually makes itself manifest to us through spiritual experience. Overcoming the dualities and seeing the ultimate Oneness of All Being is at the heart of the mystical spiritual experience.

The meaning most people seek is achieved when we find some way to connect our own lives to the unfolding of Spirit in the universe. That might sound like a rather difficult task, but, in fact, it comes through a recognition that we, like all other aspects of Being, are manifestations of Spirit. Some will add here that Spirit is consciousness becoming self-conscious through the evolution of human beings. Spirit manifests through us and is in need of us. Our ultimate meaning, as my teacher, Abraham Joshua Heschel, used to say, is to be an answer to a cosmic need. The closer we get to experiencing our lives as service to this calling, the closer we get to experiencing a sense of meaning and purpose in life.

We don't have to *do* something, we have to let ourselves *be* the fullest beings that we can be—and then we will be in touch with our spiritual identity as manifestations of the ultimate Being of the universe. Then our lives will be an answer to God's need for us (an answer to the Biblical question that God first put to human beings:

"Where are you?"). The greatest joy in life comes from being able to answer that question, being able to recognize ourselves as part of the Unity of All Being, to recognize the foundation of our Being in Spirit, to dedicate our lives to making its purposes our own, to overcome the false consciousness that sees us as separated, lost, and on our own with no higher goal than to take care of ourselves. Though we can never be truly separate from Spirit, we can experience deep alienation by not realizing our connection and by attempting to create that feeling of connection through all kinds of partial and substitute gratifications for the fundamental need to be connected to Spirit.

It all sounds so heavy and serious. But, in fact, the recognition of our connection to Spirit is a state of bliss. We recognize our part in Being when we see that we are manifestations of love, goodness, joy, and creativity. Spirit is in our being, but is also so much more than us.

Well, you can see why words are so inadequate here, and why spiritual people say, "Have the experience, encounter Spirit through developing a spiritual practice, and forget the words."

I've often wondered why people write long books about something they believe is fundamentally inexpressible in language. In my case, this book is not primarily about defining Spirit, but about why it matters to the world and why we should notice that the matter in the world is filled with Spirit. Although we may have trouble defining Spirit, we can attend to it and incorporate that attention into a way of being in the world. And doing so can lead to wonderfully fulfilling experiences. Conversely, building a social world based on the denial of Spirit can cause tremendous pain.

So come out and play. Because serious as this book may seem, it's all about playing with God/Spirit as She manifests Herself in infinitely complex and wonderful ways through you and me.

If you still fear that by joining in this playful venture you may be leaving reason behind, remember Blaise Pascal's notion in his *Pensées*, that Reason's last step is recognizing that an infinity of things surpass it.

one

The Evolution of Spirit

We are opening up in sweet surrender to:
—deep humility about the limits of our knowledge
—unusually profound states of experience
—a sense of the uncanny
—intuition of the whole working in concert
—compassion for each segment of the whole as part of a
  far-reaching self-love
—a paradoxical state of relaxed trust and animated
  engagement
—a sense of surrender into a greater awareness
—the luminous lovelight of the One

Rabbi David Wolfe-Blank

How to Have a Spiritual Experience

I can tell you how to have a spiritual experience, but I can't guarantee you'll have one, any more than I can guarantee you'll fall in love with someone to whom I introduce you, though that person might be the most loving, warm, funny, brilliant, and generous person you've ever met.

Get yourself to a place outside in nature where you can see at least twenty stars in the night sky. Close your eyes and breathe in deep breaths.

Focus your attention on your breath. Notice your thoughts as they race through your mind. But then refocus your attention on your breath.

Tell yourself over and over, "I am one part of the consciousness of the universe, a manifestation of the Unity of All Being." Continue doing this for fifteen minutes. Bring an alarm clock set to go off in fifteen minutes so you don't have to keep opening your eyes to see how much time has elapsed. Allow yourself to sink into the experience as you notice how your thoughts are rushing toward everything else other than your own breath and on this simple statement "I am one part . . . " and so forth. When you catch your mind wandering, don't scold it. Instead, gently return your attention to your breath and to this one sentence focusing on how you are part of the consciousness of the universe.

After fifteen minutes of this focus, open your eyes. Imagine that you can see yourself where you are sitting. Now, imagine that you are going up in a slowly ascending balloon and yet able to look down on the Earth and see your physical body standing where it is.

Notice yourself standing at a particular point on planet Earth. See what that point is. For example, I would see myself standing in a courtyard in San Francisco, and as the balloon went up a little farther, I'd notice that I was standing very close to the Pacific Ocean. As the balloon went up farther, I'd notice that I was on the North American continent, and yet all the way down there, on the side of the Pacific, in Northern California, in a backyard in San Francisco, there I am. Now see yourself standing there, wherever you are, and notice that you are on a planet that has been slowly turning all day, first toward the nearest star we call the Sun (which is a million times bigger than planet Earth). Try seeing the Sun as one million times the size of Earth, and see where you are in relation to it.

Notice that as you were living your very important life all day long, the planet was spinning, and that it is also moving slowly around the Sun.

See where you are on this planet and become aware that you are sharing this planet with six billion other human beings who are also looking up into heaven from time to time and noticing where they are. Become aware of how you and they must appear from way up high—a planet filled with six billion egos, each one shouting "Notice me! I'm so important! I'm the one who really counts!"

Imagine that you can see all six billion people jumping around and yelling for attention—and recognize how the human ego gets out of control and loses its sense of proportion. From the distance of many thousands of miles away, see yourself down there with the other six billion, all exhausting themselves by frenetically pursuing their lives and imagining that they absolutely must accomplish their tasks quickly. People have less and less time, because they "must" accomplish everything now, and doing so is so deeply important. Notice how many people are driven by this frenetic need—everyone calling out for attention.

Now, notice that our sun is one of millions of stars in this galaxy, and that our galaxy is one of fifty billion galaxies.

Notice where you are in the universe. Try to imagine yourself as one of the manifestations of the consciousness of the universe, and as part of the totality of all things, a momentary explosion of God energy, a momentary embodiment of the spiritual energy of the universe and of the Force of Healing and Transformation.

You know that in somewhere between twenty and seventy years from now, you and everyone around you will be in the ground, and a new generation will look up and see the marvel of the universe. But this is now, and this is your moment to join with the billions of other humans and countless other life forms that are at some level of awareness, noticing grandeur and joining in the universal song of thanksgiving at being alive and being able to see all this marvelous reality. So, allow yourself to experience how incredible it is to be alive.

If you can, do this every night for three weeks in a row, all the while telling yourself, "I am one part of the consciousness of the universe, a manifestation of the Unity of All Being."

Whenever your conscious attention wanders, gently bring it back to focus on the incredible grandeur of the universe.

Once you succeed in quieting your own mind down enough so that it can focus on your breath for fifteen minutes, you'll find that in the course of those three weeks you will have a spiritual experience.

The Marvel of Creation

Everything that has ever happened in the history of the universe is the prelude to each of our lives. Everything that has happened from the beginning of time has become the platform from which we launch our lives.

We are the heirs of the long evolution of Spirit. Each of us is the latest unfolding of the event of Creation. Our bodies are composed of the material that was shaped in the Big Bang. And so, too, our spirit. The loving goodness of the universe breathes us and breathes through us, giving us life and consciousness, and the capacity to recognize and love others.

Each stage in the development of the universe incorporates and transcends that which went before. It has been so from the earliest stages in the formation of galaxies, to the emergence of solar time for our particular planet, through the geological development of the Earth and the emergence of biological reality, until we ultimately emerge into human time, or history. Each stage of history, in turn, makes further developments possible, which finally bring us to the present moment.

That evolving reality has been understood through much of recorded history as an integrated and mutually interacting web of body, mind, soul, and spirit. When we faced problems in our human reality, we can often understand those problems as dysfunctions in the way these different levels of reality interacted with each other.

Recognizing One's Place
in the Unity of All Being

Jewish tradition relates the story of a rabbi who sought to understand his place in the universe. To keep a balance between too much grandiosity and too much self-diminution, he had two notes, one for each of his two pants pockets. One note read: "For me the world was created." The other note read: "I am nothing more than dust and ashes." The task of the rabbi is our task: to integrate these two messages and keep them in appropriate balance.

"For me the world was created." The grandeur of creation comes to full expression in the creation of human beings. Complexly magnificent, able to be conscious of ourselves, able to transcend that which *is* and to move toward what *ought to be*, human beings were "created in the image of God" and reflect the universe's greatest outpouring of love and generosity.

But also, "nothing more than dust and ashes." We are part of the totality of all that is, and we are ever arrogant when we see ourselves as somehow better than everything else, as having the right to use everything else for our own ends. We are here on the planet for a brief moment, and for much of that time we are deeply enmeshed in foolish schemes to perpetuate ourselves for eternity, imagining that if we amass enough power or control we can somehow live forever.

Emancipatory Spirituality offers a different kind of immortality, not a promise that our own individual personalities with their specific sets of memories and experiences will last forever, but the immortality of being part and parcel of the totality of all being. To appreciate this second kind of immortality, we need to reach a fuller awareness of our place in the universe and our identity as manifestations of the totality of all that is.

We are what Ken Wilber calls "holons," entities who are simultaneously separate beings, seeking to maintain our own individual existence and parts of something much bigger than ourselves. In the contemporary world, it's easy to understand the consciousness of ourselves as separate beings, but it's very hard to develop a sense of ourselves as part of the Unity of All Being.

The Western intellectual tradition tends to encourage us to see the world as a collection of individual things, separated from each other, and then tries to figure out how they might interact. Much of our language contributes to this sense of separateness because it was developed to break up nature and our visual field into objects that could be used or shaped by human action.

But this isn't the only possible human goal. There's another way of thinking, one that stresses the fundamental interconnectedness of all being, one that starts with the premise of totality and moves from there. To understand the world from the standpoint of its fundamental unity, we need to transcend the language that was created to serve a different and narrower purpose. It's difficult for words to capture our intuition or perception of "the totality of all with all."

I sometimes think of our individual consciousness as a liver cell in a complex body. The liver cell understands what it can take in, given the limited consciousness a liver cell can have. It has some inkling of connection to other liver cells, and probably some notion of a larger consciousness of the entire body. But it can't imagine a larger interconnected reality with a consciousness of the totality that is filled with love and pours out its generosity to all of its parts.

When a liver cell gets out of balance with the rest of the body, we get a destructive expansiveness in which certain cells start to crowd out neighboring cells. We call that condition cancer. Cancer is the perfect analogy for individual egos that lose their sense of balance and begin to expand themselves at the expense of others.

In some spiritual traditions, the solution to this problem is to obliterate the individual ego. The ego itself is seen as the big problem, so the solution is to overcome it.

Emancipatory Spirituality, however, does not seek to obliterate the ego, but to put it in balance with the rest of the universe. In our society, we are in great need of this kind of rebalancing. Our society is full of people who go around saying "I am a self-made man or woman. I did it myself and therefore I deserve more money or power or recognition than anyone else." Many people say that because they were spiritually wounded, because they have been deprived of recognition and love, or because they never had the experience of being in a supportive community. It never occurs to them that the science and technology, the phone lines and the paved streets, the automobiles and airplanes that they use, even the conceptual distinctions and the language they draw upon were not built by them but by others. Instead, they need to puff themselves up to defend against their feeling of aloneness and their certainty that they cannot count on others. Said often enough, the myth of the self-made individual starts to take on the dimension of common sense in contemporary capitalist societies.

But look a little closer. Emancipatory Spirituality teaches that every one of us is standing on the platform of thousands of previous generations of human beings. We inherited the wisdom, the language, the categories, and the work of the past.

Even as I write this, I have to remember that the food on my table, the shelter over my head, the computer in front of me, and the language and categories I use are the products of a planetary economy and tens of thousands of years of human effort. That economy has been made possible by all of humanity's previous experiments with forming larger and more inclusive cooperative enterprises. You and I are the beneficiaries of the goodness of tens of millions of human beings who struggled to get information, who developed techniques, tools, systems, words, and institutions. It was out of their love for each other and for the future of the human race that we can now live in peace, ease, dignity, security, affection, and harmony.

Here is one spiritual exercise that each of us needs to try every day. Take anything in your life—a musical instrument, a computer, a car, a piece of fruit that sits in your home but was grown far away, a television, a phone line, a book. Now try to imagine all the steps that needed to happen between the moment that human beings began to evolve and the moment you were able to have this thing in your life. If you ask what knowledge those who brought this object into your life had to have, what those who developed that knowledge had to learn from previous people who developed their knowledge, you will quickly be overwhelmed by the amount of cooperation through thousands of years that made all the things that populate your daily life possible. Try this exercise with a different object or aspect of your life every day and you'll soon see how much each of us is a beneficiary of the goodness and cooperation of past generations.

And that's what the universe is—a vast system of cooperation. Though many contemporary social institutions teach us to see others as enemies or potential rivals for scarce resources, the truth is that we live in a world in which the basic principle is one of cooperation.

My Hawaiian friend Morty Breyer taught me to recognize this in our own bodies. In his words: "My lungs with their system of bellows, branching, and oxygen exchange membranes; my circulatory system with its tubes, valves, and pumps; my nervous system with its wiring; my digestive system with its juices and absorption linings; my sensory systems with their lenses, keying sites, and tympani membranes; my movement systems with their structural members, hinges, and rigging tendons; all of these and much more do not occur anywhere in the internal structures of any of my cells, nor in the life of any cell that preceded it. The beautifully cooperative actions of all of these systems with their common goal of preserving and empowering me, their organizational creation, developed over a long period of the evolution of animal life with the ultimate desire to cooperate on a vast scale. And we human beings have similarly built human technologies and cooperative organizing strategies just like the cells built within us."

Or think of DNA and the way, when damaged, it reorganizes itself. The individual parts work together to reveal the astonishing interconnectedness of Spirit.

What makes this cooperation possible is the force of love. Each of us was a product of the love of the universe pulsating through our parents. Though many of us think about how our parents were not as loving as we needed them to be, the fact that we are alive at all is testimony to the interaction between their loving and the loving manifested in social institutions that made it possible for children to be fed, housed, clothed, and protected.

The Possibilities Created by the Legacy of Love

On the platform of embodied love we have received from the universe we can create our world afresh. We are poised to take the next step in the evolution of human consciousness. To do that, we have to be aware of all that has gone before.

Human beings were never truly isolated or thrown into the world alone. That existential picture, described by the German philosopher Heidegger, is a further elaboration of the philosophers of early capitalism like Hobbes and Leibniz, who saw human beings as isolated nomads who forged contracts to enter into community only to avoid the war of all against all. Ironically, this war of all against all may be a good picture of what it's like to live in our contemporary "looking out for number one" society. It was seldom true of human life throughout most of our history.

Much of human history has been the history of smaller groups beginning to see common interests and ties to larger groups, first as clans, then as tribes, then as peoples, then as nations.

The next stage of human history requires that we take the next step in the evolution of consciousness and begin to see ourselves as one—as deeply connected, sharing one planet.

The idea of our fundamental interconnection with each other and with nature was already articulated in the Bible when its Prophets warned that without a society based on justice, peace, love, and caring, the whole world will face ecological catastrophe. From the Bible's perspective, we commit a global sin by allowing injustice and lack of love toward the stranger and our neighbor to persist. And its message is clear: You cannot act immorally without global consequences.

The next stage in the evolution of our spiritual consciousness will be facilitated when we internalize the awareness that you and I are deeply linked to the other six billion human beings who share this planet. But more than that—we are interdependent with all the other creatures who are traveling with us on spaceship Earth, and beyond that, with all life throughout the universe.

Here I think that the human race has a lot to learn from Biblically based religions. The central message of the Jewish Torah, the Christian Bible, and the Muslim Koran is that we were born from God's love and the love that permeates the universe, and that we have every reason to see each other as created in the image of God, as embodiments of God, and to treat each other as such.

When I talk of God, I am talking about YHVH (mistranslated in the King James version as Jehovah, but actually four letters that Jews never pronounce precisely because they do not signify a specific being, but a world process, a God-ing, or, as David Cooper put it in the title of his book, *God Is a Verb*). YHVH comes from the root HVH, the Hebrew word for "the present tense" and the Y, which indicates the future. What the word really means is "the transformation of the present into that which can and should be in the future." In this sense, God is the Power of Healing and Transformation in the universe—and the Voice of the Future calling us to become who we need to become.

The word "God" has accumulated so much authoritarian and patriarchal baggage that many people find it impossible to believe in the God they were taught about as children. Part of my reason for using the word Spirit throughout this book has been to avoid those associations. But if we think of God as the totality of all that is, was, and ever will be, as seen from the perspective of its evolution toward higher levels of consciousness and higher levels of loving connection, then many people who do not believe in God can still come to see the universe from this Spirit-oriented perspective.

Looking at the world in this way, we can each understand ourselves as one of the billions of ways Spirit has chosen to pour its love into existence. We are at once a manifestation of all the love of the universe, and an opportunity for the universe to manifest greater loving, cooperation, and harmony. This is what the angels meant in the Psalm when they said, "What is Man that thou shouldst think of him or the son of man that thou shouldst take account of him? But you have made man just a little lower than the angels." And yet, we are also, as the Psalmist proclaims, ". . . like a passing shadow, like a dream that vanishes."

While we are here on Earth, we have an incredible opportunity to recognize and rejoice in the Unity of All Being, to stand in awe and wonder at the glory of all that is, and to bring forward as much consciousness, love, solidarity, creativity, sensitivity, and goodness as we possibly can.

Developing and refining this kind of consciousness is a central element in what it means to develop an inner life. And this is one of the central aspects of spiritual practice.

When Spiritual Wisdom Lost Its Path

". . . some tragic falling off
from a first world
of pure light . . ."

Robert Hass

To the best of our knowledge, human beings have always responded to the universe with awe, wonder, and radical amazement. Religious and spiritual consciousness evolved in a variety of ways, but until the past three hundred years, it was always a major fact in the daily lives of ordinary human beings.

The need to celebrate, to rejoice in creation and in our own existence, and to connect what was perceived as an inner spiritual reality with the outer spiritual reality of the universe seems to be pervasive throughout all cultures and societies.

The memory of a spiritual golden age seems encoded in the human psyche. Great epic literature from around the world—from Greek mythology, to the Scandinavian Edda, to the Bible—recall an early paradise when we knew that spirituality was present in all things and all actions. And most contemporary movements, even movements we find distorted or misguided, seem to hearken back to some lost paradise. Spiritual oneness cannot be "objectively verified," but our literature, our music, and our current yearning for spiritual connection seem to recall a shadowy past when the intuition that All was One played a much more powerful role in human life.

What we do know about the spiritual lives of ancient peoples teaches us that ancient spiritual wisdom frequently involved a sense of the individual's connection to the totality of Being. Whether that was expressed in the Hindu notion that "atman is brahman" (the individual soul and the universal soul are one) or in the language that each individual is "created in the image of God," the intrinsic connection to the Unity of All Being was a central part of ancient spirituality. With that spiritual wisdom came an equally powerful sense of connection among human beings, a sense of solidarity and shared common purpose.

I do not want to suggest that the meaning of this ancient experience is what I want to return to by renewing our spiritual traditions. The meaning of this oneness, and how it is experienced, is significantly different in those who have gone through other stages in the development of human consciousness. The lionizing of indigenous societies seems off base to me for this reason: there are many elements in the consciousness of earlier societies that need to be incorporated and transcended, not romanticized as the goal of spiritual development.

Nevertheless, these earlier moments, memorialized in the literature, folk legends, and cultural legacies of many ancient peoples, help us understand why the emergence of class societies was such a shock, and why many religious and spiritual traditions had immense credibility in part because they managed to perpetuate some of that earlier sense of unity and connectedness whose absence in the daily life of class societies was painful and traumatic.

One of the interesting facts of human history is that when people conquer or oppress other human beings, they often feel a strong need for some kind of ideological framework to tell them that these others are really Other, that is, not really "like us," not really human at all, something else, something lower, something that somehow requires oppression. This kind of self-deception is necessary because of the almost instinctive awareness each of us has of our deep ties to all other beings, an awareness that has been increasingly repressed over the past four thousand years and needs to be repressed in order for people to function in societies that do not treat everyone with equal respect.

But once this domination started to happen, spiritual traditions were altered and warped. Instead of the spontaneously joyful celebration of the universe and of each other, organized elites began to shape spiritual life into forms that justified or even supported class domination. Over the course of a few thousand years, religious communities lost much of their original spiritual foundation.

This couldn't happen overnight. People's strong spiritual intuitions sustained a deep understanding of the value of every other human being and of the preciousness of the earth. The very idea of "owning" the earth violated the sacred traditions and memories of this earlier spirituality.

So religions were developed that preserved the consciousness of awe and wonder at the glory of the universe. They thus sustained the feelings of unity and connectedness that have given the world its beauty and enchantment for most humans. In their stories and in their rituals, religious and spiritual traditions taught people about solidarity and caring, about hope and joy, about the obligations to community and the need to find one's own path.

Yet at the same time, the religions that emerged in the three thousand years between 2000 B.C.E. and 1000 C.E. were shaped to meet the needs of the ruling elites of the society. The more they fit those needs, the more they were forced to forget or marginalize aspects of the original spiritual insights. So religious traditions became increasingly ritualistic and spiritually lifeless. To accommodate themselves to the established order they focused more and more on demands the gods made on human beings.

The same religion that could encourage and permit people to dance the joy of being alive and conscious, and incorporate the erotic energies affirming life, joy, and pleasure, could simultaneously tell people that their rulers were given sanction by the gods to run the world and to appropriate a portion of the food each family labored to create.

Similarly, within families and throughout the society, these religious systems were used to justify patriarchal rule and the subordination of women to men.

While some religious traditions sustained the memory of earlier moments in which women had equal power, and celebrated the power of female gods, most soon succumbed to the growing patriarchal order, its class domination, its justifications for unequal power, and the infliction of pain on the majority by the privileged.

Religious ideologies began to speak of pain and cruelty as endemic to the very nature of creation, embedded in the gods and in the nature of human beings. Cruelty, in short, was presented as an inevitable part of "reality."

Having begun to codify the spiritual experience of the community, religious traditions were soon shaped by a specialized class of priests and religious leaders with interests of their own, often intimately connected with the interests of the society's ruling elites. The social world and its class realities were presented as part of the natural world, unchangeable, fixed, and God-given.

People in the ancient world already knew that there was something deeply distorted in the religious traditions being imposed upon them by their own elites. So it's important not to romanticize ancient or even indigenous religious or spiritual traditions—because many of them were already quite distorted by the time they were taking concrete form some four thousand years ago. It's popular today to blame Western influences for undermining indigenous cultures, but many of these cultures had already distorted themselves by accommodating to a world of pain and cruelty and the demeaning of the other.

No wonder, then, that some people were drawn to religious renewal movements that sought to get people back in touch with the original, and sometimes quite revolutionary, consciousness that had formed the spiritual basis for the religion.

Judaism, for example, came into the world to protest the tight alignment of spirituality with oppression in the religious life of both Egypt and Babylonia/Assyria/Persia—and to testify to a very different conception of the spiritual than the one that prevailed among ancient imperial societies. On the basis of the slave rebellion recounted in Exodus, Judaism explicitly called for a redistribution of wealth and for a spiritual order that would restore the fundamental justice, equality, and dignity of each individual.

Equally important, Judaism proclaimed that "cruelty is not destiny," that the world could be radically transformed, and that what makes that possible is YHVH—the four letters that stand for the Divine as the Force of Healing and Transformation of the universe. Nothing in the world was fixed, because the fundamental creative force in the universe, the Creator of the universe, was the YHVH Force that guaranteed that the world could be transformed from oppression and cruelty to a world based on love and caring.

Yet the people who received this message and brought forward the religion of the oppressed were deeply scarred themselves by all they had undergone in the world of oppression. The history of the Jewish people became a history of asserting this transcendent message inscribed in its holy book, the Torah, and then of running away from that message and reverting to the very same patterns and systems of thought the Torah had originally been created to resist.

At times the people who proclaimed a renewal of the basic spirituality of the universe found themselves acting just like the pharaohs who had oppressed them. At times they abandoned the radical spiritual message: celebration of the Spirit must not be connected with any form of domination or oppression, but should instead be a way to reinscribe awe, wonder, and radical amazement at the center of our lives and at the core of how we build social and economic practices. Jews were supposed to be witnesses to the possibility of social healing and transformation. But frequently they abandoned this task and tried to become "ordinary people" like everyone else, making accommodations to the world of oppression and even incorporating some of its norms into their own religious lives. Even in the Torah itself there are times when the original transformative vision gets obscured and people begin to hear the voice of God speaking in a language that seems more consonant with the established wisdom of an oppressive class society than with the fiery presence of the transcendent good-ness of the universe.

The contradiction was so overwhelming that many Jews them-selves saw it, and a movement of resistors and renewalists, called *nevi'im*, or Prophets, emerged to get this renewal religion back on track.

The Prophets were met with hostility, anger, and sometimes overt violence. Yet the initial impulse to Judaism was so strong that in subsequent generations the Prophets were honored and their messages read aloud and sometimes taken to heart. Jewish history has been replete with renewal movements, including Hasidim in the eighteenth century and Reform Judaism in the nineteenth century. In our own time, I've been involved with a vibrant Jewish Renewal movement that seeks to restore the powerful and deep path of Jewish spirituality as it becomes an embodiment of this prophetic energy.

A similar story can be told about Christianity. It emerged in part as a renewal movement within Judaism, but its largest impact came from taking the Jewish renewal message and attempting to bring it to the rest of the world.

Christianity originally challenged the system of Roman power. The Roman legions had enslaved much of the known world, and their power seemed invincible. Yet Christianity identified with the slaves, with those who had been subjected to torture and crucifixion. Our God, the Christians proclaimed, had become incarnate in a human being, a Jew, who died on the cross, and transcended all that pain through resurrection to a higher realm. The real power, then, was not in the hands of those who defiled the earth with their instruments of oppression, but rather with human beings who stayed faithful to a higher spiritual truth.

Christian spirituality was a renewal of the original spiritual vision of human beings as connected to each other through love, and as loved by the universe—in short, a return to the deepest spiritual aspi-rations of the human race, which had originally been articulated in the Jewish Torah. No wonder it spread like wildfire, winning to its midst those whose experience with religion lacked this sense of outrage at injustice and hope for a world more consistent with our fundamental spiritual being.

Yet within a few hundred years, Christianity had developed its own set of priests and elites, who defanged and declawed its original revolutionary message and reshaped it to justify cruelty and inequality. But even as Christianity served to consolidate and justify oppressive regimes and humanly demeaning policies, its theology kept a transcendent vision alive and sustained hopes that stood in sharp contrast to its own social realities. Christian traditions like Quakerism and Catholic Liberation Theology have sought to keep this consciousness alive for centuries.

This same story could be told about most of the major religious and spiritual traditions of the past few thousand years, as unique as each of these traditions is. On the one hand, these spiritual traditions maintained the deepest and most liberating aspirations of the human race. Frequently they were a society's most consistent repository of hope for justice, love, and human connection. But at the same time they were guilty of some of the worst forms of oppression, and acted as cheerleaders for the oppressors.

Empiricism and the Rebellion against Distorted Spirituality

It's no wonder, then, that by the late Middle Ages many people had become deeply cynical about the religious traditions that flourished throughout the world.

Ruling elites used religion and spirituality to justify horrible crimes. It was in the name of the Christian religious tradition that native peoples around the world faced murder and sometimes extinction, that millions of women were burned as witches, and that Jews were expelled from country after country and subjected to periodic assaults, rapes, and murder. Though it's popular today to stigmatize Western religious traditions as particularly venal, the reality is that Eastern religions often played a similar if less extreme role in the inner lives of their own societies.

Such realities foster cynicism. It was clear to many that despite all the religious rhetoric, the people who used the mantle of religion were doing so for their own narrow and selfish purposes. Over the course of a thousand years, more and more people began to see this selfishness as the underlying reality of religious institutions.

The anger that many people developed toward their own religious traditions was, ironically, based on the deep spiritual insights that they had learned from these very religions: the Unity of All Being, the sacredness of all creation, the obligation to be stewards of the earth, the intuition that justice and love, sharing and nonviolence should be the basis of religious practice. Religion was the only voice in public discourse that acknowledged these spiritual insights, so when religious institutions stopped paying attention to these ideas, or used these words as a cover to justify a social reality that contradicted the religious message, many people became cynical about the very ideas of the sacred, of holiness, of soul, and of Spirit. Existing religions frequently were the farthest thing from embodying the spirituality that had originally engendered them.

It's important to note that this disillusionment began to fester as soon as religions began to function as handmaidens to power, and that the explosion of anger at religion and cynicism about Spirit in the sixteenth, seventeenth, and eighteenth centuries was the culmination of a process that had its roots in the *formation of class societies four to five thousand years before.*

To make a class system work, even in the miniclass systems of the city-states, people had to learn to think of other people as not fully entitled to love and respect. In much the same way, class societies transformed our relationship to the earth. Instead of seeing ourselves as living in harmony with the earth, we began to believe we had the right to conquer it and use it for our own needs without regard to the needs of other life forms.

In this context, spirituality was necessarily a protest against class societies. But tragically, class structure was quickly able to dominate the spiritual life of the community and make it an adjunct to class rule rather than its enemy.

This process was gradual, and it was frequently resisted, but over the course of some two to three thousand years, a distorted religious reality lost touch with the original impulses of spirituality.

Inevitably, this kind of spiritual distortion starts to produce cynical people. And cynical people fit well into despiritualized religion. Indeed, some of the most cynical became leaders of religious communities, manipulating the language of religion and spirituality until even they found it hard to distinguish between what God wanted and what made them feel good at the moment. It's hard to convince merchants and traders not to put their own interests above the needs of their community when they see this kind of behavior even from religious leaders.

In the emerging towns and cities of the fourteenth to eighteenth centuries, spiritual light was beginning to dim. Anger at the contradictions and hypocrisy of the religious establishment began to surge. If holiness was about burning the heretics at the stake and crusades were about killing anyone of a different faith, if religions lavished wealth upon the few who seemed oblivious to the fate of the poor, then, many people concluded, the spiritual must either be a delusion or at least something best kept out of the public sphere and away from political power.

The articulators of this disillusionment were supported particularly by a group of traders, bankers, and small artisans. Because people involved in these activities sought opportunities to sell their wares and "do business," they came into conflict with Church laws. Based in part on Biblical constraints on selfishness, the Church had instituted a set of laws that called for a "fair price" for goods and a "fair wage" for working people. Buying and selling were prohibited on Church holidays, which often numbered as many as a hundred days a year in addition to Sundays, when all work was forbidden. Numerous other "constraints on trade" flowed from principles of Biblical justice that put dampers on the merchants' strivings for unlimited wealth.

As more merchants, artisans, traders, bankers, and small-time manufacturers began to see their common interests, they became a new class. They talked about their shared interests in terms of "freedom," which in this case meant freedom from any constraint by the Church or by the secular feudal authorities. This talk about "freedom" had immense appeal to ordinary people who were looking for some way out of the oppression of feudal society.

So the merchants became the vanguard in the struggle against institutionalized spirituality and the often oppressive demands of the feudal community. This was a gradual process. At first, the merchants sought to create space for their economic freedom within the religious paradigm. They were among the earliest converts to Protestantism, because within Protestantism, the many different denominations allowed greater freedom of expression and freedom to differ from whatever the Church, the religious community, or the political community was telling people was the official line. Most important, Protestantism encouraged the merchant class and released them from the constraints of Church law, with its demand for "fair price" and "fair wages" for employees.

Within these spiritual communities of protest, the activities of merchants and bankers were given much greater latitude. Freedom to dissent and to have one's own opinion were no longer seen as threatening to the community and to the spiritual domain. And yet, most of these protesting communities became just as oppressive. Before long the Protestants themselves were burning witches at the stake, and the people who had sought religious tolerance and freedom were becoming intolerant toward others.

Many people began to feel that the only way they could have the freedom to make their own choices was to eliminate any spiritual demands whatsoever. I can't say I blame them. Living at a time when all forms of oppression were justified by existing religious orders, these people felt that the only way they could be true to their own deepest selves was to break free. Rather than argue that the realm of spirit was being misused, increasing numbers of people began to challenge the whole way of thinking that the dominant forces of the old order were using to justify their increasingly tenuous hold on power.

The merchants, bankers, and their allies had reached a point where they could offer people something the old spiritual order could not: tangible material goods. "Taste the food, smell the perfume, see the gold, touch the products—all of these things that we can bring you are real. Seeing is believing. The spiritual people can't offer you that. If you can't see it, or hear it, or discern it through any of your five senses, then it's 'non-sense.'"

A whole new theory of knowledge emerged. Forget about your intuitions and the experience of your heart. Knowledge is science. That's all.

This way of looking at the world is based on a narrow empiricism. It claims that things are only "real" if they can be objectively verified by our senses and confirmed by others who experience something similar under similar circumstances. Anything that does not conform to this picture is understood as literally *non-sense*. If a statement cannot be either verified or falsified by some conceivable set of observations, it is dismissed as meaningless.

What a powerful club to use against the old order and its religious and spiritual props! Instead of having to say, "I am not sure you are using your spiritual insights in the right way," the rising class could say: "It's not that your spiritual interpretation is mistaken, it's that spirituality itself is a false premise. You've based your whole system on something you can't even prove exists. We have seen how the wars between religious communities have caused so much pain and hurt in the past. Now it's time to boot all the religious communities and all religious and spiritual language out of the public discourse. It can't be proven, and it's never produced anything but bad feelings, antagonisms, and irrational hatred. Let us, instead, have our public life governed by the scientific worldview. Using that criterion, we can easily see that spirituality may deserve a private sphere. It may even be protected there as long you stay clear of the public sphere and don't try to win others to your religious or spiritual perspective."

Moreover, compared with many religious traditions that had sacred texts that could only be interpreted by priests or sanctioned religious leaders, the claims of this scientific worldview seemed truly democratic: everyone could have access to scientific claims; they rest on sense observations anyone can have.

In retrospect, it's easy for us to construct a counter-argument in support of the spiritual order. It *too* is equally accessible to anyone who opens his or her heart to the glory and wonder of creation. But this kind of argument couldn't be made at the time. The official spokesmen and defenders of the spiritual order were committed to a hierarchical order in which only they had access to spirituality, or, in the Protestant world, only those who shared a certain set of beliefs about God were able to access "Him." *No wonder, then, that the baby was thrown out with the bathwater. The bath attendant insisted that the two were really one and the same.*

We Lost Too Much When We Lost Spirit

I feel certain that if I were faced with the narrow choices available to people in repressive religious communities, I too would have wanted out. Who can blame someone who feels a deep emotional revulsion upon seeing a community use the language of Spirit, God, love, or community to force all people into a narrow mold and repress their ability to think for themselves? In these situations, what people are rejecting is not a true *spiritual order*, but I can't blame them if they can't hear that at a point in their lives when they are first finding their way to their own voice and their own experience.

It's important to acknowledge how exhilarating it was for human beings to free themselves from the shackles of a spirituality gone awry. In fact, I believe that Spirit was moving through those who denied the existence of Spirit, and that the revolution that they created was a powerful advance in human life. Or, as Ken Wilber teaches, the Enlightenment, with all its limitations, was itself a stage in the development of Spirit, and one that was absolutely indispensable for being able to reach a higher level of spiritual consciousness.

But there are also significant costs to the way the human race moved beyond the forms of spirituality that had been available under feudalism. Instead of incorporating and transcending spirituality, the empirically verifiable knowledge developed in opposition to feudal oppression was morally challenged. In overthrowing the spirituality of the past, the advocates of a new scientific empiricism insisted that the very terms of ethics could only be subjective, and perhaps not much more than expressions of personal emotions. "It's good to be honest, caring, and respectful" really didn't mean much more than "I personally like honesty, caring, and respect, though I don't have any right, of course, to tell you what *you* ought to like."

Governing the process was a metaprinciple of tolerance. People were free to have any moral or ethical judgment they wished, just as they were free to choose any ice cream they wished or to root for any football team, as long as they were tolerant of other people's right to make their own choices.

For the newly emerging class of merchants, bankers, manufacturers, and others, this approach made perfect sense. It mirrored the economic marketplace that had become the dominant force of the nineteenth and early decades of the twentieth centuries. The market offers a wide variety of options for individual consumers. Those consumers are free to choose whichever products please them. Manufacturers are free to market these products and consumers are free to purchase them or not.

If, for example, you can find a market for tobacco filled with nicotine, nobody has the right to tell you that you are doing the wrong thing. If it causes cancer, well, some people choose to take that risk.

It's only been in the last few years that this kind of thinking has been combated by some lawsuits against the cancer merchants, and even so, the cancer-causing products are still marketed to tens of millions of people. People get to make their own choices, freedom to consume becomes the highest shared value, and people are free to do whatever they want within the boundaries of their incomes. The consequences for society, however, have not always been so great.

Knowledge and Human Interest

The theoretical foundation of scientific knowledge is not any sturdier than the foundation of ethical and spiritual knowledge, which often gets dismissed as "merely subjective."

True, the empirical method "works" in the sense that it has given us information that has enabled the human race to dominate and control its environment, making it predictable, making it safe.

Yet, in recent decades, a growing number of people have challenged the alleged objectivity of scientific knowledge.

Science, these critics argue, often constructs as much as it describes, shaping a reality to fit its categories. There are no such things as "facts," but only perspectives on reality. We approach the world with particular tools, and what we discover is what those tools allow us to discover.

In my view, this critique has its limits. After all, if science is limited by the perspective of those who practice it, then a critique of this scientific perspective is similarly limited—it's just another perspective, and it may not be valid for those who don't share the perspective. That's the thing about relativism—it always undermines its own claims.

Nonetheless, the critique of science has an important element of truth: it requires us to historicize "the facts," to understand that when we approach reality we usually do so from the standpoint of some interest that we have, something we are trying to understand about reality or something we want out of reality. The tools we bring to the task are the ones that are relevant to this preexisting interest.

In *Knowledge and Human Interests*, the German philosopher Jurgen Habermas argued that different forms of knowledge develop when we try to dominate or control nature than, for example, when we try to build effective communication between people seeking to live together in peace. The criteria for what counts as knowledge in the sphere of science turn out to be quite different from what counts as knowledge in the sphere of building communicative competence between human beings.

This is not a matter of denying the legitimacy of science, but rather of acknowledging that science enables us to acquire a specific form of knowledge within the context of a certain set of legitimate human interests. For example, building an effective plow or a bridge that won't collapse are perfectly legitimate human interests. But it takes a different kind of knowledge to determine whether or not to trust a potential business partner or to develop a shared commitment to a community's goals.

Throughout most of recorded history, humans have not sought solely to dominate or control nature. We have also sought to respond to the world with awe, wonder, and radical amazement at the grandeur and mystery of Creation. It is this interest, an interest in awe and wonder, that has generated a different form of knowledge: spiritual knowledge.

In developing spiritual knowledge, human beings have paid attention to spiritual intuitions and insights, some of which have come from inside and some of which have seemed to come from God, nature, or some other transcendent source.

When cynics respond by calling these claims delusional, what they usually mean is that these kinds of claims cannot be verified through scientific criteria. But here the cynic is making a "category mistake." The claims of one form of knowledge cannot legitimately be used to refute the claims of another.

Ten million people might agree that the waterfalls at Yosemite National Park are "beautiful" or that "Adolf Hitler was an evil man," but neither of these claims can be verified by science. They belong to a different kind of knowledge. It's a category mistake to invoke the criteria from one realm to another realm in which they could not possibly apply.

Science without Ethical or Spiritual Vision: Scientism

When scientific thinking moves beyond the sphere of scientific discovery and becomes integrated into the way we think about the rest of our daily lives (including how to best use what we've discovered through science), we get a new class of scientists, engineers, and cyberspace experts who can produce almost any product but who rarely have the conceptual tools to deal with questions like "How does this product serve the common good?" or "What will the consequences be for others if I develop the products or techniques or methodologies I'm being paid to develop?"

The divorce of scientific knowledge, and eventually of all forms of contemporary knowledge, from an ethical and spiritual foundation made it possible for some of the most incredibly brilliant people to serve very evil ends. In the twentieth century, it became commonplace to discuss the ways that German scientists and engineers contributed their talents to the "efficient" extermination of the Jews. At every level, from those who drove the trains to those who developed the gases for the concentration camps, it rarely occurred to the practitioners of contemporary forms of rationality to ask whether their "efficiency" was ethically appropriate.

The division of science, technology, indeed of "rationality and efficiency" from any substantive ethical position made it seem inappropriate, even unprofessional, for people to be asking these kinds of questions. The same goes for those who engaged in developing weapons of mass destruction or lesser weapons that were used to kill and maim hundreds of thousands of civilians in struggles throughout the world. In fact, the question really had no "appropriate" place in public discourse, since ethics itself was considered merely a matter of personal subjective emotions.

We face the same problem in the twenty-first century on a global scale. The economic marketplace offers us endless opportunities to consume, but little opportunity to understand the ethical, spiritual, or ecological consequences of our consumption.

But there are consequences. If we consume product X made up of raw material Y, we may find that in thirty to forty years the earth will have no more of Y, and an entire ecosystem, or even the entire climate of the planet may be dramatically changed.

But even if we did know that a particular set of corporations was, say, using up the world's energy resources at a pace that might lead to widespread scarcity and crisis in thirty to forty years, we would have no vehicle for raising this question in the public sphere. Science has no categories for verifying whether it is "good" or "bad" to exhaust a particular resource. So, we will be told, our concerns may be entirely legitimate as a personal matter, but we have no business bringing them into the public sphere, which should focus on less subjective issues.

The same has been said about our discussion of beauty, justice, and love. None of these are objective, so none of them really fit into the discourse of the public sphere.

This is what I mean by saying that the baby and the bathwater got thrown away together. A world that takes ethics and morality, spirituality, beauty, justice, and love and puts them all outside the public domain becomes a society that has lost its enchantment and become one-dimensional, in the wonderful phrase of Herbert Marcuse.

The cynic might say here, "Well, that's the breaks of living in a world based on rationality. It's still the best possible system with human nature the way it is."

But this turns out not to be true. We can do much better. We don't have to legitimate a system that destroys the life support system of the planet. We don't have to tolerate a system in which tens of millions of people die each year of malnutrition and hunger-related diseases, and in which one out of every three people lives in poverty (roughly two billion people). How rational is it to have a world that produces huge amounts of pain and suffering and that is destroying the possibility of survival for future generations?

So much for the cynic's implicit contention that scientism has produced the best of all possible worlds. But what about the contention that to accept the scientistic picture of reality is what rationality demands?

Well, that doesn't hold either.

The deep dark secret of the ideology of scientism is that it is all based on a very flimsy foundation: the assertion that statements about reality must be intersubjectively validatable through sense experience.

When you look at that worldview, you might ask the same question that it asks of every other assertion: what data *could* validate or verify its truth. It quickly becomes apparent that there is no such data, nor could there be. The criterion of truth being asserted by contemporary descendants of the empiricists turns out to be without foundation according to its own criterion of truth.

There is no verifiable data that can validate the statement that all truth must rest on verifiable data, just as there is none to validate the notion that ethical judgments should be held in a mutually tolerant way. In other words, scientism itself is another faith, its own foundation just as tenuous or just as solid as any other spiritual or religious tradition.

Don't Discard Science

People who have been victims of terrible mistreatment justified as the "inevitable product of the triumph of rationality" are delighted to discover that scientism itself can be challenged by its own criterion of truth. In the last century, science became so clearly a handmaiden of destructive forces that it lost some of its credibility, at least among those seeking a more ethically coherent world. Scientists worked feverishly to assist Hitler build his concentration camps and empower his armed forces. Other scientists have contributed to the technology that is rapidly destroying the life-support system of our planet.

In the contemporary world, a small elite of wealth and power has been able to harness science to its own narrow goals of domination and control, not only of the physical world but of human society as well. Using the prestige built up through centuries of admirable scientific and technological advance, this elite claims that the current way we organize our society—including the way we distribute wealth and power—and our current way of relating to the natural world are all consequences of science and scientific rationality.

Contemporary science has often been structured to ask the questions being financed by corporations and governments who often have their own selfish or venal agendas. Most corporations are not seeking to promote the accumulation of knowledge, but the accumulation of wealth, and government often seeks to fund the projects that will increase its own power or the wealth of its friends in corporations. These agendas then determine which particular scientific research gets funded.

In this world, the scientific enterprise is skewed to serve the most powerful.

That, of course, is precisely what happened to spirituality in the precapitalist period. Spiritual people need to have the same compassion for the scientists, engineers, and cyberexperts who have had their lives and intellectual interests dominated and distorted by the powerful. Just as we insist that the core spiritual understanding is valid even though it was appropriated to serve distorted purposes by ruling elites, so we must have compassion for science and see the validity of the enterprise even though it frequently serves distorted purposes in the contemporary world. Science needs to be freed from corporate and governmental control and funded for its own sake, not for the sake of what established interests it can "efficiently" serve.

There has been a mistaken tendency among contemporary spiritual seekers to denigrate science. But this is a fundamental error. Science has a very powerful and important role to play in human affairs. Its methodology and its discoveries are appropriate for the questions it asks.

What is not appropriate is when science turns into scientism, empiricism, or some other "ism" whose goal is to claim exclusive power or exclusive right to define "knowledge." We need a sense of balance between the kinds of knowledge we can achieve through science and through other forms of knowledge. The task of a spiritually sensitive person is not to reject science, but to reject scientism.

Science has often reduced human suffering and toil. If its results are not used that way, the fault does not lie with science itself. *Science* is a form of knowledge, a way of approaching reality. But *scientism* is an ideology that claims there is only one way to approach reality—through the empirical method based on a narrow notion of what kind of experience is legitimate. Scientific descriptions of reality are not the same as scientistic assaults on other approaches to reality. Science should not be discredited just because it has been so widely and destructively misused.

On the contrary, the kind of spirituality that is emerging today can be an ally and champion of the scientific enterprise. It can recognize that true science often asks important and valuable questions of reality.

There are many scientists today who recognize that they need to validate the realm of the sacred. In an ingenious argument in his posthumously published *Ritual and Religion in the Making of Humanity*, anthropologist Roy A. Rappaport argues that understanding how the sacred is embodied in spiritually oriented rituals may be indispensable for the survival of the human race. "In a world where the processes governing its physical elements are in some degree unknown and in even larger degree unpredictable, empirical knowledge of such processes cannot replace respect for their more or less mysterious integrity, and it may be more adaptive—that is, adaptively true—to drape such processes in supernatural veils than to expose them to misunderstandings that may be encouraged by empirically accurate but incomplete naturalistic understanding."

In *The Return to Cosmology*, Stephen Toulmin suggests the need for a postmodern science that would reconnect with some of the elements that used to be called "natural religion." These were considered illegitimate in a post-Cartesian program that radically separated mind and body and saw the scientist as a detached observer. Contemporary thinkers recognize the impossibility of detached observation, because the observer always affects what is being observed. These thinkers recognize that living systems have subjective as well as objective characteristics and that studies of ecological systems are inevitably interventions into those systems. A postmodern science would recognize the validity of subjectively derived knowledge and would be guided by moral values as well as scientific methods. It would help us see the world as an integrated and ordered whole, concerned with the world's unity. As Rappaport summarizes, postmodern science would be an enterprise "in which both those who seek to discover natural law and those who seek to understand the nature of meaning and its fabrication are reunited within a world which they do not merely observe, but in the creation of which they participate and which they strive to maintain." Or, in my language, postmodern science would embrace an overt commitment to Spirit.

Yet it's important for people to not feel that Spirit is "real" only if it can be validated by science. Science may have to do a lot of "catch up" before it can fully acknowledge the realm of Spirit, but those of us who seek a world that can contain and adequately express our spiritual being need not wait for the approval of scientists. Far more important that we respond to the inner truths of Spirit as they emerge through our own spiritual practice.

Globalization and the Web: The Latest Idols of the Marketplace

Don't expect people to be immediately open to the realm of Spirit just because they see that science is unable to really provide a firm foundation for building our world. When people leave the religion of science, it is often to worship at the altar of an only slightly different idol: the religion of globalized technology.

During the years surrounding the turn of the millennium, this new religion has been particularly successful in delivering its message: the miracles of technology, coupled with the collapse of the Soviet Union and the opening of the entire world to unimpeded capitalist penetration, have created a brave new world of international humanity joyously linked together through the World Wide Web. Our meaning and fulfillment will come through our Internet connections. In this new world, borders disappear, the nation-state comes to an end, and we are on the verge of a new epoch in human history. The

Internet seems to promise the ultimate expression of the miracles of science happily linked to an expansion of our material well-being. (Now we can buy things we never imagined before, and do so without ever leaving our homes.) How can we be unhappy with a science that can so easily fulfill our material needs?

Globalization is certainly a reality. Global capital crosses boundaries, taking little, if any, account of the economic sovereignty of the individual nation-states. As Israeli geographer David Newman points out, "The McDonaldization of the world's landscapes which allows my Bedouin neighbours in the Negev desert of Israel to order a take-away burger and fries and take it back to a shanty town encampment which is still fighting to get a paved road and piped water from the government, this is 'true' [sic] globalization of capital. So too is the sudden appearance of a North American out-of-town shopping plaza, including such corporate names as 'Toys R Us,' 'Office Depot,' and the 'Home Center' where, until just a year or so ago, camels continued to wander the desert surroundings. ("The Lines that Separate Us: Borders in a 'Borderless' World." TIKKUN, forthcoming.)

Globalization's cheerleaders note that the dissemination of information through cyberspace, e-mail, and other electronic media means has broken down the ability of governments to restrict information to their people. Instant information through the Internet and cable TV accelerates the process of turning the world into a "global village."

There's no question that world markets are expanding, just as they have been expanding for the past five hundred years. And there are few impediments to the rapid conquest of the globe by high-tech communications.

But no matter how much a small percentage of the world's population enjoys the Information Superhighway, the majority of the world's people continue to live in conditions of subsistence and poverty. There are hundreds of thousands of refugees worldwide who do not have jobs or any way to feed their families.

Nor has information ended ethnic oppression or the desire of the previously oppressed to have separate and independent national boundaries. Ethnic cleansers in Kosovo came from the highly "wired" and technologically sophisticated Serbian society. Israelis have the highest rate of cell phone usage in the world, but managed not to hear about the systematic torture of Palestinians or the outrageous behavior of West Bank settlers.

As David Newman points out, "a globalized world is not a multicultural world. It is one in which uniform standards are imposed by a small elite upon the rest, normally for their own economic benefit. It is a world where a relatively small number of powerful governments and corporate companies have succeeded in imposing a post-modern version of neo-colonialism, without the need for military intervention, on large parts of the globe who do not yet have access, and do not yet enjoy, the levels of technology which are being churned out by Microsoft on an almost daily basis. It is a world whose standards are being reduced to the plastic, lifeless, non-caring control of chips and satellites, while the human dimension and the rights of the individual are pushed aside. It is certainly not a world without borders, but one in which some borders have become more permeable and open to trans-boundary movement, while others have remained as closed and as sealed as ever before."

Globalization is not spurred by a new desire for global democracy and an understanding of our common human fate, nor by a desire to overcome millennia of demeaning "the other." Rather, it is fueled by the globalization of selfishness, the desire of major corporations to find new markets for their products and their information.

That does not mean that there are no positive aspects to globalization. There are. But as we will see in chapter four, unless the globalization of capital is balanced by the globalization of Spirit, the world may face irreparable environmental damage that could ultimately end life on this planet.

The globalization of information may increase democracy, but it may just as well increase the homogenization of world cultures in ways that reduce our lives together to shopping in a global strip mall on the Internet while we have almost no physical contact with human beings who are different from us. The chance encounters that we have with "the other," "the stranger," and those who share radically different perspectives when we enter public space can be dramatically reduced when we do all our shopping, information gathering, and possibly a major part of our work on-line. We may leave our homes for selected entertainments and vacations, but if an increasing amount of our work is done on-line, we may never encounter anyone whose ideas or presence might subvert the ideas we've been taught in our increasingly mechanized and standardized-for-the-objective-tests educational systems. And as the worldwide Net increases the speed at which we process information, more and more people become tied to demands for higher levels of productivity, the distinction between work time and home time diminishes, and people report that they have less free time today than they have ever had. And with increasing speed comes a decreasing ability to concentrate on any one thing for any length of time. Sustained thought becomes a strain; following an argument through from beginning to end seems pointless to people who are used to having answers pop up immediately on-line.

So before jumping to worship the salvation offered by the Net and by globalization, we might want to consider the ways these technologies, with real and important benefits, may have equally powerful downsides that increase the possibility of our being enslaved rather than liberated.

When you get right down to it, the religion of globalization and high-tech worship is just the latest embodiment of an older form of idolatry: the worship of things and the attempt to make the accumulation of material goods the standard for a good life.

Spiritual traditions have always posed a powerful critique of that vision, insisting that having more does not mean being more. Rather, those involved in the world of Spirit have a very different message: we already have enough, we can share what we have and we will be more fulfilled doing so than if we continue to accumulate more for ourselves without regard to the well being of others. The goal of contemporary life need not be to find new markets, but to discover new opportunities to rejoice in the grandeur of the universe and new moments to experience the love that surrounds us and give it back. Let's assess the networked society by that criterion: Has it increased our capacity for love and for awe?

The cynical voice inside us is likely to object: "People don't really want the spiritual goodies you are describing; what they really want is more material possessions and wealth. That's why people cheer on the globalization of capital and why they feel so much hope when they learn of technological advances. People will never change this world and make it more spiritual, because they want more material. So forget this pretty talk and get real."

Much of the rest of this book will answer this kind of criticism. I will show that people really would want a very different kind of world, only they don't believe that is possible. And that belief that a different world isn't possible is the central force binding us to a world that we don't really believe.

In the next chapter, I'll tell you why I've come to be much less convinced by the dominant and supposedly sophisticated cynicism that tells us that nothing fundamental is ever going to change. The short answer is this: Most people have deep spiritual needs, and those needs provide a foundation for a progressive transformation and healing of American society once they are connected with Emancipatory Spirituality.

two

LIVING IN A SPIRITUALLY DEADENED WORLD

Connecting to Spirit

We have a higher level of material consumption than ever in human history. People have more things than ever before. Life has increasingly become focused on the acquisition of these things. Selfishness and materialism are presented as the central cultural wisdom of Western society. Anyone who acts by other standards is seen as incredibly naive, even self-destructive.

People who have spent all day at work thinking in terms of the bottom line come home shaped by this experience and by this vision of "common sense." More and more they find themselves surrounded by others who, in the words of a common complaint, "only care about themselves and can't really be trusted at all." No wonder. For the most part, they've spent all day in a work world where the only thing that counts is "the bottom line," and those who succeed are those who are best at maximizing the bottom line of money and power.

Live in a world based on money and power and you soon find that all relationships get corroded. Nowhere is that crisis of spirit more manifest than in our loving relationships and friendships.

Few people sink to the depravity represented by the television spectacular "Who Wants to Marry a Multimillionaire?" but almost everyone is affected by the cynicism about love and commitment that abounds in a society in which money, power, and fame are seen as the only trustworthy reality, and love and caring are seen as romantic fantasies or New Age slogans.

No wonder, then, that today people feel they can depend less on friendships than they once could. When friendships are based on a market model, people give care and support to each other only if they can expect a good return on their investment. We've lost the sense of solidarity that as friends we'll care for each other even in moments when it's unlikely the favor will ever be returned (for example, when one party is sick or incapacitated).

Most intimate relationships take on this same marketplace quality. People shop for relationships on the Internet and the singles columns, and try one person after another to find the "right fit." The right fit, however, becomes the person who can best satisfy our own needs. Commitment increasingly becomes something like a rational assessment of who among the pool of people who may find us attractive will best satisfy our needs and take care of us. We've learned to be rational maximizers of self-interest, so these market calculations often dominate the way people treat each other in the world of dating. Yet the more self-interest becomes the bottom line in romantic commitments, the more people grow insecure about their marriages, never sure that at some point that their spouse won't find a better deal.

Hence a societal crisis in families. Family is the one institution that is still supposedly committed to caring for its members without regard to how well they do in the economic marketplace. No matter how far the family falls from this ideal in practice, it is still the only institution left that even bothers to articulate a value different from that of the competitive marketplace. No wonder, then, that people have become deeply distressed as they see their family lives weakening and families falling apart all around them.

No wonder many people seek a spiritual framework for their family lives that could be an alternative to the market calculations I've described. It is only in our spiritual heritage that we are guided to see human beings as embodiments of Spirit (in Biblical language: as created in the image of God) and to respond to them as such. We value them *not for what they can do for us, but for who they are as manifestations of Spirit.* When we look at another human being in this way, we see a creature who elicits awe and wonder, a living miracle just like ourselves. It's the absence of this consciousness in the marketplace of relationships that makes people feel so insecure and so much reduced to commodities.

No wonder people intuitively grasp that something major is missing in their lives. But without any framework to help them think this through, many people don't quite know how to identify what's missing. They will reach out to anything that offers some sense of meaning and connection to something beyond themselves and beyond the accumulation of money, success, security, and power.

People will identify wildly with a sports team, or become part of a nationalist or religious community, or proudly wear tee-shirts of a company they work for, a product they consume, or a cultural hero with whom they can identify. They will fill stadiums to dance together and listen to music; they will spend endless hours on a computer trying to find connection to others through web sites and chat rooms; they will identify themselves with political parties whose actual programs they have never heard or do not understand; they will animatedly discuss movies or television shows that seem to offer the possibility of linking to others; they will grab onto nationalist or religious chauvinist communities that promise some framework of meaning; and in a zillion other ways in daily life, they will reach out to construct some meaning that transcends the logic of the competitive marketplace.

I encountered this hunger for meaning in the occupational stress groups that my colleagues and I ran for thousands of middle-income working people over the past two decades through an organization called the Institute for Labor and Mental Health.

You might not think that spiritual needs are relevant to the world of work. But the thing people most frequently miss at work is the ability to connect their work to a higher purpose and to interact with others in a loving, caring way. I call these concerns spiritual or meaning needs. The deprivation of these needs produces what we call alienation at work and in society.

Trusting "Ordinary People"

It took me a long time to realize what an elitist set of ideas and perceptions I was given as I grew up in a middle-class family, ideas that were reinforced at the elite universities where I earned my PhDs. I learned to think of myself as somehow different from "ordinary people," as someone on a higher moral plane.

Most of the people I met in intellectual, academic, or liberal circles seemed to feel that religion and spirituality were for people who were culturally and intellectually retarded, for people who couldn't handle the world and hence "needed that sort of thing." The very idea of "needing" was seen as a sign of being weak, undeveloped, retarded, because, of course, people who are cool can stand alone without "need" of anything or anyone. It was these "ordinary people," I was taught, who were such jerks that they got duped by right-wing fascists; adopted racist, sexist, and homophobic ideologies; and clung to religion and spirituality because thinking in a clear and rational way was beyond their capacities and scared them too much.

It was with this elitist attitude that I first conceptualized my role as a psychologist when I began to do research on "working-class consciousness." I wanted to understand why working people were leaving their traditional roots in the liberal and progressive world and becoming more responsive to right-wing politics. I assumed that this could only be some form of pathology and I wanted to learn about it.

Imagine my surprise, then, when I discovered that "ordinary people" (the term itself now sounds elitist to me) were far more aware and complicated than most intellectuals had allowed themselves to notice. I had looked for pathology, but what I found instead was a deep and significant yearning for spiritual purpose in life. Working with middle-income people whose jobs were not high-paying or "fancy," I learned the following: Most people have a real need for meaning and purpose in their lives, a meaning and purpose that could transcend the selfishness and materialism of the competitive marketplace and root them in something with transcendent significance. That need is so great that people will seek to fulfill it in whatever way they can.

This astounded me because I had bought into the notion that "middle America" was governed by a narrow materialism. In fact, the leaders of the labor movement itself claimed that all "their" workers cared about was money—and that explained why workers only came to meetings during contract negotiations.

But what I discovered was something quite different, namely, that ordinary working people in America, the ones who went to the mall and who sat in front of their television sets, were just as concerned with meaning as anyone else, including any of us who consider ourselves intellectuals or agents of social change.

Connection to Spirit is as essential as oxygen. It's a basic need.

Yet, we have taught ourselves to see people as a bunch of isolated machines driven by the need for food, sex, and power. We have acted as though we could cut ourselves off from our Divine essence as manifestations of Spirit. We have built social and economic institutions and have raised children as though we did not know that we are part of the spiritual order of the universe and that our hunger for spiritual connection is every bit as urgent as our hunger for food.

My fellow psychotherapists and I set up the Institute for Labor and Mental Health to study the psychodynamics of American society. I learned in my work with middle-income Americans, people who used to be called "working class," that we cannot maintain our separation from Spirit, nor from each other as expressions of Spirit, without great pain. In fact, our separateness has always been an illusion, but we have learned to see ourselves as separate and that has shaped our experience of "reality." It's been a painful reality. Sometimes almost unbearably so.

Psychologist Abraham Maslow posited a "hierarchy of needs," suggesting that we must first satisfy our material needs and only then address our "higher" needs. While this account may apply to people who are literally starving, for most others it is deeply mistaken. Throughout history, human beings have frequently been willing to sacrifice material well-being for the sake of spiritual connection and ethical purpose. Rather than thinking of material needs as the foundation and the spiritual dimension as a kind of accessory, we should understand that spiritual needs are equally real and equally essential to our being.

What happens to people who live in a world in which Spirit is being denied?

The short answer: we end up living very distorted lives.

And this applies just the same to everyone, no matter how much money they have, no matter how much power. There really is no "they" and "we" in the realm of Spirit: "they" and "we" are one. What I knew about myself I learned to be true of many, many others in this society: although people certainly care about their economic well-being, it is not all they care about, and often it is not the central thing in their consciousness.

If working people fought for more money in the world of work, it was often because they had become cynical about securing workplaces in which they might find meaning and spiritual nourishment—not because they had no such need.

To be realistic, they had come to believe, they had to keep their hunger for meaning and spiritual fulfillment out of the public sphere.

So they went to church, even though there was no money to be gotten there, and did not go to union meetings (because there was no meaning to be found there except during negotiations when they could fight for more money). People used their unions to fight for more money not because money was all they wanted from life, but because it was the only winnable compensation they could get for a life they felt was being wasted all day in meaningless work.

No wonder, then, that many of these people responded to the Right. However irrational the Right's solutions might appear to be, it at least seemed to notice the problem of the decline in America's ethical and spiritual sensitivities. And no wonder they resented their own union leadership. Yes, they were happy the unions were there for them as insurance companies that put some constraints on arbitrary power from management at the workplace. But though most unionized workers were glad they had their unions, just as they were glad that they had auto insurance companies, they felt no closer to their union leadership than to their insurance brokers, and they were equally unlikely to reveal to either the deep concerns in their lives.

It never occurred to the liberals or progressives that people were responding to the Right at least in part because it was speaking to some real and legitimate human need that was excluded from the liberal and progressive agenda. When I personally tried to explain this to the national leaders of the AFL-CIO, I was told explicitly that these issues were of little interest. Yes, they might be willing to use spiritual language or music at a picket line or during a strike, but no, they would never actually talk about challenging the materialism and selfishness of the world of work. For union leadership, as for much of the liberal and progressive movements, the whole notion of "spiritual" is so deeply identified with right-wing ideology, New Age flakiness, and the memory of coercive religious communities that they have been unable to imagine themselves opening their movement to spiritual concerns and the radical challenge to contemporary economic and political arrangements that an Emancipatory Spirituality presents.

Yet my colleagues and I could not close our ears to what we were hearing; and what we were hearing made it clear that the reason why many Americans were not able to trust the progressive social change movements is that although they often found themselves agreeing with these movements on a variety of economic and political issues, they felt misunderstood and unseen by these liberals and progressives who dismissed spiritual issues as reactionary or who simply seemed tone deaf to the inner life.

Most of the people who attended the training courses we offered in how to deal with occupational stress were initially extremely uncomfortable discussing spiritual issues. It's easier to talk about sexual perversions or childhood abuse in contemporary America than to publicly discuss one's inner spiritual life. It took many weeks of creating safety for people before they would open up and discuss these issues on a deeper level.

Yet eventually an amazing thing began to happen in the occupational stress groups that my colleagues and I ran at the Institute for Labor and Mental Health: as people sat in the room with others and heard their stories, they could recognize that others shared the same spiritual hunger they feared to fully acknowledge.

The people who came to these groups were not from a milieu in which therapy or introspection was the "in" thing. Often, they came only after being assured that they could learn valuable communication skills and that by coming they were not identifying themselves as "sick" or "in need of professional help." They only felt comfortable sharing their stories in the most superficial ways possible until they began to understand that their personal pain was connected to the larger framework of the deprivation of meaning in our society.

I want to tell you some of their stories to show you how these issues play out in the daily life experience and lives of people who have little in common on the surface.

I've changed the names of group members, and in some cases I've changed the stories or added details to further hide people's identities, but I received their permission to tell you some of their stories because they are so illustrative of the ways that Spirit Matters in our daily lives.

Joan Sharpen

When Joan Sharpen began therapy with me in 1979, I had only been seeing clients for five years. I was still a little wet behind the ears. I was amazed at the disparity between the strength she projected to others and her inner sense of worthlessness.

Joan was a shop steward in her union local: her task was to represent her coworkers when they filed grievances against their supervisors. She worked in a large corporation in which she processed data on a high-power computer network. Some of her coworkers were responsible for interpreting this data and making it relevant to the sales staff.

Since I had been trained as a psychoanalytically oriented therapist (with all the latest refinements and modifications), I was inevitably drawn to looking at Joan's childhood. Not surprisingly, I discovered plenty of childhood sources for her low self-esteem. Her parents divorced when she was eight, and though they fought over custody arrangements, when Joan actually arrived at one or the other of their homes, she was often ignored or given very little real contact.

Outwardly, both parents proclaimed love and caring, but inwardly Joan reported feeling little real involvement from either parent. She perceived herself as an outsider whose presence was cherished more for the deprivation it caused the other parent than for any intrinsic value or worthiness in herself. Joan did her best to get her parents to recognize her for who she really was as a person, but they never seemed to notice Joan, only a "good daughter" who could reassure them that she wasn't too badly hurt by the divorce.

Joan excelled in school and in extracurricular activities. In high school she became a cheerleader and a member of the "popular crowd," but inwardly she felt lonely and unloved. By the time she was a high school junior, she was having sex (and imagining she was getting love in return) with some of the more popular boys on the high school sports teams, though she carefully nurtured a public appearance of sexual squeamishness and made sure not to date more than one boy from any given sports circle. Joan felt that she would only be recognized by others if she "put out" for them. She attended a state college and did reasonably well in mathematics and statistics, areas she believed would lead to a good job.

When she was first hired by the corporation in which she was working, she imagined that she might make it to the top. But after eight years of slow advance, she had resigned herself to a series of merit raises for the rest of her life—certainly not a meteoric rise to the top.

Joan told me she was depressed about her job situation and had little energy for the rest of her life. A psychiatrist at the company's "employee assistance program" had prescribed antidepressant medications, but these made no difference at all.

After seeing Joan privately for some time, I referred her to one of the "occupational stress and family support groups" I had created at the Occupational Stress Center.

These groups met once a week for two and a half hours. They were designed not for people in crisis, but for people who were dealing with ordinary levels of stress in their jobs or their family lives. We soon discovered that there was no way to separate the issues of work and family life: if we wanted to understand what was going on in personal life, we had to understand what was going on in the world of work as well. So we began to ask people about their experience at work.

No one had ever asked Joan much about the details of her work because no one much cared. For Joan and her colleagues—as for most working people—it was routine to boast that "I don't let it get to me" when they spoke of the demeaning and boring situations in which they worked. Joan was part of a high-tech firm that employed hundreds of engineers, scientists, and technicians. She was highly skilled herself and often came up with innovative insights based on the data she was analyzing. But her supervisors showed little appreciation for her work. Even ideas that Joan felt confident would have translated into higher profits for the company won her little more than a perfunctory nod. Her supervisors treated her as though they were doing her a huge favor to employ her in the first place and acted as though the workers in Joan's division deserved little respect. Though Joan knew she was smart and skilled, she felt unrecognized and unappreciated.

Eventually, Joan stopped applying herself at her job, since she saw little chance of actually using her intelligence in a creative way or in a way that would be of value to others. She doubted the social value of the consumer products her firm was producing. She knew intuitively that her work was meaninglessness to her and she doubted it was in the long-term best interests of the human race either.

A Hunger for Meaningful Work

Over the course of the next ten years, my colleagues and I interviewed and worked with thousands of working people from a wide variety of workplaces: From autoworkers, machinists, and Teamsters to computer technicians, engineers, nurses, secretaries, teachers, social workers, government employees, lawyers, doctors, TV cameramen, architects, scientists, flight attendants, military personnel, sales personnel in large and medium-size stores, and many unemployed people who had previously held skilled jobs.

We had not expected what we heard: that work was frustrating not just because workers felt powerless to control the agenda, but at some more basic level because work did not serve any higher social good. People wanted more than "making it" in "the rat race." Spiritual meaning, not money or power, was the thing they were missing—and they made no bones about how painful it felt to be "wasting our lives" for no purpose except "the almighty paycheck."

Louise Glenn

Louise Glenn was a doctor at a major health maintenance organization. She worked in the perfect profession for "making a difference," and indeed Louise could tell of many specific moments in which she had been able to see her work as "serving humanity" and, since she was religious, as "serving God."

Yet most of the time, Louise told us, she was serving the profit motives of a company that constantly looked over her shoulder for "the bottom line." Louise talked about the days before managed care had taken over, longingly recounting the times when she had been able to spend enough time with patients to find out what was happening in their lives.

Louise had been one of the doctors who had opposed national health insurance, fearful that it would limit her freedom. Now, she acknowledged, she wished she had been more open to those "radical ideas," because what happened subsequently had made things far worse than a national health-care program ever could.

She had imagined that governmental bureaucrats would restrict her freedom. But now she found her freedoms constrained by the private sector in ways that were far more severe. The insurance companies that governed medical "managed care" neither knew nor cared about her clients' needs.

Louise now found herself in situations where she knew that she was not serving the best interests of her patients. She didn't want to quit her job because she still felt she was doing some good. But she also did not want to feel that she was selling out the needs of her patients. Louise did everything she could not to let the financial interests of managed care affect her work, but she often felt that the pressure to see more clients in less time ensured that every act of healing and care she engaged in was significantly flawed.

Louise found herself spending an inordinate amount of time trying to convince HMO managers that she was not giving "too much treatment" and that she was not suggesting "too many collateral services" for her patients. Fellow doctors had already internalized the demands of management and were no longer conscientious about the ways they restricted themselves in their dealings with patients. For them, Louise reported, it had become "the way things are done here, a routinized and constricted way of delivering health care."

Those who remained aware of the distorting aspects of how the HMO prevented them from giving good medical care talked about finding another workplace, but they were aware that HMOs like theirs were becoming more and more prevalent. Their colleagues in private practice often complained bitterly that they faced these same dynamics in another form: private health insurance companies had begun to require that each medical procedure be given prior clearance by their own bureaucrats in order to be approved for insurance payments. "I wanted to make a meaningful contribution to society when I went into medicine," Louise told me, "but instead I think I'm finding that doctors are really indirect employees of large corporate conglomerates or insurance companies."

Louise was facing a deep spiritual crisis: a conflict between keeping her job and honoring her desire to have her work connect to a higher spiritual purpose.

Although few clients in our groups were surprised when they heard stories like this, it took them several weeks before they were ready to acknowledge that this was a spiritual crisis rather than simply "the way it is." Whether they came from the high-pressure workplaces of Silicon Valley, from San Francisco's financial district, or from factories building automobiles or creating cutting-edge fashion, everyone told of corporate structures in which decisions were made primarily on the basis of what might generate corporate profit. Ideas about how their capacities and skills might be used to solve societal problems were systematically discounted.

What *did* surprise most of the people from the corporate settings, however, was that they heard similar stories from professionals such as social workers, teachers, computer and electronic engineers, and scientists—people who seemed to have a great deal of self-determining power in their work. Yet even these professionals reported a growing regimentation and narrowing of freedom. Over and over again members of our occupational stress groups identified meaningless work as a central aspect of the stress in their lives.

Many acknowledged that they themselves hadn't known how upset they felt about the absence of spiritual purpose in their lives until they started to talk about it. But once they started, they could tell us in considerable detail that they had been feeling these things for a long time but had "tried not to think about it, because, hey, what's the point? Nothing's going to change, so what difference does it make if I feel this way?"

"Well, everyone bitches about work," some might say in response to all this. "People just don't like to work." Yet we found, quite to the contrary, that when people feel that their work is serving a socially valuable purpose, when they believe that the way they are doing things is the best way to do things, most of these people find their work exhilarating, no matter how hard it is.

It is when the work in question *fails* to serve a goal that we can believe in, or when it is obvious that the way things are being done is not the best or even the most rational way to do them, that we tend to seek personal compensations for the time we feel we are wasting, either in the form of getting out of doing things, higher pay, or less willingness to contribute our attention and brain power to the workplace.

Corporate administrators have sometimes tried to co-opt the hunger for meaning by offering management schemes aimed at increasing "participation," most of which are actually schemes to increase corporate control by providing the facade of listening to people.

Workers quickly see through this manipulative intent and show little interest in this kind of illusory participation. Meaning can't be supplied by corporate rah-rah, though some people will glom on to their corporation the way others glom onto their local athletic team as providing them with something beyond themselves to believe in. Yet ultimately all of these partial fulfillments don't satisfy.

The smartest contemporary advertisers speak to this lack of satisfaction in their ads, encouraging people to believe that if they would only consume some particular product, they would find the elusive meaning that is absent in so much of their lives. Ironically, the very people who are producing these pseudosatisfactions and market manipulations are themselves equally hungry for the meaning whose absence they cynically manipulate, but since they also believe that their hunger for meaning is unrealistic and impossible to satisfy, they feel they might as well participate to their own advantage in the cynical manipulation of meaning-oriented media images.

Self-Blaming

Let me return to Joan and her coworkers.

Joan understood that her frustration was widely shared by her coworkers. For that reason she had volunteered to be an (unpaid) shop steward for the union—the person who represented her coworkers when they brought grievances against management. Yet deep down Joan believed that she deserved the lack of respect she was getting from her supervisors. She would speak in detail about mistakes she had made that had kept her from being more successful in the world of work. She spoke of not being smart enough, of not having tried hard enough, of being ensnared by fantasies of having various men take care of her (which she quite smartly tied to her own lack of self-worth as a child), and of being someone destined to have a rather uneventful and useless life.

In the stress group, Joan's recognition of her tendency toward self-blaming broke an invisible wall. It soon became clear that every single member of that group (and of every group we ran) was nurturing a self-blaming story that helped him or her account for why work was so frustrating and pointless.

Most had bought into the meritocratic fantasy that in this society you could make it if you really tried. Hence, if they hadn't made it, hadn't found work that was fully satisfying, they had nobody to blame but themselves. It was a society based on merit, and their frustrating lives proved that they lacked merit.

Anger that might have been externalized as a source of struggle to change things was internalized as self-blame.

But there was a deeper despair that sustained their self-blaming. Many working people hold the pathogenic belief that everyone will always care only about themselves and will never be motivated by anything higher than self-interest. Though many personally experienced the world from the standpoint of awe and wonder, they felt embarrassed about this dimension of their lives. They looked forward to trips to the country, sometimes to visit a national park, or to hunt or fish, or to "vacation," not only because they didn't feel fulfilled in their work but also because in these country settings, or standing at the edge of the ocean, they could reconnect with their highest sense of the universe and their place within it and not fear that somehow they would be seen as crazy for having such "unproductive" and "useless" thoughts. Many people firmly believe that their own spiritual yearning for some higher meaning and purpose is a personal idiosyncrasy that makes them appear weird or crazy or at best wildly unrealistic and immature.

That's why it's hard to get people to talk about their spiritual yearnings. After her experience in the Occupational Stress Group, Joan began to talk about these issues with her coworkers. At first she was greeted with cynicism. But she persisted, and when she spoke to her coworkers privately, she learned that they were not cynical about the desire to have some spiritual purpose at work, but about the possibility of ever achieving that purpose in the world as they knew it. When Joan talked about the common good, her coworkers felt she was wasting their time, or even mocking their deepest but hidden selves—precisely because they felt so bad about living a life in which their work would never be about anything more than serving the interests of the powerful.

They dealt with this repressed desire for spiritual meaning by splitting it off from their public life—where they imagined they would only be humiliated and disappointed if they spoke about their hunger for meaning—and allowed it to resurface in private life. In private life, this hope for meaning could be channeled into a hope for a meaningful relationship that might compensate for the wasted hours of work, or a religious life that would provide the meaning they despaired of finding at work. But Joan's coworkers had repressed their awareness of this need so fiercely that it was only because of her years of building trust with them that they eventually opened up to her and went beyond talk of wanting more money to talk of wanting more meaning. A sociologist or pollster interviewing these workers would never have learned about this aspect of their being.

Deadening the Mind to Repress the Memory of Work

Frustrated from a day without spiritual connection or meaning, many people come home from work filled with unconscious rage, sometimes at the workplace but more often at themselves because they feel deep shame at doing work that feels alienating, frustrating, meaningless, and spiritually dead.

To cope with this shame and anger, people look for ways to forget what they've been going through all day. Very few people want to tell their spouse or their children what they've been feeling, not only because they imagine that no one would really want to hear it, but also because they feel so embarrassed at having to stay in a workplace that seems so distant from their own hopes about what their life might have been about.

A recent television ad for a Web-based worker-recruitment service taps into this feeling. It has a group of children talking about what they want to do when they grow up. Ironically, one after another talks about some kind of alienating and meaningless work. The viewer is supposed to recognize immediately that no child would ever have wanted the kind of work that most people face today, to recognize this in themselves, and then to sign on to the relevant web site to get more information about how to get different work.

But most people will not be able to get different work, or if they do, they'll find that the same spiritual vacuity prevails in their new workplaces as well. Knowing that, most people give up by the time they are in their mid-thirties.

To forget the spiritual vacuum they've faced all day, many seek mind-deadening mechanisms. The specific forms vary from individual to individual and from subculture to subculture, but all are designed to blot out the pain that is the inevitable consequence of living in a world that systematically denies our spiritual needs.

The more stressed they are by powerlessness and meaninglessness at work, the more likely people are to head straight for a drug, some alcohol, or the television. But healthy activities, too, can serve to repress the pain of working in situations where our desire for meaning is stifled. Sports, aerobics, politics, religion, and social life are all used to repress the memory of work without Spirit. Though these activities are perfectly wholesome in themselves, they are often used in a fre- netic, frantic, and "addictive" way to deaden the negative feelings we (inappropriately) direct at ourselves for not having more fulfilling lives.

The pervasive abuse of alcohol and drugs in our society is one indication of a major spiritual crisis. What we discovered in our stress groups was that the combination of a sense of meaninglessness at work and the self-blaming that occurs when people internalize meri- tocratic theories often produces an overwhelming desperation to escape with "substances."

The literature on drug abuse, alcohol, and mental health scarce- ly acknowledges the question of meaning, much less the problem of meaninglessness at work. Imagine for a moment what might have happened if someone had said, "Maybe there's some connection between what people experience all day at work and what they try to escape from when they go for drugs or alcohol?" The trouble is, that kind of question doesn't get asked. It's considered too subversive; it could lead to real change. So very little money is given to research it.

We hypothesized that if we could increase our clients' sense of meaningfulness or decrease their self-blame, we would see a decrease in alcohol and drug consumption. Since we did not have the power to increase meaningfulness, we could not test that part of the hypothesis. What we could do was to decrease self-blaming. To do this, we needed to provide a context—namely, our occupational stress groups—in which middle-income people could discuss these issues directly, learn about the ways they had nurtured self-blaming stories, find support for getting back in touch with their own spiritual insights and sensitivities, and engage in activities aimed at increasing their sense of power and efficacy in the world of work.

To accomplish this, however, we needed to challenge the ways most people in our groups had learned to think of themselves as isolated individuals. In short, we had to validate their spiritual and ethical desires, helping them to overcome their inclination to marginalize those desires or place them in a "private" or "religious" sphere that had nothing to do with their work or public lives. We had to encourage them to feel that they had a right to the meaning-centered lives they wished for but imagined were impossible.

And that's exactly what we did. We focused on spiritual empowerment, allowing people to reconnect with their deepest spiritual goals. We soon saw tremendous healing taking place in front of our own eyes. To test this out, we secured a National Institute for Mental Health (NIMH) grant to do "pre," "post," and "post-post" interviews, using "objective" measures. We found the following: There was a statistically significant decrease in the use of drugs and alcohol by people who went through these groups. Not only that, but our clients became increasingly adept at using existing social support systems to buffer the worst aspects of their stress. They showed an increase in their sense of personal efficacy, a decrease in physical and mental health problems; and a measurable increase in productivity at work (confirmed by informal interviews with the supervisors of group members).

Do you think these powerful results stirred a considerable amount of interest in the scientific community or the government? Not at all.

The strong correlations we demonstrated between the spiritual crisis in the society on the one hand, and the health, mental-health, alcoholism, and drug abuse problems on the other, were not something people in positions of authority wanted to know about. One official at the National Institute for Mental Health calmly explained to me that I was raising the kind of issue that not only would not be appreciated by higher-ups, but might actually lead to a reduction of funding for the entire NIMH. The scientific community had no categories with which to understand what we were talking about when we discussed a sense of meaninglessness at work—because what was "meaning" anyway? (I wrote my results up in my book, *Surplus Powerlessness: The Psychodynamics of Everyday Life and the Psychology of Individual and Social Transformation.*)

Today, millions of dollars are poured into research schemes designed to uncover what personal factors make people susceptible to drug or alcohol abuse. If we can pin our social problems on individual pathologies, chemical imbalances, genetic makeup, or other personal factors, then we can avoid questions about what we need to change in our economic or political life. Hence, a researcher trying to gain funds from a university or a governmental institution must show that she doesn't have any political, spiritual, or religious agenda (like being interested in promoting meaningful work). She is not going to raise questions that challenge the funders of her research, and she's not going to suggest that somehow there's something deeply wrong in our society.

There may be workplaces where some of these changes are happening or where a new opening is taking place toward spiritual life. But to the extent that it happens, it is often of a very narrow sort of spiritual openness that directs our attention away from social transformation or changing the way we work, the products we produce, the way our products either support or undermine ecological sustainability, to developing a spirituality that is entirely internal and personal. We may be encouraged to meditate or to do yoga or even to pray. These practices, healing as they are, will not fill the vacuum of meaning in our souls unless they are part of a larger effort that changes our relationships with one another and the world—and changes the "bottom line" of the world of work. Meditating for fifteen minutes will not offset forty hours spent manipulating others for self-advancement or company profit any more than it will offset the devastating psychic impact of knowing you are producing goods that are using up the world's precious resources, destroying the environment, or encouraging people to be profligate shoppers and mindless materialists. What we discovered in our work with thousands of "ordinary" Americans was that *spiritual healing must address the spiritual healing of the entire society, not just the internal lives of isolated individuals.*

Yet even on the personal level, some change and healing is possible. Joan Sharpen finally got up the courage to share her feelings about Spirit with some of her fellow shop stewards. To her surprise, after an initial skepticism, they responded with interest and respect. Gradually, she became an influential advocate for a spiritual awareness as part of union life.

Louise, too, benefited from these discussions. Once she started talking openly about the problems in the medical profession, some of her coworkers responded, and within a few months they had put together a group of health professionals concerned with the same issue. Although they started with discussions of health-care reform (because it seemed more "concrete" to them than just discussing spiritual transformation), eventually they began to follow the direction outlined in chapter six and moved into the realm of fantasizing about what a healthy system could be like. Some of the suggestions that came out of that group appear in chapter seven.

The very ability to name the problem (the ethos of materialism and selfishness as manifested in corporate globalization) and to name the solution (a new bottom line of love and caring) was so empowering for Joan and Louise that it made it possible for both of them to become more confident in their personal lives as well as effective agents of social change at work.

The Narcissistic Personality
and the Psychodynamics of Selfishness

Let me tell you about Shawn Sanders, a young man who had "made it" in the corporate world by the time he was thirty-six. When I first began to see him in individual psychotherapy, Shawn had just broken up with his wife of three years. In fact, this marriage was the fourth significant relationship he had had, each one lasting approximately the same amount of time.

Shawn was a charmer. He had worked his way to the top of a small corporation, then moved into a senior position in one of America's Fortune 500 companies. He had been careful to make time for his personal needs. Since taking his current job as a senior vice president, he assured me, he had been working out every day at the corporate athletic facilities, and then coming home before 7:00 PM, so he could spend the evening with his wife, an attorney at an important law firm.

Shawn was bursting with self-confidence about the importance of his work. Every day, he told me, millions of Americans used and depended on the product his firm produced. Not only that, but they were using his firm's product and not that of the competition because of his sage marketing ideas.

Shawn's former wife, Allison, had respected his accomplishments, just as he had respected her powerful position at a major corporate law firm. Moreover, she was beautiful, and she knew he thought so. He had loved to go out with her, to show her off to his friends and bring her to corporate parties and gatherings.

Allison had complained that Shawn had never really shown her much caring. True, he was proud of her. But what he was proud of, she told him once, was her accomplishments at work. She felt that he never really asked much about the details of her work (which, he explained to me, was "just corporate stuff—boring to me and, I thought, boring to her too"). Nor, she complained, did he ask much about her feelings or seem to care about what upset or moved her. Shawn told me that when she had said things like this, he had immediately moved into his problem-solving mode, trying to figure out what he could do to get her out of those moods that he described as "depressed and depressing." Shawn came up with all kinds of strategies. He would arrange for fancy vacations to Caribbean or Hawaiian island resorts. "We even went to Russia once," he told me, "because we wanted to experience the excitement of a market society being built on the ruins of socialism. We had a great time, buying all kinds of things dirt cheap, making a few investments, and bringing home some dynamite art."

When not vacationing, Shawn and Allison would often spend their weekends buying things. They bought antique furniture, they bought "the very best food available anywhere in the world," and they often took trips to the country, looking for the perfect weekend country home.

Shawn was amazed that Allison had complaints—their life together was so full of activity, socializing, and planning. He simply could not understand why Allison was unhappy with him, or what he was doing wrong. But he had decided he needed therapy, because every one of his relationships had ended in the same way—with the woman leaving him because he was, as one former lover put it, "too self-absorbed."

"I'm so successful at work," Shawn complained, "I don't know why women don't stay with me. The amazing thing is, I can go after and win almost anyone—once I even won a woman who was already married. But what I can't seem to do is make them stick with me. And that's so unlike me. At work, I never lose a client. I always figure out what they want, and give them something close enough so they want to stay with me."

For Shawn and for many people in the corporate or professional worlds, the problem of meaning arises in a different way than it does for Joan Sharpen and her coworkers. Increasingly, corporate and professional people find that success in the world of work requires that they develop personalities geared to selling themselves and selling their products: they must manipulate the consciousness of others and make themselves into commodities for sale. Shawn was a genius at this, and it was this talent at figuring out what people wanted and then giving them something "close enough" to which Shawn attributed his rapid rise.

The dynamics of the competitive market reward those who are best at getting others to want what they have to sell. Increased productivity is perceived as coming not only from the production of more goods but from the involvement and manipulation of people's attitudes. Hence, people in the corporate world are increasingly required to develop personalities that fit the latest management fad or the latest theory of what it takes to be a success.

Outside the corporate world stand an array of professionals who market themselves directly to the public: the lawyers, psychotherapists, doctors, dentists, accountants, architects, writers, and soothsayers, all of whom must win their clients' personal trust before they can sell their services. Selling their personality becomes increasingly important.

Shawn's success was partly a product of having a "naturally likable personality." But he had also done a lot to cultivate his style so that it would be effective in the corporate world. Like tens of thousands of others, he had enrolled in endless classes, growth groups, seminars, and other activities aimed at shaping himself into a person who could get others to want what he wanted, to want to be with him, and to want to buy whatever he sold. By the time he was twenty-seven, Shawn told me in an offhand boast, he was "the smartest manipulator in the whole company."

The people who are most effective and successful at manipulating others become the corporate leaders and seers; the rest of the corporate world honors them with high pay and accolades. Over the course of the past half-century, the Western world has seen a dramatic increase in the number of people like Shawn. Typically, they are self-absorbed, manipulative, "charming," clever, persuasive, and domineering—we call this condition narcissism.

In its extreme form, narcissism becomes a character disorder that appears in psychotherapy practices and hospital wards. But most narcissism is "garden variety" and shows up not in psychotherapy clinics but in boardrooms and professional offices, and again in the bedrooms of so many "successful" people. Narcissistic qualities are widespread and well rewarded in the contemporary world, and they contribute dramatically to the crisis of meaning.

Narcissists frame their lives solely in terms of satisfying their own needs. This might work for them if having material success and recognition actually could made them happy. Unfortunately, it doesn't. Narcissists often find themselves unable to fulfill their own immediate needs—largely because they need others. When they offer others—who need recognition and love—little more than the opportunity to be manipulated and controlled, the people who originally fell for their charm and seductiveness become disillusioned and eventually leave them, just as Allison left Shawn.

Underlying the pain of narcissism is a social order that rewards the very behaviors in the world of work that are so detrimental to building loving relationships in personal life. To function effectively and justify manipulative practices, narcissists develop a set of beliefs that sustain them: everyone is alone, disconnected from others and from the universe. We live in a world with no higher purpose or meaning, a world that can offer us nothing but the chance to take what we can and use what we can to our own advantage. To people who suffer from this pathogenic belief, it is inconceivable that the world could be friendly or populated with people who actually desire connection to some higher meaning. It is very difficult for them to imagine a universe that tilts towards goodness and nourishes love.

These pathogenic beliefs have been presented as "common sense" for centuries. Today they are reinforced by thousands of columnists, news analysts, movie and television script writers, and by a large group of intellectuals repeating the mantra of meaninglessness, narrow self-interest and the impossibility of altruism with the same intensity others reserve for their religious beliefs. To most, the question of whether this kind of society is good never arises.

The ideologues of the status quo insist that, in the words of *New York Times* columnist Tom Friedman (commenting on the globalization of capital), "there is no alternative." The current reality, the unfolding and further development of the ever-expanding pursuit of material goods and money, the shaping of the world to the requisites of the competitive market, simply is reality, and nothing else will ever happen. The dynamic energy of markets will, they acknowledge, change everything—and they are almost filled with awe at the incredible wonders technology has in store for us in the twenty-first century. But they imagine that the only sacred permanence is the permanence of selfishness and materialism in a limitlessly expanding competitive marketplace.

These high priests of a self-satisfied materialism do not even acknowledge spiritual traditions that teach the radical impermanence of every social arrangement. From a spiritual perspective, the only thing that is permanent is God's love for all, or, in secular language, the Unity of All Being and its manifestation as love and goodness. And the most fundamental question is always, does this social arrangement make it easier for us to manifest Spirit? But for the narcissists of our time, spiritual issues have nothing to do with "the real world" and have no possible connection to the problems they face in their personal lives.

These themes have been part of human history since the emergence of class societies ripped apart the fabric of trust and created the sense of betrayal that has permeated human history ever since. But through most of human history, there was a counter-tendency, rooted in the spiritual experience of each individual and in the spiritual institutions of society. Those spiritual institutions supported a sense of obligation to take care of others and a sense of trust that you yourself would be cared for in turn.

The assault on Spirit in the past few centuries has caused a decline in the capacity of those spiritual institutions to develop an ethos of caring or a common understanding of the link between our individual lives and the totality of the universe, with its spiritual, ethical foundations. To the extent that spiritual consciousness has been marginalized, narcissism has become a "common sense" way to survive in a competitive market.

The decline of our confidence in spiritual life takes an immediate toll on our personal lives. Whereas the family was once part of a religious, national, or political community, today each individual family or couple is forced be its own center of meaning, providing for many the "meaning of life" that was once provided by larger communities of meaning. Under these circumstances, expectations for each relationship grow exponentially, until they are expected to compensate for a world that in many other respects has failed to provide meaning and purpose in other arenas. Under any circumstance, being subjected to scrutiny and expectations that far exceeded the capacities of even the most healthy, loving, and supportive family would be an almost impossible burden for a relationship. But in the context of world of work that fosters narcissistic personalities and people filled with frustration and self-blame, we have an almost guaranteed formula for family breakdown.

Talking about these issues helped Shawn get a perspective on his life. But his quick acceptance of this perspective and brilliant articulation of it worried me. I knew he was an excellent "pleaser," and now he was doing his best to please me and others who shared this perspective. So, although on the surface Shawn was a star student, I was never convinced that he was open enough to really let in the full importance of what he was learning. There are many cases where I doubt that insight is enough—what is really needed is a reworking of deep thought patterns, which may require an extended process of spiritual therapy. Shawn didn't have time for that, and our society doesn't provide the funding, so I have no confidence that the momentary insights he seemed to "get" would last long or change much.

Nor do I want to give the impression that spiritual practice or spiritual therapy can by themselves rectify the problems I'm discussing. Quite the contrary. In presenting life stories in this and the next chapter, I am trying to demonstrate how the societal deprivation of spiritual fulfillment tends to generate people who are deeply hurt and in pain. Although I will present some aspects of spiritual practice in chapter ten, and though I believe that people who have a deeper understanding of these issues can take some important steps toward spiritual health, the fundamental thing I learned in my work is how very deeply distorted we all get by living in a society whose very definitions of rationality and productivity are fundamentally Spirit denying. More and more people are moving beyond individual solutions and beginning to ask how to build a society on a different foundation precisely because Spirit Matters so deeply, and because individual repair can only go part of the way in rectifying the damage caused by internalizing the ways of thinking and being generated in a materialist, individualist, and narcissistic social world.

But let me return to their stories.

The Crisis in Relationships

Joe Katz was a successful attorney in his thirties when he first started psychotherapy with me. He had come because he wanted to understand his difficulties in sustaining a relationship with a woman. Joe did not fit the negative stereotypes of an aggressive lawyer. He spoke softly, and when he talked about his relationships with women, each relationship lasting approximately three weeks, he spoke with tenderness and sensitivity about each woman's needs. But Joe was never satisfied.

Although his generation worries about AIDS, Joe assured me that he used condoms, got tested for AIDS several times a year (in order to reassure potential partners), and that the women he dated were "not the type" to be heavily at risk. Suddenly, quite casually, he mentioned that he had slept with seventy women since he had broken up with his first long-term girlfriend at age twenty-seven. Joe used a combination of "personals" in various newspapers and several computer-dating services to find possible partners. He earnestly assured me that he wanted a long-term relationship, but there were problems with each woman he met.

I did not doubt that the women he met were imperfect. It is highly unlikely that anyone is going to enter the world of dating and find partners who do not have some real limitations or "flaws." Anyone brought up in a society that valorizes selfishness and encourages narcissism is going to reflect some of those values in their personal lives. Thus the search for the unflawed mate will be an endless one, because no such critter exists.

It's not that Joe didn't experience pain in his frequent breakups. Each relationship began with a genuine enthusiasm that gave his partner a sense that "this was really serious." So when Joe suddenly withdrew, they were often quite startled and hurt. And Joe himself felt badly about his frequent changes in partners. But, he told himself, "why should I stick with someone who I know has significant difficulties, when every week I see so many single women in various public places, read their appeals for a partner in the 'relationships classifieds,' and know that if I just have the courage to keep on looking, I'm more likely to find someone appropriate?"

In the supermarket of relationships, the idea of "working through" difficulties has diminished appeal. The notions of loyalty and commitment somehow seem as outdated and irrelevant here as they do in the economic marketplace, whose ethos sets the standard for the rest of life.

Joe was an unusual case, because he saw his behavior as a problem. For millions of young people, Joe's behavior is just "the way it is."

Couple this "marketplace of relationships" and consumer mentality with narcissism, stress, and self-blaming, and it no longer seems surprising that, over the course of the last half of the twentieth century, advanced industrial societies have witnessed a dramatic increase in the rate of divorce.

But the divorce rate tells only part of the story. The insecurity that people experience as a result of the dynamics I've discussed permeates most relationships, including those that never show up in divorce statistics. The divorce statistics do not include the millions of loving relationships that end each year but do not involve legal divorce because they never involved legal marriage.

In a world governed by the thought patterns of the market, love relationships become unstable and difficult to sustain. Yet all people are faced with the reality that if they play by different rules, rules of trust, mutuality, and commitment, they are as likely as not to find themselves on the short end, being taken advantage of by someone else who has assumed that *they* had to play by the ruthless and narcissistic rules of the world of work.

Love, of all things, should operate by a different logic.

That different logic is the logic of the Spirit. The less awe and wonder in our lives, the less we are able to see each other in anything but instrumental terms—and the more most people feel alone and scared.

When the world loses its connection to Spirit, the amount of pain increases. Spirit Matters—in every aspect of our daily lives. In looking at the lives of Joe, Shawn, Joan, and Louise, I could see how very deeply it mattered that they lived in a world where their needs for meaning were systematically frustrated. Many of the tensions they experienced as "personal problems" were actually manifestations of social pathologies generated by the peculiar way our society denies and represses Spirit. Had they lived in a world in which the "common sense" was to see other human beings as embodiments of the sacred, if the culture of their work world and the larger society had encouraged them to develop an awareness of themselves as part of the Unity of All Being and to feel successful to the extent that they manifested their ability to be loving and caring, had they been surrounded all their lives by others who were as concerned about them as they were about others, had their communities supported them in assessing their lives in terms of the evolution of the consciousness and goodness of the universe, their particular relationships would have been very different and their lives would have felt far more meaningful.

However, we don't yet live in a different world, and one important reason is that we hold pathogenic beliefs in the impossibility of building a different kind of world, a world in which spirituality would be more central to our lives. Ultimately this belief brings us deep pain and unhappiness. Yet most of us feel a certain loyalty to it—it's one of the things we learned to "believe in" as we grew up in this society. So in the next chapter, I want to look at some childhood dynamics and to understand more of the factors that contribute to our intense commitment to a belief that makes us feel so bad.

A Spiritual Exercise

Next time you are at work, or at a social gathering, try the following exercise:

Look at every single person, one by one. See each one as embodiments of God, one of God's many faces.

Become aware of the many resistances you have to seeing others as embodiments of God.

Are you focusing on all the "faults" of these others? You know that you have "faults" as well, but that doesn't make you any less an embodiment of Spirit.

That's the point of the realm of Spirit—being an embodiment of God's presence is not based on how much your looks conform to the media's standard of beauty or how well you'd do on some allegedly objective test of performance, how much money you have, how clever you are, how charming, or how sweet.

There is nothing you have to *do* to become an embodiment of Spirit—you already are. And so is everyone else. So, pay careful attention to all your resistances to seeing others as the embodiment of God's presence. What are the feelings that come up? What makes this so hard to do?

Has somebody taught you that your real value is that you are so different from others in some respect or other—and that it's only the ways that we are different that make us really count? Well, that belief itself is part of what spiritual practice seeks to overcome. You are certainly valuable in your uniqueness. But you are also valuable for what you have in common with everyone else—your ability to embody and emanate Divine energy.

Once you realize how wonderful it is to be an embodiment of Spirit, it may be easier to do this exercise. Instead of having your head filled with the many "faults" we are all such experts at finding in each other and in ourselves, let your head fill up with what is so wonderful about each other person.

Try it every day for five minutes. It will dramatically improve your relationships with everyone. And it will make it much easier for them to see *you* as an embodiment of God's presence. Though this exercise is no substitute for changing the world of work and the dynamics it engenders, it's a useful first step to protect you from some of the worst impact of the market's debilitating and pathology-generating "common sense."

Joe tried this out one time on a date with a sharp-witted woman named Kara. When he shared his dating woes, Kara wasted no time in pointing out that Joe wasn't perfect himself. Joe told me his first instinct was to say, "I don't need another ball-breaking woman in my life—I'm out of here." But then he remembered my suggestion and tried it: he looked at her as a manifestation of God. "I didn't even know what that could mean the first time you told me to try it," Joe confided, "because I don't think I believe in God anyway. But I tried it, and amazingly I started to feel like a different person. And Kara seemed like a different person too—which is why I decided to stick it out." The last I heard from him, Joe and Kara were arguing frequently but were still seeing each other and, according to Joe, the relationship was very serious.

three

LOVE, MUTUAL RECOGNITION, AND SPIRIT—
THE PSYCHOSPIRITUAL DIMENSION

"Humanity will not perish from want of information, but only from want of appreciation."

Abraham Joshua Heschel

We are loved by an eternal love that has sustained the universe since its inception. Each moment in the evolution of Being was necessary for us to be alive and aware today. In our bodies, in our nervous systems and brains, lie traces of eternity. The chemicals that compose us were part of previous configurations. Our blood pulses with the dim awareness of fish, frog, and mammal. The generosity of the universe is present within us, making our particular existence possible. We are the recipients of the loving energy of the universe, so powerful that it brought about the attraction between beings that ultimately led to our own conception and birth.

We are manifestations of the Unity of All Being, a moment in the development of Spirit, part of the consciousness that pervades All Being. And our lives feel meaningful to us to the extent that we can connect them to the highest calling we have, a calling to more fully manifest Spirit in our lives.

At the same time, we inherited another reality: the intense anxiety of parents who had internalized the fears and concerns of the competitive market. That anxiety is so pervasive that liberal ideas of school reform today are built around notions of school testing. "If only we could get those schools to produce students who will perform well on objective tests, we will be assured that they will have the skills to succeed in an increasingly competitive world market."

Today, many parents are already worrying about whether they can get their children into the right preschool, which will teach them skills to get into the right grade school, which will teach them skills to get into the right college, which will teach them the skills to get into the right graduate or professional school, which will get their little toddlers into the kind of job where they can be economically secure. Many children must contend with these parental and societal anxieties just at the moment when they are first coming to self-awareness and first able to fully experience and consciously affirm the love and goodness of the universe.

Spiritual Connection and Childhood

In infancy, our lives were made possible by the goodness and generosity of those around us. It's not only that we could never have survived as infants without others to care for our material needs. Experts on infancy tell us that children who are not picked up, held, and given loving energy literally die—infants need that connection to others.

From early infancy we are fundamentally connected to the wonder, marvel, and grandeur of the universe. We are filled with overwhelming love and trust for those around us and for the marvel of creation. We see ourselves reflected in the eyes of our parents or caregivers, and it is this recognition that helps us develop a sense of who we are.

We are drawn to others and to the world. We feel connected to all other beings, to strangers, to animals, to plants, and to the totality. We find it difficult to distinguish between ourselves and the world, feeling our Unity with All.

There are no atheists in infancy. Every child connects with the awe and wonder and marvel of creation. And almost every adult has unconscious memories of these moments of pure love and joy, memories that contribute to our ability to face life even when our actual situation is overwhelmingly scary or painful. We've all had early years in which the Goodness of Being was manifested in a powerful way, and our memory of those years helps to sustain us today.

There was never a moment in this process, then, when we were separate beings detached from the totality. From the moment of our inception, we were connected to and dependent on our mothers, who in turn were dependent on the larger social infrastructure to provide them with adequate food, shelter, and safety. We did not emerge from the womb as independent beings, but as deeply interdependent beings whose entire history to the point of birth had been shaped by the physical, emotional, and spiritual states of the women who carried us. We experienced a primal unity with the nurturers and with the nurturing we received from the universe.

Much of this infancy and early childhood period is lived without language or categories, so the memories are not easy to store or reclaim.

Language distances us from these earlier experiences. For much of human history, language has been particularly helpful when we had narrowly defined goals concerning physical safety and material comfort. Language pointed us to the aspects of our physical environment that could be most helpful to our survival.

Language at once empowered us and disempowered us.

It empowered our physical survival.

But there were parts of reality that language had a hard time capturing—the aspects of things that do not repeat themselves in a predictable way, the things we experience internally, or that are part of all of our experience and not just one segment of it.

Language has always seemed completely inadequate when we try to express our experience of unity, goodness, radiant beauty, and the mystery of all that is. We have an intuitive sense of the world that goes far beyond anything that language can capture. And for much of human history, we have connected to this intuitive sense through dance, art, music, and ritual celebration.

I certainly don't want to fall into the fallacy that Ken Wilber describes when he writes of spiritual people who glorify primitive states of consciousness before people had any categories or capacities to differentiate one aspect of existence from another. As Wilber correctly points out, the unity sought by the mystics and spiritually grounded people today is not a return to this earlier state, but to a higher state of consciousness that incorporates and transcends all previous stages in human development.

Wilber insists, however, that earlier stages are not rejected but are incorporated even as they are transcended. Earlier forms of connection to spiritual reality have never fully left us. They provide an important, although primitive and underdeveloped, taste of what spiritual reality is all about.

Unfortunately, for most of us this earlier childhood spirituality was never fully experienced or gently transcended—it was repressed. As children, we did not simply "grow out" of our spiritual consciousness, we were forced to repress it. The anger and hurt that come from this experience must be overcome if we are ever to reconnect with our higher spiritual potential as adults.

In our society, the process of acculturation often comes at a terrible price: the loss of contact with important aspects of reality. Instead of transcendence and inclusion, we get pathological development in which earlier stages have been forcibly abandoned rather than lovingly incorporated.

A Different Childhood Story

Let me tell you a different story than the one you may have learned in Psychology 101, a story about the psychospiritual dynamics of childhood. It's not meant to replace Psych 101, but to supplement it—to use a different language to attend to parts of our experience that psychology does not address. Every story about the psychodynamics of childhood is, in part, a useful myth. So consider this account that focuses on Spirit:

We start our lives filled with love for All Being and a powerful connection to the glory and grandeur of all that is. But we quickly have to deal with a family and social reality that have been deeply scarred and distorted. It is in relationship to that distorted reality that we begin to form a picture of ourselves on a conscious level.

Long before we were born, our parents learned to function in a world that never gave them the recognition and sense of connection and spiritual safety they deserved.

Many of our parents felt underrecognized. Even those who "objectively" may have grown up feeling good about themselves for being "successful" often feel that they are being rewarded for something external, not for who they really are.

Moreover, our parents were socialized in a world that taught them to deny their own childhood spiritual intuitions. The luminosity of their world was replaced with a narrower goal-oriented consciousness. Slowly and painfully they succumbed to this "reality" as presented to them.

Over the course of decades, our parents learned to protect themselves from their own disappointed hopes for spiritual fulfillment. Usually by the time we appeared in their lives, they'd become "mature" enough to not expect much of the world, and hence they dulled their own emotional and spiritual aliveness. Many succumbed to the low-level depression that faces most people who have lost their spiritual connection.

But this isn't the only message we get from our parents.

Our parents never *totally* lost their own spiritual awareness. Usually they unconsciously but ferociously held on to a deep desire for meaning and connection, and to memories of moments when they felt that meaning and connection.

Filled with these conflicting impulses, many parents are unable to see their children as manifestations of the love and goodness of the universe. By the time they become parents, most people have lost their ability to be fully alive and consciously present to their children. No wonder they are unable to be witness to the miraculous sacred energy embodied in this vulnerable and needy infant. Inevitably, they bring their own pain and emotional deadness to their encounters with children.

Parents often hope that their children will somehow make their own pain more bearable, that children will give them a sense that life is worth living, or that the children will succeed where the parents failed. So, they look for their child to be entertaining, cute, beautiful, charming, talented, smart, better at sports or at relationships with other children, and so on, than they were themselves. When you have these needs clouding your vision, it's hard to see the miraculous even when it stands right in front of you embodied in this other being. The great tragedy for so many parents is that, if they allowed themselves to see their children as they really are, they would get tremendous pleasure from that experience. But since their vision is clouded by their own pain, they often feel a desperate need to fix their children or get them to be different, always, of course "for the children's sake."

Parents often bring their children a powerful message that the world is an unsafe place in which others will hurt you unless you constantly protect yourself.

Hoping to protect us, our parents sometimes act as agents of the larger repressive social order, insisting that we focus our attention in the most narrow ways, ridiculing our "childhood fantasies," and teaching us that it's important to not be "babies" but to grow up and give more attention to those parts of our experience that might be useful in the larger society and less attention to those parts that seem merely private fantasies with no particular value in relationship to "doing well" in the larger society.

Long before we get to school, with its established mechanisms of spiritual repression, its array of tests, standards, and emotional hoops through which we must jump, we are taught not to daydream, not to doodle, but to "pay attention."

Some parents actually say this kind of thing, but most communicate it in a much more unconscious way. The alienation, insecurity, and sense of danger they feel gets communicated. Parents don't necessarily teach an explicit message of cynicism or depression, but they act cynical or depressed. Children carry their parents' cynicism, unhappiness, or anxiety, repeating the cycle in their own lives. They may sense a parent's fear of anything outside a narrow range of "success-oriented" behavior. Given the omnipotent ways some children think, many immediately try to care for their parents by staying inside the contours of thought and feeling that make their parents feel safe. Indeed, the joys of remaining connected to spiritual life may trigger a sense of guilt that the child is somehow abandoning her parents and hurting them by having pleasures unavailable to them. The natural altruism that children feel leads them to want to take care of their parents, and their own self-protective desire makes them want to have a happy parent. Both of these dynamics prevent children from pursuing spiritual and emotional aliveness that would take them beyond their parents' understanding or capacity. Far safer to shut down one's own intuitions and awareness than to find oneself in overt conflict or subtle but distinct misalignment with one's primary caregivers.

To the extent that parents are aware of giving these kinds of messages to their children, they may tell themselves that they are communicating a caution based on real love and caring. They don't want their children to suffer the pains and frustrations that they themselves experienced when they were too hopeful, too spiritually alive, too loving, and too aware. They don't want their children to be as cruelly slapped down by "reality." Alice Miller's brilliant study, *Thou Shalt Not Be Aware*, describes some of how this operates, though she does not apply the analysis fully to spiritual awareness.

No wonder, then, that parents are already scheming about how to get their kids into the right preschool that will get them started on the road to success. These parents know that it really will make a difference to their children's future success in the market if they can "focus" on accumulating the skills that will be rewarded in our educational system. Parents don't consciously want their children to unlearn their spiritual sensitivity, they just want them to pay attention to "what's important"—and of course, it's "for their own sakes." It's because they genuinely love their children and want them to have good lives that it's important for them to ignore those aspects of their inner lives that distract them from what is going to be rewarded in later life.

The point is not to blame these parents, who correctly believe that their children will have easier lives in this society if they are more financially successful. Rather, it is to notice that each of us has faced a massive assault on our spiritual consciousness from our earliest years, an assault that was all the harder to resist, because it was done unconsciously, yet with the best of intentions.

But no matter how well intended, the denial of our spiritual reality is a source of immense pain.

Peter Gabel has identified our hunger for mutual recognition and the ways it often gets distorted into what he calls "misrecognition." Children are faced with the deepest form of misrecognition—the misrecognition of their own daily experiences. They learn to ignore sources of joy and nurturing and to attend instead to something many fail at, namely the development of validatable skills. The rich, textured luminosity of the world begins to fade as children turn their attention toward the narrower band of experience that might win them the caring and support they so desperately need.

Children intuit that this recognition, while absolutely necessary in order to get the attention and support they need from their parents, comes at a price. They are recognized as someone other than who they really are. In short they are misrecognized.

And yet this misrecognition is all the identity they are offered. It seems far better than nothing, but it comes with enormous pain. Or with a depressive certainty that this is all that is possible without causing their parents immense pain.

It's not uncommon, then, for many children to express frustration and rage as they feel increasingly misrecognized. While some quickly and cheerily adapt to the misrecognition that is offered to them, fearful of the consequences of not providing their parents the immediate gratification they so obviously need, many others take longer to adjust to the messages and conflicting expectations they pick up from their parents.

The anger, frustration, and rage children sometimes express often seem, from the standpoint of parent or outside observer, to be unprovoked, or "merely" expressions of infant or early childhood frustrations without definable cause. Yet that anger or frustration is often the natural expression of profound loss, as children learn to extinguish, repress, or minimize their spiritual connection to the joy of being alive. You may be a wonderfully sensitive parent and still find that your children are going through this process. They are up against a massive Spirit-denying socialization. Don't blame yourself, but don't blame your child either.

It's when children have repressed their rage and become "mature" that they begin to manifest the low-level depression that has become the near-universal experience of people who live without the joy of spiritual connection. So parents who allow children to express their anger rather than repress it often find that their children become less depressed.

All this may sound a little too incongruent to some of us. Spiritually sensitive children? Parents who divert their attention? Doesn't this belie the "dark truths" of children's aggression and cruelty?

Some of the most honored psychological theorists of our time claim to have discovered an innate tendency toward hurtful and destructive behavior—a discovery cheered by those apologists for the current social order, who wish to discredit any criticism of the current ethos of aggressive competition and mutual hurtfulness.

The ideologues of contemporary society imagine that they have confirmed some fundamental truth about human nature. In fact, what they've discovered is that the pain of misrecognition and disconnection can be transmitted from the instant of birth and perhaps even prenatally in the way a parent relates to a fetus or newborn child—and this produces angry, aggressive, or destructive behavior in children. Again, the task of parents is not to blame themselves or blame their children, but to focus their energies on changing the aspects of our social reality that encourage us to be emotionally and spiritually dead.

Young children spend an extraordinary amount of energy trying to be who their parents, teachers, and classmates want them to be. To do this, they must make the painful adjustment to a world that values them not for who they are, but for what they do. The terrible irony is, the more children struggle with demands that they "succeed," the harder it is for them to meet those demands.

To the extent that children are in such pain, they have trouble focusing on what their parents, playmates, or teachers really want from them. Their own inner drama—trying to construct a way of being that internalizes and takes seriously the demands of parents to be "unreal"—begins to overshadow their ability to be present to the others around them.

All this shapes how a child presents herself to others in the preschool and early childhood environment, which in turn shapes how others respond to her.

I've watched little children enter play groups or child-care centers at age two and bring these pains and upsets with them, acting them out on other kids.

Most toddlers have already begun to internalize the complicated messages of misrecognition and disconnection from their parents. Some have already learned that they are safest hiding their sense of wonder at the universe or their playful and joyous attitude toward life. Others are still in the midst of learning that repression, but sometimes an inspired teacher or playmate can help them hold on to the most hopeful and spiritually alive parts of their being.

There are some children fortunate enough to have parents who understand this process, who do their best to offer a message that counters the message of hopelessness and spiritual repression. It's rarely either/or. Most parents end up being somewhere on a continuum between the two extremes: simultaneously giving messages of hope and despair, communicating spiritual validation and also spiritual negation.

This whole picture will only make sense if you realize that I'm describing a set of tendencies. How these tendencies play out in any given family will depend on many factors, including the life experience, work realities, psychological awareness, and spiritual resources of any given parent. There is a huge spectrum of options and subtleties to how these dynamics actually play out in any given family. What I'm talking about may be very present or only slightly present, with all kinds of gradations and combinations possible.

So, let's return to this psychospiritual story and see what parts fit your experience or help you understand the experience of others around you, even if you are one of the lucky few to whom this story doesn't apply at all.

Most children do their best to cover up their inner turmoil as they struggle to be good little boys and girls who fit into their families, their play groups, their child-care centers, or their schools. They do their best to take care of their parents, to stay loyal to them, and to make sure their parents are as happy as they can be made to be.

No wonder, then, that most children try their best to distance themselves from the pain they feel at being misrecognized and at having to give up their connection to the spiritual dimension of their own experience. They learn to develop a pleasing external personality for the benefit of parents, teachers, schoolmates, and friends.

The child labeled "dysfunctional" is often the child who has not learned how to cover up the pain and anger. But those who have learned to develop a pleasing external personality do so at a high price: a distance between their inner sense of self and an outer self. The painful part is that these "successful" children often feel that no one else is really seeing them. The part that *is* recognized and rewarded is a counterfeit, not their real selves.

Each of us has an internal identity, someone different from the external self we present to others. But since it's that external self that gets the validation, many of us end up believing that our inner selves are not really valuable or deserving of love. We've had to hide this inner self, and we often imagine that the reason it must be hidden is because it is so undeserving. Yet this is "who we really are."

No wonder, then, that we are in no rush to claim that part of ourselves in any public arena. Many children begin to imagine themselves as fundamentally unlovable, and they fear that if they were to show this "real self" to others, they'd experience torturous rejections and misrecognition all over again.

One of the central dimensions of that inner self is the part of us that was connected to the grandeur and mystery of the universe. The overwhelming beauty, the mysterious yet powerful interconnectedness and unity of it all, the feeling that the world (or God) was directly speaking to you, the joyful sense of being connected and part of it rather than separate—these are among the original spiritual intuitions and intimations that still are dimly present in the unconscious memories that help constitute the inner self. Yet, alongside these spiritual intuitions are the memories of ridicule, cynicism, and withdrawal of love that were associated with our childhood attempts to stay connected to that reality.

We need therapists of a new kind, therapists who have been trained to be sensitive to this loss of connection with spiritual life.

Few of us are ready to talk about the spiritual reality that is so intrinsic to our inner selves. It's often far easier to articulate the ways that our parents rejected us, much harder to recall and reclaim the spiritual parts of our being that were lost in the process of accommodating to the expectations we faced at home and at school.

The only place where it may feel safe to begin acknowledging these feelings is in the context of religious institutions, spiritual communities, or groups that have been officially designated to deal with these issues. In spite of everything, people still retain scraps of that early spiritual connection. Often without knowing why, they feel drawn to these spiritually defined spaces—churches, synagogues, ashrams, and mosques.

And yet, when we get there, most of us are afraid to go too deep on this path. We find it safer and more comforting to listen to spiritual leaders who talk about spiritual issues but who do not actually seem to lead lives of spiritual connection. It feels so much less threatening to be in spiritual contexts where Spirit is only *barely* present, and where we do not have to reencounter the fear and trembling that sometimes accompany the mystical reality of existence. We want to reconnect to the lost childhood experiences of connection spiritual aliveness, but we simultaneously fear that connection, unconsciously remembering the pain we went through as we felt compelled to give it all up.

So, we get this paradoxical reality: spiritual and religious communities that simultaneously elicit our spiritual memories and yearnings, yet fail to actually provide a safe enough place for us to fully reconnect with that part of our being. No wonder, then, that people are simultaneously drawn to these spiritual institutions and frustrated and disappointed in them.

The Denial of Desire

Spiritually wounded as we are, we continue to seek recognition from each other, as well as reconnection with the awe we felt as children when we intuited the wonder of the Unity of All Being. But these quests are systematically thwarted, not only by the inability of others to recognize us, but by the wounds from our childhood experiences.

As my colleague and close friend Peter Gabel points out, we often settle for distorted forms of recognition, even if doing so actually makes us accomplices in the denial of our deeper need for authentic recognition.

The cumulative effect of being misrecognized over the course of a lifetime has a significant and detrimental impact. We become depressively certain that if we make ourselves vulnerable to others, they will reject or misrecognize us once again, and restimulate our painful past experiences of misrecognition.

Fearful that we will be rejected should we approach others with our fullest and most open selves, we instead create a held-back position that denies our desire to be more fully present to each other in a community of equals. This inner reserve at once protects us and ensures that each person will frustrate every other person's desire for a fuller and deeper connection. Because they experience our absence, people conclude that it would be useless to reach out to us, and so each of us ultimately presents a withdrawn self.

As Peter Gabel said at TIKKUN's Summit on Ethics and Meaning, 2000, "in every social interaction, we pull for real recognition in spite of our simultaneous paranoid effort to ward off the very thing we most desire."

We are constantly torn between our loving instincts and our fearful inclination to act in the most self-protective and closed ways possible.

We were so burnt by our disappointments when we tried to reach out to others that we are extremely reluctant to try again. Gabel has noted that when we peer out from the withdrawn and disconnected place inside our heads and look at the way everyone else is acting, we often feel hopeless about the possibility of breaking through each other's alienated behavior. We walk down the streets and watch as people avert their eyes, unwilling to connect or acknowledge that they are going through the same thing we are, that their desire for connection is also being suppressed. We watch as people carefully and skillfully play out their assigned roles, acting as lawyers, doctors, police officers, salesclerks, waiters, telephone installers, construction workers, postal clerks, computer experts, Wall Street investment brokers, and so on. They all seem to know their parts and seem to want to have so little connection with anyone else. So, since each of us peers out at different times, for each of us the others seem to be "behaving correctly," while our own hopes to reach out and be "real" with others seems utopian and fanciful.

The only way this can be overcome, Gabel says, is to provide each other with a series of reassuring experiences in which we can be together in safe contexts, recognize each other's fears, and work to give each other confidence that we will remain truly available to each other, truly committed, and truly willing to sustain support as each of us goes through our moments of withdrawal, doubt, and paranoia.

Even on a one-to-one basis, providing these experiences of confidence is extremely difficult, given all the psychological baggage each of us carries, not to mention our tendency to deny our desire for this connection, even to ourselves—out of fear that it simply can't happen. But it becomes much more difficult still when we try to get *groups* of people to sustain this sense of hopefulness. At almost every moment in a group experience, someone feels insecure or paranoid, which in turn makes all the other people in the room feel scared and wish they could withdraw into their own personal lives. If you've ever been in a group trying to accomplish some political or spiritual goal, you will often find people acting in scared and destructive ways—and you will find yourself wishing to escape, give up, and distance yourself from the whole thing because the disappointment at things not going smoothly and gently seems to be at such variance with your original hopes for the possible connection and shared values that led you to be part of the group in the first place.

Take a moment to think of your interactions with people yesterday. How many people did you write off as people from whom you can't expect very much? How often did you have to adopt a protective stance toward others in the expectation that opening up to them would only lead to vulnerability and possible hurt? How many times did you avoid contact with others because you assumed they wouldn't want any more closeness and that they had better things to do with their time? I raise these questions not to suggest that you are doing something wrong, but to underscore that each of us can't avoid these dynamics, that this is what it means to live in a world where we pass warnings to each other to keep our distance and stay in our protective shells.

Sad as it is to realize, the process of mutual distancing starts in grade school. Children arrive at school hungry for the recognition and connection that they got in a partially distorted fashion in their own families. Yet they do not enter child-care centers, kindergartens, or grammar schools *tabula rasa*, or with an empty slate—they have already learned how to hide themselves, how to fear others, how to expect that they will not be really seen. So, they approach each other with a whole mix of hopefulness, loving energy, fear of rejection or misrecognition, anger, and confusion. Where any given child stands on this spectrum of emotions will have been shaped by all that has happened to her up to that point.

Even the best intentioned teachers and child-care workers seldom have the capacity to sort out, much less fully unravel, the complex knot of turbulent emotions that kids present when they show up in school. Nor will the behavior presented in the classroom be obvious in its meaning and roots.

For example, a withdrawn child who doesn't show much interest in connecting with others may be showing the roots of her own trauma at misrecognition at home. But she might also be involved in an inner spiritual focus that needs to be nurtured rather than disrupted. Unless her parents and her teacher work together to unravel the meaning of the behavior, they could easily diagnose a "problem" where valuable internal work was actually taking place. It's important not to romanticize this situation or construe spiritual life when a child is actually showing withdrawal or depressive alienation as she protects herself from the anxiety and frustration of misrecognition. Even as some children experience a higher consciousness, others are just showing evidence of the damage they have sustained at home and at school. In today's climate, where many families and schools deny their role in the damage, these children may soon be treated as though they have an organic dysfunction and handed a prescription for Ritalin.

Figuring out exactly what is happening with any given child requires the kind of time and attention most child-care workers or grade school teachers simply cannot be expected to have when they deal with so many children. Children bring their anger or anxiety from home into the little "public arena" of the day-care center or the grade school. As children, many of us assumed the roles that confirmed to others that we really were the kinds of people we imagined others thought we were. Our fantasies of how we were seen often become self-fulfilling. To the extent that we imagine others are going to like us, they tend to like us, and to the extent that we imagine that they won't, they don't.

Most schools have children cooped up inside buildings that allow little contact with nature, much less the celebration of it. If they do get to go outside, it is more often to participate in competitive sports than to commune with the glory of creation. The young person who does the latter will be seen as an oddball, soon to be ridiculed by teachers and fellow students alike.

Nor is school a safe place to share pain and anger. Show pain and you'll be ridiculed as a "crybaby." Show anger and you'll be considered a threat to the authority of the teacher or the safety of fellow students.

In fact, the most powerful lesson students will learn in their early years at school is this: *Don't be emotionally or spiritually real, hide what is going on inside.* Your feelings and your spiritual intuitions have no business here—take them elsewhere. This is "public," and in public we don't deal with this sort of thing—it's your private affair. Deal with it at home.

It's not so difficult to see how this is conveyed even by well-meaning teachers. It's not only that teachers will dismiss students' doodling and daydreaming or their desires to dance, sing, run, or be alone in a beautiful natural setting as a waste of time, never imagining that those moments might be the most creative and genuinely educational experiences the student will have in school. It's not only that the need to control a class requires that teachers discourage students from acknowledging feelings that might, once unleashed, lead to deep and troubled waters (including questions about how the student is being parented). It's not only that teachers today are discouraged from hugging students, or showing any spontaneous empathy at all.

It's more than all that. The very structure of our school system comes with a series of unspoken mandates like "stay away from Spirit" and "stay away from anything that might lead to challenging the parenting being done, unless you see explicit signs of physical or sexual abuse." Teachers risk their jobs if they allow themselves to be emotionally attuned, loving, and spiritually alive in the classrooms.

What is more distressing is that it is usually the children themselves who are the worst enforcers of the norms of the spiritually barren and emotionally empty public space. Having suffered the sting of parents and teachers who demanded that they "grow up" and not "act like babies," which children quickly learn means "don't be emotional and don't be spiritual," youngsters are quick to tease others who show the very behavior they were forced to abandon themselves. The teasing is a way of reinforcing their own inner controls and of expressing the anger they felt when someone quashed all that was spiritual, special, or strange inside them.

Thus begins the tragic process through which we all enforce on each other a denial of that which we want most in the world. By the time we enter high school, we are all experts at repressing our spiritual and emotional truths.

It makes no sense to blame the spiritual repression of the world on others without assuming our own part of responsibility. In every interaction with each other, we either reinforce that repression or permit people to lift it. Usually, since both messages are conveyed, both feelings are present. But the relative weight of one part of the message versus the other depends both on the history of our whole lives and on the specific levels of hopefulness or despair we feel at any given moment.

But this is also the good news. There's no big conspiracy out there keeping everything in place. We ourselves are making and remaking the world in every interaction. And we ourselves may ultimately be able to transform it all and help our entire species reach higher levels of emotional and spiritual reality.

Sounds easy to say. A spiritual awareness can lead us to a recognition that our entire human community could take the steps forward to build a whole new way of being together, replete with love, commitment, caring, celebration, and joyful restructuring of our society in ways that would protect the environment and provide work that was fulfilling. But in my therapy work with teenagers and young adults, I've learned that it was far easier for some of us in the 1960s to envision social change than it is for teens and college students today.

Without the foundation of solid intact families, many children growing up in the 1980s and 1990s reported feeling that they had no secure ground under their feet. Unlike the children of the 1960s and 1970s, who felt powerless against an oppressive external structure, many children growing up in the 1980s and 1990s felt they had *too much* power. Many grew up in flawed, frustrating stepfamily situations, or with single parents who felt so guilty and insecure about having failed to provide "a normal family" that children became burdened with having to take emotional care of the parents.

Even intact families suffer from a sense of not having done enough, known enough, or been cool enough to give their children what they needed to make it in the competitive market. Far from empowering children, this feeling leads many to fear their own destructive potential and to feel guilty that they might inflict more pain on their vulnerable elders.

In the 1980s and 1990s, movies like *Home Alone* portrayed babies as superinflated giants, whose innocent movements might destroy all around them, or as sages who couldn't trust their parents and ran things for themselves. With AIDS threatening that sexual urges could be literally deadly, teenagers and twenty-somethings of the 1990s began to suspect that their own sexual and rebellious impulses were simply too dangerous and had to be repressed. The resulting depression has generated a surge of self-destructive nihilism, which might yet form the psychic foundations for an American fascism.

While young people in the 1960s swayed to "Imagine" or "Blowin' in the Wind," their children adopted songs like the Sex Pistols's "No Future" or Nirvana's "Smells Like Teen Spirit" as generational anthems. Many identified with music with a passion that bordered on religious, and as the music industry grew increasingly corporate and consolidated, they reacted as bitterly as their spiritual forbears did to the institutionalization of religion. For young people in the 1980s and 1990s, music, nihilistic as it was, provided community and connection. Concerts served almost as floating meetings of a twelve-step program (regrettably without the follow-up and continuity that make twelve-step so useful).

The world feels far more confusing to these young people than it did to those who grew up in the 1960s and 1970s. The only voice of authority that speaks with confidence (unconflicted about its right to authority) is the voice of the market, channeled through the media, that treats children as consumers, valued according to how much they can buy. The implicit message in this pseudomeritocratic society is "if you can't afford it, you're worth less than someone who can." No wonder, then, that the pressure to "make it" becomes almost overwhelming.

Losing Spiritual Energy
and Meaning in Daily Life

When Samuel Hughes became my client in psychotherapy, he was a middle-management executive in an Internet firm that sold innovative uses of the World Wide Web to businesses.

Samuel described himself as depressed.

The problem, he told me, was that he had missed the 1960s. He was a child when the last major demonstrations occurred in the early 1970s, and he always felt he had missed something spectacular. In the late 1990s, he was a successful "yuppie" executive in his early thirties, clearly on the way up, with an attractive wife and two young children. But he felt depressed.

"I'm a Republican and a conservative now," he chuckled, "but I want you to know that when I was younger I had a glimmering that I might have been attracted to the movement.

"Still, I kind of suspect that you guys did a lot of damage. Most people I know think the sixties failed miserably, and the legacy was a lot of families breaking up and a lot of unhappy kids. In fact, the truth is my parents broke up, too, and I felt pretty resentful. Sure, they were pretty conventional types who never got involved in politics. But that's precisely the kind of people who never would have broken up before the sixties; they would have stayed together. But you guys in the sixties made it legitimate for people to 'do their own thing,' and that's what the problem was. So I'm not going to make that error with my life. My family is going to stay together.

"But meanwhile, though I've fought my way up to a great position in a growing and expanding investment firm, I've experienced a decline in my energy level. And I'm worried about that, because this job takes a tremendous amount of energy to just keep going. And now that I'm supervising other people, including, would you believe this, some people who are older than me, I just feel depleted and de-energized.

"I got involved in the mayor's commission on urban renewal, and I thought that would really help me in my firm, because some of our innovative electronic technologies might be useful to the construction industry—and anyway, I thought I might do some good, kind of in the way that I can, not in the way of making big changes, but getting something real to happen on the local level. Unfortunately, the struggles on this urban renewal panel with community groups make me sick. I hate to see people standing in the way of progress. But somehow I've been losing steam at work, and I need to figure out why."

How could Samuel, someone who virtually personified the economic boom of the 1990s, suffer from depression?

I couldn't help but hear Samuel's story as exemplary of the story of so many other people in this society—a story of people desperately seeking to find some corner of meaning in their lives.

But like so many others, Samuel experienced much in his daily life that depleted him of hope and undermines his potential for spiritual or emotional connection.

Every morning, Samuel reported, he woke up full of energy, ready to take on life's tasks. But he was soon assaulted by the television, which was always running during breakfast. A struggle often ensued with the kids about whether to watch cartoons (which, he pointed out to me, are filled with violence) or the news (which is similarly filled with violence). Either way, Samuel got the message that the world he was about to enter was a dangerous place. Or as he put it, "Everyone is alone and out for themselves in this world. Nobody has a sense of principle."

At one of our sessions, Samuel described walking from his fancy apartment to the bus. He frequently passed a homeless person who asked him for spare change to buy breakfast.

"Is this guy taking me for a ride or what?" Samuel asked me. He didn't want anyone taking advantage of him. But he knew that homelessness was not always a choice, and that many people simply can't get jobs, don't have friends or family to financially back them, and after a while have nowhere to go but the streets.

I asked him to explore his feelings more. Samuel told me that he felt like he had to close his feelings down every morning, because he hated to think about this or that homeless person and what it must be like for them at two or three in the morning, alone on the street or sleeping in an alley. Sometimes he has actually imagined bringing someone home, even as he realized how dangerous that would be. But in the end, he always decided he'd be better off not even thinking about it. In fact, he reported, it made him angry to see all these people. He wished the mayor would clean up the city and put them in jail or push them out of the city. As he said this, he became energized and lifted his voice. Then, suddenly, he calmed down.

I asked him whether he had noticed that his voice had been raised in intensity when he said this. He did. In fact, he said, he had recently become interested in some conservative political movements, because they were addressing the problems he saw all around him. Liberal solutions hadn't worked; he wanted to see conservative solutions tried.

I understood that Samuel was testing my openness to him by *not* performing in the way he had performed for his parents and for everyone else in his life. And I did my best to let him know that he would be safe in having any political attitudes he wanted. My goal was not to convert him to a specific ideology but to allow him to feel the kind of recognition and caring that had been denied him for most of his life.

My own view is that conservative politics are often an outgrowth of the pathogenic belief that human recognition will always be impossible. You can't undermine that belief with a rational argument until people have an *experience* of recognition that starts to dislodge their cynicism and pessimism. Liberal and progressive politics have their own pathogenic set of beliefs: that spiritual reality is purely personal and has no possible place in our public lives together and that most people outside of the small liberal elite are really just out for themselves and can't be trusted to support a just and loving social reality. Interestingly, both sets of beliefs lead to the conclusion that all people really care about is their material well-being and that you can't really trust others.

But on another level Samuel was telling me that he was unhappy having to confront the pain of another person and feeling powerless to do anything about it. The solution that was available to him—actually bringing a homeless person to his home—seemed too risky and scary to him. At one point in his life, he would have supported a massive governmental program to build enough housing to end the problem completely, but no one in the liberal world had even proposed that—all that liberals wanted to do was to get enough money for the homeless to keep them fed while they remained homeless and hopeless.

If there was no compassionate solution on the horizon, Samuel could side with another solution—"get these people out of my face." He was cheered by a mayor whose public charisma allowed him to get away with a policy of ridding the city of the homeless by making their conditions increasingly harsh.

Yet, as he turned away from the homeless man each day, Samuel had to withdraw from the caring part of himself, to cut off part of his feelings and repress his outrage at a world that failed to care for its own. And cutting himself off from others had been part of his life since childhood. Rather than seeing himself as connected to others, Samuel had gone through a set of experiences that reinforced a sense of himself as alone in a world with no meaning beyond "making it." His depression was, in part, a reflection of the disconnection he experienced from the Unity of All Being. Though Samuel scoffed at the notion of having spiritual needs, his crisis was, in fact, a direct reflection of the deprivation of Spirit in his daily life.

Samuel frequently used public transportation to get around the city. He recounted his experience visiting a Central American country, where everyone spoke to each other on the buses. He was so impressed that the first day after returning home he had turned to two people on the bus and attempted to start a conversation. Their icy silence and frightened looks were enough to remind him that people could easily think him crazy or dangerous if he sought to penetrate the self-protective walls of indifference most people build around themselves as they enter public space.

Samuel's work had been particularly stressful over the past year. His firm, though growing stronger financially, had decided it needed to increase productivity. Samuel was charged with either getting more creativity out of some of the people he supervised or getting rid of them.

"Frankly," he told me, "I don't have a clue what they actually want me to do. The people I supervise are doing a hell of a good job. How can you force creativity? But I have to tell them that they should be bringing in better ideas, even though I can't tell them how, or what's wrong with what they're already doing. It makes me feel crazy. But I do identify with my firm, and I do understand that in the kind of competitive world we live in, profits have to be maximized. Under the circumstances, it pisses me off that these people I supervise aren't more creative."

Samuel was annoyed that his firm had turned down some potential uses of the Internet that might have been socially valuable. Although he understood why his superiors had concluded that there might be too much risk involved and not as high a return as other possible applications the mushrooming Internet technologies offered, he was frustrated nonetheless.

Nonetheless, he reminded me, the firm was in business to make money. "I learned a long time ago that idealism has no place in business until after we've assured our profitability. Many of the people working with me in Silicon Valley think Internet technology can save the world—but I've learned that when push comes to shove, decisions aren't really made on the basis of how to save the world, but on how to grow the company." I shouldn't forget, Samuel assured me, that this firm made contributions to good charities with some of the profits they accumulated each year.

Things got particularly rough when Samuel had to reduce his staff by three. He hated having to choose whom to fire, and he hated having to tell them, since he didn't really believe they were incompetent. Samuel felt increasingly angry at his own staff, in fact, angry at all the people he worked with. For years he had made a point of implementing the best techniques of management/employee relations. Some of the people he supervised were lower-status professionals, some were clerical workers. He had made a point of keeping the lines of communication open, he had implemented some techniques he learned from Total Quality Management, and he had adopted other mechanisms to ensure that he was aware of the needs of "his" staff.

Samuel worried and wondered why he had a dull but aching awareness of rage. He dismissed his feelings as "inappropriate" and did his best to keep them under control. He had been taking a variant of Prozac, and that had made it possible for him to get to work each morning. But he continued to feel angry and de-energized. He worried that his own boss might notice this and that this could have very negative consequences for his career.

Samuel didn't feel comfortable discussing his feelings with his wife. She was a "superachiever" like he had been, and part of their partnership was based on the idea that they both liked to "work hard and play hard." He was afraid all that might be undermined if he told her of his downward spiral. Sure, she loved him, he acknowledged, but he wasn't so sure she'd continue to love him if he "became a different person," namely someone who no longer really felt so inclined to "make it," someone who couldn't keep his energy up. The last thing in the world he wanted, he told me, was to end up in a divorce. His parents had done that number and it was such a disaster he'd do anything to avoid it. But lately he was having trouble keeping his motivation going, even for his marriage.

The more Samuel told me of his work situation and his daily life, the more it sounded like a spiritual crisis rooted in pathogenic beliefs about the impossibility of love, solidarity, and caring and about the inevitability of a system that gave profit priority over human needs.

Samuel had felt devalued and underrecognized as a child. Though he'd done all he could to please his parents, he kept imagining that if he'd done just a little more he could have kept them together. They both seemed to like him, particularly when he did well in school.

He hated most of the stuff he studied in school, he told me, except for his classes in English and history. ("But that stuff with imagination doesn't earn you a living," he reminded me.) His early inclinations to be a painter or novelist had been banished from his mind by the time he reached high school. He had concentrated hard, done well, and eventually gotten into a top undergraduate school with the most advanced computer technologies and theories. Finally, he had cleverly combined that training with a graduate degree in business.

He had particularly blamed himself for his parents' divorce. His younger brother was badly hurt by the split, and Samuel felt he had let his brother down by failing to keep their parents together.

As he explored his childhood, Samuel began to see that both his parents had suffered crises of meaning as well. Their relationship had been based on an "alliance of interests" just like Samuel's was. True, his parents had been against the war in Vietnam and for civil rights, but this had played no actual role in their daily lives, which had been devoted to advancing their careers. (His mother had been a school-teacher who was trying to become a principal, his father a successful business executive.) His parents had grown apart, particularly after his mother had become interested in the emerging women's movement and the father had grown more conservative and gotten involved in opposing Affirmative Action in hiring.

"It wasn't that they had political arguments. They just didn't have much to say to each other. Dinner and evenings were spent watching television. To me, they both seemed lonely. I only wish I had been more entertaining; it might have made them want to stay together."

Samuel *had* been entertaining to his bosses at the corporation where he worked, just as he had tried to be for me, his therapist. He believed that his charm had kept him employed when others had been laid off a few years before. But now Samuel couldn't remember any of the jokes people liked. His quick wit was no longer apparent to others in his life. "I'm just not charming anymore."

Samuel had desperately sought recognition and genuine contact all his life, but he had learned over and over again that such contact was not available, or could only be available if he performed, created a "charming" external personality. But now he was having trouble putting out that charm. Still, he told me, he felt proud of having made so much of his life. He was part of a firm that "knows what it's doing" and "makes waves and gets taken very seriously" in the world of high finance. In fact, his position with such a prestigious firm made it possible for him to get the appointment to the city housing commission that was involved in urban renewal.

In the past, when I was involved in social change movements, many of the people I knew might have seen Samuel as "the enemy." He was a well-paid business executive with conservative views who exercised control over people who might have been my clients in an occupational stress group.

But I could look at Samuel spiritually and see him as more than just an economic and political category. I could see him instead as a living human being whose own needs for recognition and meaning in life had forced him into a role that some of my associates in the liberal world would have reasonably labeled "oppressive."

When I looked at Samuel, the executive, I also saw Samuel the victim of a meaning-denying reality. His depression was one of many possible manifestations of the impact of a systematic deprivation of meaning. I saw him as an embodiment of God energy, and though I might not have agreed with his life choices and political stances, I couldn't help but feel immense compassion and caring for him.

"But," you might object, "this is somebody who earns high pay and high status for pushing other people around. He doesn't even seem to hear the cries of pain from the people he supervises when they tell him 'ouch, you're hurting me,' so why should we be so sympathetic? What's so spiritual about him?"

Well, don't misunderstand me. I never sympathized with the specific choices Samuel made. But I did feel love and caring for him as a human being and as an embodiment of the God energy that is manifested in everyone on the planet. And I witnessed him suffering. Samuel hung on to that job because he felt the need for meaning and purpose that was partially satisfied by identifying with his firm and with a technocratic elite that "knows what it's doing."

In some ways, Samuel was deeply addicted to his fantasy of belonging to a group of younger managers who were going to take over the world and make things more rational. According to Samuel, the young people in Silicon Valley and all over cyberspace, were "truly changing the world." He was part of this, he assured me.

True, this group never met or talked to each other in these terms. But the fantasy that there is such a group, connected internationally through the World Wide Web, and that he was part of it, provided Samuel with some sense that his life had meaning. From the standpoint of that imagined community, he had the right to fire people in his firm, even if they didn't do anything wrong, because "the future" required it of him.

Even as he fired people who had done nothing wrong, there was a part of him that wanted to invite a homeless stranger into his home and offer him shelter. There was a part of Samuel that missed the idealism of the 1960s, a time he scarcely remembered. He was in a state of spiritual crisis because he wanted to be part of something larger than himself, a group of people who really were committed to changing the world.

"Why doesn't Samuel rebel, become part of a progressive political movement?" you might ask.

The answer is that *there is no movement that even begins to address his concerns or that wouldn't make him feel like a bad person*, except the most conservative movements, to which he might well be attracted.

Samuel's political connections got him an appointment to a position of some prestige in his city—the citywide housing commission—and in that role he played a part in shaping the city's plans for urban renewal. He was particularly resentful of the local alternative news weekly that criticized the urban renewal projects and worried about the "Manhattanization" of the city.

For decades, minority community activists have told stories of how their economically poor but culturally rich minority neighborhoods were "renewed" into commercial centers or into anonymous high-rise condominiums, where wealthy people could ignore each other into perpetuity. For these minorities, urban renewal is a "meaning eradicator" that undermines real communities which, though poor, provide people with genuine connection.

Yet Samuel had never heard this story. When he heard testimony from advocates for minorities, what he heard was a bunch of left-leaning lawyers talking about the "rights of the poor." And Samuel was fed up with people who were always claiming "rights"—from his children who wanted the right to watch drivel on television to his employees demanding rights in their jobs that he had no power to provide. No one even tried to explain the experiential impact of urban renewal to Samuel's commission. The lefty lawyers never talked about the hunger for meaning and purpose that was partially satisfied by the street culture that urban renewal would eradicate. What Samuel heard instead was a series of harangues about the rights of minorities to determine their own future, and from Samuel's standpoint that "right" had to be balanced against the "rights" of other groups in the society who wanted to live in a different kind of city, one that didn't have "urban blight."

It never occurred to the community activists that Samuel might also have a desire for meaning and purpose in his life, much less that they both suffered in an impersonal and alienating society. Not that this would have provided them with an immediate basis for an alliance. They might still be far apart on how to address the specific situation they were in. But not worlds apart. Had they shared a common language, one based on affirming spiritual needs, Samuel might have understood why his own solution, namely giving people money to assist in relocation, was not adequate.

The language of "rights" that the attorneys used helped reinforce Samuel's image of the poor as a group of independent egos seeking to maximize their own self-advantage. This vision made it impossible for him to see the protesters as a community of people linked to one another through love, caring, meaning, and purpose that could not be replaced by relocation funds.

But my point here is *not* about finding the best strategy to "reach" Samuel. Rather it is that Samuel is caught in the same crisis as an economically displaced person who might one day meet Samuel's wife and child on the street and rob or assault them. Of course, not all forms of victimhood are the same. The suffering of a wealthy white male, such as Samuel, is vastly different from that of a physically abused and homeless African American woman. The suffering and hardship are not equal. But Samuel's suffering is no less real.

Samuel felt attached to his electronics firm because he got

recognition for his work. It wasn't the recognition he needed to satisfy his soul, but it was as much as he ever experienced in any other part of his life, as much as he imagined he ever could get. This is how it works for most people: we imagine that these partial satisfactions are all we can achieve, and we cling to them desperately.

When I asked him why he was willing to stay in a life that offered such limited rewards, Samuel replied that he was making the only rational choice possible. He simply saw no alternative. Without a visible spiritually oriented social movement working toward a less materialistic world, Samuel felt his only option was to maximize his own advantage.

It never occurred to him that the absence of a spiritually oriented social movement is not some "fact" to which he must accommodate, but rather the result of choices that he and others keep on making every moment of their lives.

There is no "external reality" that makes all this alienation and spiritual deadness happen. There are only tens of millions of people who daily recreate the institutions and social practices of their lives, imagining that they "must" do what they do, and thus recreate the entire fabric of an alienated society filled with people who suffer deeply from the deprivation of Spirit.

When we began to talk about this, Samuel immediately remembered a childhood experience. In third grade he overheard his "best friend" talking to someone else and mocking Samuel's joyful expressions about how beautiful the weather and the world was on the warm California days when nature was sprouting around them.

"That kid is full of shit," the other kid said.

Samuel had gone to the boy's bathroom, hidden himself in a stall, and begun to cry. His friend, he realized, couldn't be counted on, wasn't really his friend. And he felt deeply alone.

Though his parents would not split up for another seven years, he could already feel an absence and lack of connection at home. Until that moment, he had looked forward to school as a place where people really cared about him. Now he felt that no one cared.

He emerged from the bathroom stall determined never to let himself cry like that again. And he would never tell anyone about how great it was to see all the beauty around him.

He never did. After that he lost faith that others would be there for him when he needed them. So, for Samuel, it would take lots of work before he could be open to a spiritual movement that was about caring for others. Opening his heart to such a spiritual movement would bring him back in touch with his painful memories of childhood betrayal.

Samuel's story is very common in one form or another. So many people struggle with the same internal conflict—a fierce need to be in a very different kind of world, matched with a pathogenic belief that nothing can ever change. We are trapped in this conflict as long as we make a commitment not to let ourselves be vulnerable to the humiliation of hoping and finding yet again that our hopes are not realized.

It's no surprise to me that Samuel reported that he had never again been overpowered by the beauty of the world. Our loss of connection to awe and wonder is deeply linked to childhood hurts, and many of us are reluctant to even begin to open up again for fear of reexperiencing those painful moments. So I wonder how many people who are deeply cynical about Spirit are unconscious of the moments in their own childhood when they went through experiences of shame or humiliation that made them feel they needed a cynical veneer to protect themselves from ever acknowledging a connection to the oneness of being or the awe, wonder, and loving feelings it generates again.

I still see Samuel in therapy, and he read an earlier draft of this book. After doing so, he started reading the books I recommend at the end, and from there he plunged into a wider program of reading spiritual thinkers. Although most of the issues in his life remain unresolved, the more he read the more his depression began to lift. As he heard other stories of people trapped by the ethos of the marketplace, he began to develop a more compassionate attitude toward himself and his own situation and became less critical of others as well. He now reports to me that he is accumulating spiritual wisdom, and our sessions together have moved from a focus on his personal psychodynamics to a discussion of spiritual issues and spiritual practice. He has attempted to follow many of the specific ideas articulated in chapter ten. And he reports feeling more centered and grounded in his life. He still argues with me about politics, but he also has begun to talk about using his finances in a socially responsible way. We've discussed how he might protect his children from the impact of this society's materialism and selfishness at a time when there is no social movement that embodies spiritual consciousness. And recently he spent a weekend volunteering at a homeless shelter! For him, that's been a major step.

What is even more of a major step is that, through his exposure to the world of Spirit, Samuel has begun to try to understand the tensions and hurts in his life as a child. For the first time, Samuel has been able to see himself as a hurt little kid and to reexperience some of the pain that he felt in a context where those memories do not overwhelm him. He has begun to develop a sense of compassion for himself, and even for the boys who made him feel so bad that day in third grade. He even dared to imagine how he himself could become less cynical if he found other people who could open themselves to awe and wonder, so he wouldn't feel so "out of it" (his words) as he opened to Spirit.

I remain hopeful that his newly emerging compassionate awareness can be nurtured and widened to include many more people in his psychic universe—though I do not want to minimize the incredible challenges he faces in the development of his inner life as long as his work situation rewards him for being insensitive to others as long as his employers would probably fire him were his sensitivity to become too prominent in his corporate decision making. But I do want to insist that even people whose financial interests remain squarely on the side of a spiritually deadened status quo have the capacity to respond to a spiritually sensitive message of social transformation—because their spiritual needs are rarely fulfilled and this generates a pain that no amount of money can heal.

We Are NOT Stuck

Jennifer Cantor was an African American lawyer who had graduated from the New College of Law in San Francisco and who had gone on to become a legal services attorney. When I met her, she was a partner in a law firm specializing in class action suits that raised important human rights, health, ecological, and consumer rights issues.

Jennifer was proud of her work and of her commitment to social justice, but she was a bit unhappy with the fact that she had little time left to pursue a social life. She came to me after I became the rabbi of a synagogue in San Francisco and told me of her interest in converting to Judaism. She felt that the ideas she had encountered in TIKKUN magazine were so close to her own that she wanted to be part of such a community, and she imagined she'd find that in my Beyt Tikkun synagogue.

I explained to her that she didn't have to convert to Judaism to be part of the movement of people seeking to transform our society, and that the Emancipatory Spirituality emerging today is not confined to any particular religious or spiritual tradition. In my view, there are many different paths, and no one of them has a corner on spiritual wisdom.

Jennifer persisted, telling me that in all the years she had gone to an ashram to experience Buddhist meditation, she had never felt the sense of community that Judaism seemed to offer. Although she felt emotionally comfortable in her own Baptist tradition, she couldn't accept Jesus as a God, nor even as more God-like than other human beings. I urged her to retry her own community, but after a few months of retrying, she returned to me. I agreed to start her on the course of study that would eventually lead to her conversion.

In the course of our work together, Jennifer was excited about Judaism's focus on social justice, loved the rituals and the community celebrations of Shabbat (the Sabbath), and met a man with whom she could share her future Jewish life. But she was completely resistant to anything that had to do with God or spirituality. Her previous meditation practice and her current enthusiasm for Shabbat had to do with, in her words, their powerful impact as "technologies of inner peace." But when it came to thinking of the world in terms of awe, wonder, and amazement, or of a realm of Spirit that could not be defined by science, Jennifer took exception. "The world is just a random assembly of material facts, and that's all there is," she told me resolutely.

Jennifer had belonged to a left-wing organization several years before. Though she'd ultimately concluded that the group was "so self-destructive they'd never get anything together," she continued to faithfully articulate its hostility to spiritual issues. Though she had come to seek conversion, she was certain that once she opened the door to God or the realm of the Spirit, there would be no way to stop her from sliding down "a slippery slope" to archconservatism, Christian Coalition politics, or other groups she viewed as racist, sexist, or homophobic.

Jennifer knew that many members of my synagogue were just the opposite—people who were deeply committed to progressive politics—but she insisted that she need not believe in God or Spirit to join. And technically she didn't. She wasn't the only synagogue member who loved the sense of community and the religious celebrations but who did not really share any of my ideas about God or the realm of Spirit.

It took several months before Jennifer would reveal the source of her resistance to spiritual ideas. She had actually been quite active in her church as a girl and felt that it was the one place where people respected each other. In high school, kids were always "trying to score," and much of life was a sexual meat market in which a young woman was evaluated by how sexy she looked. It was different in church, where the robes hid everyone's sexual identity and protected young women from being sexually objectified. Imagine Jennifer's outrage, then, when, at age fourteen, her best girlfriend revealed that the minister of her church had sexually assaulted her. Jennifer had been sickened by the story and felt personally betrayed by God. Such a God was either evil or didn't exist. Jennifer turned to politics as the only way to fight the evil all around her.

As an attorney, she pursued a classic progressive strategy: use the court system to protect the rights of clients. But in recent years she had grown less and less optimistic about what she was accomplishing, despite the fact that she often won powerful judgments for her clients. She saw many other progressive lawyers winning similar victories, but none of this good work seemed to add up to a social movement to change things. In fact, she noted, people had become more and more conservative in the past two decades, despite the fact that there were so many good grassroots organizing projects taking place and so many good people were involved in important progressive work. She knew the standard lefty explanations: that corporate power was now being exercised through powerful media that delegitimized any voices outside the pro-capitalist mainstream and made people feel that they would not be taken seriously if they called for deeper social change.

But why, she wondered, had people not stayed together and commit-ted to each other in a movement that could challenge corporate power? She intuitively felt that there was something missing from the Left's analysis.

I urged her to stop thinking about other people as "the other," and to place herself within the question rather than outside of it. What made it hard for her personally to be part of such a social change movement? Perhaps, I suggested, if she knew what stopped her, she might be able to understand what stopped others.

In the resulting exploration, Jennifer came to realize that the fun-damental thing stopping her was a deep sense of distrust of others, a distrust she had acquired through her childhood. She was afraid to believe that others could transcend their own conditioning and build loving, caring communities. For that reason, she didn't want to be part of any movement that required that kind of belief. In fact, she sud-denly realized, believing in social change is really like believing in the Unity of All Being, like believing in God. It's just another belief sys-tem, a belief that things can really change.

Precisely!

I often talk of God as "the Force of Healing and Transformation in the Universe," the Force that makes the transformation from "that which is" to "that which ought to be possible."

It's no surprise to me that people who can't believe that there is such a Force will find it hard to believe that the world can ever be fun-damentally healed or transformed. If they rely on "the evidence" (that is, the history of everything that has happened up until now), they can find as much tragedy as hope.

True, there has been remarkable progress toward the elimination of slavery and a growing consensus on the value of education, free-dom of conscience, individual liberty, and equality. But one might also point to the Holocaust, the use of nuclear weapons, the global-ization of capital and the resulting impoverishment of many sectors of the world, and the insensitivity toward the environment that threat-ens global destruction and use all of these as arguments for why things have simultaneously been growing worse.

The way we look at the world—either as friendly toward healing and transformation, or as random, indifferent, and possibly evil—is not determined by "the facts," but rather by an orientation toward the facts that might well be called "a matter of faith." To see the world from the standpoint of the development of Spirit is a faith choice just as seeing it as little more than a jumble of random and indifferent facts is a faith choice.

But it's easier to choose the faith of random indifference than of a loving and generous Force of Healing and Transformation if your own experience has been that of hurt and betrayal. Growing up in a society where there is so much betrayal and mutual disappointment leads many of us to a deep cynicism. That cynicism, in turn, makes it very difficult to be open to the realm of Spirit.

Of course, I've talked about this cynicism as though it were directly produced by our experiences. Yet, most people's experiences have been far more ambiguous than this. We've had many moments of hurtful betrayal. But many of us have also experienced moments of caring and nurturing. In fact, in order for most of us to have survived to adulthood, the balance of the universe had to be more toward nurturing than toward hurtfulness.

One would have to be naive and foolish to deny the hurt and betrayal we've all experienced, but it's equally misleading not to notice that most of us have experienced acts of tremendous generosity and goodness—from friends, neighbors, parents, family, community, or random strangers.

Why don't we pay more attention to those?

When we see kindness, goodness, or generosity in our own lives, we often interpret them as strange exceptions rather than as confirming a more hopeful perception about human nature. We tell ourselves that, "sure, the people I know are decent and caring and would never intentionally hurt others, but my group is really a special set, unlike most people." We have no intellectual framework upon which to hang the experiences of altruism or love, so we bracket them in our consciousness as somehow "on the side" rather than as central realities of life.

It takes an act of faith, a leap toward belief in the Spirit and a rejection of the dominant cynicism of the contemporary world, to begin to believe that the goodness and generosity we've personally experienced are not exceptions, but are the underlying reality of our spiritual nature.

In fact, it is precisely this leap of faith that is necessary for loving relationships to work. No matter how many times we've been disappointed by previously failed connections, people continue to make this leap of faith—to believe in each other, to hope, to trust, and to work out a life with a partner. And those leaps of faith into love are the beginning of the dynamic that makes the triumph of Spirit possible. In fact, loving another person is at once a manifestation of Spirit and a way to make Spirit stronger and more present in the world.

The alienated world is not merely imposed upon us. It is something we recreate every day through our own levels of despair and depression, through our certainty that nothing fundamental can change, and through the cynicism that closes us off from the realm of the Spirit. I've called these pathogenic beliefs, because the more we believe our own cynicism and despair, the more we help create a world in which our worst fears come true.

But leaps of love are hard to take and hard to sustain. That's why spiritual practice is so important. Spiritual practices are designed to teach us to attend to the world with a loving yet fully honest awareness of what is. This is not a rosy-colored pretense that everything is just as it should be. The world is filled with pain that can be overcome, and we have a role in healing and transforming it. Healing is truly possible, it has been happening, and we have a real contribution to make. To notice this is to make a major step toward finding meaning in our lives. We don't have to be grandiose about what any one of us can accomplish. As Rabbi Tarfon used to say, "It is not upon you to finish the task, but neither are you free to ignore it." To look at the world as it really is requires noticing the specific contributions you can make, and then to make them, confident that if we each do this we can together heal the planet. Every act of love and kindness counts.

Jennifer fell in love with someone in our congregation, but for a long time the relationship was very rocky. Jennifer felt that her partner frequently ignored her "rights." One day she heard me talking about the Jewish conception of relationship as one that rejected the paradigm of "contract" (as in: we two make a contract to trade concessions to each other in return for benefits we receive) and instead saw God as the necessary ingredient and the third partner in every loving connection. To see ourselves and each other as sitting in God's presence, to incorporate God's intentions for us as best we can understand them, to become alive to Spirit as the guiding force of our lives, as the purpose for being together in loving relationship—these ideas gave Jennifer a whole new framework for understanding her partner. If her report is to be trusted, the less she focused on every minor infraction of her rights, the more her partner began to attend to the major issues that had previously seemed too much a product of Jennifer's litigious mind. I'm not a champion of religious attitudes that covertly tell women to learn to subordinate their will to the person taking on a male power role in families, so I cautioned Jennifer that believing in God's presence did not mean submitting to the power or control of one's partner. She reported to me that once the whole framework of "who has most power" was overcome, she actually felt herself "winning" much more, getting her way far more often, and caring far less about whether she did or didn't.

After this relationship began to develop greater solidity, Jennifer became open to other spiritual practices. It was our community's loss that her partner found a job a few thousand miles away and Jennifer moved to keep the relationship strong before most of the people in our synagogue even got to know her. But I feel hopeful that she will be part of the emerging movement for Emancipatory Spirituality.

A Spiritual Practice

To the extent that we allow ourselves to see ourselves and each other as manifestations of the universal spirit of love, the scarcity model (that there's not enough love to go around) starts to recede and we become more and more aware of the love that surrounds us and is part of us.

Take five minutes each day to focus on the following: in what area of your life has the universe poured out its love and goodness to you and why haven't you allowed yourself to fully notice? Think about your childhood and the people who helped sustain you or support you. Think about friends in grade school or high school or in your work world. Think of your neighbors or members of your church, synagogue, mosque, or ashram. Think of the people you can count on to do the small things that make your world work as well as it does.

Then, allow yourself to think of the chain of goodness and love that sustained them. See how you are surrounded by people who have been the beneficiaries of the goodness of the universe. Each day focus on someone or something different that has brought you love and goodness.

Then focus on something good that you bring to others or to the world. It need not be some dramatic accomplishment. It could be as humble as a way you smile at others, a way that you attend to someone who has done something on your behalf. Thank that personal way that you are alive to the trees and flowers, or a way that you sing or paint or garden and bring beauty into the world. Appreciate the way that you too are an embodiment of the universe's goodness and love.

A Scientific Postscript

In their *General Theory of Love*, Thomas Lewis, Fari Amini, and Richard Lannon, amass considerable data from neourodevelopment, psychopharmacology, neonatology, and experimental psychology to argue that our need for loving connection to others is hardwired into our physiology. As they put it, "people cannot be stable on their own—not should or shouldn't be, but can't be. . . . Total self-sufficiency turns out to be a daydream whose bubble is burst by the sharp edge of the limbic brain." That the universe has designed us to be lovingly connected to each other is a manifestation of the fundamental love that is constantly undermined and subverted by a society based on the ethos of selfishness and materialism. Conversely, the Emancipatory Spirituality I will describe in chapter five is meant to be a healing both on the individual and social level that will enable us to live in congruence with our deepest needs. What Lewis et al. demonstrate in their physiological conclusion that relatedness and communal living are the center of human life is that there is no division between our spiritual needs and our physiological needs—they are one.

four

ECOLOGICAL SANITY REQUIRES
SPIRITUAL TRANSFORMATION

*"The world is just a little place, just the red in the sky
before the sun rises, so let us keep fast hold of hands, that
when the birds begin, none of us be missing."*

From *The Collected Letters of Emily Dickinson*

In the last few chapters, I've spoken a lot about how the deprivation of Spirit has had a devastating impact on the quality of our lives. I believe that this suffering will ultimately open many of the most skeptical people to spiritual concerns. However, Spirit Matters in an even more urgent way: the upsurge of Spirit is the only plausible way to stop the ecological destruction of our planet. Even people who have no interest in a communal solution to the distortions in our lives will have to face up this ecological reality. Unless we transform our relationship with nature, we will destroy the preconditions for human life on this planet.

Denial can only go so far.

For all my daily meditation and spiritual centering, there are times when I watch television, particularly the local evening news, and I want to scream: "When will all this craziness stop?"

• The weather reports are increasingly filled with floods, droughts, and other environmental devastations. Or they depict extremes of hot and cold spells. The television newscaster typically makes some comment to the effect of "imagine that" or "wow, isn't that interesting" (or sad, or depressing, or upsetting to see so much pain), and then moves on to the next item, never stopping to talk about global warming and its tremendous impact on our lives, unless there is an equally powerful statement by some pro-corporate scientist who is willing to make a statement about how the concern about climactic changes is misguided and unproved, and probably just the work of people with some irrational fear of "progress."

•Occasionally, you'll get a report on how there has been an increase in cancer or heart disease in a given area, but rarely is there any discussion of which corporate policies have generated which environmental diseases. Groups that make these links are rarely reported. I know of one group that regularly leafleted hospitals with a message about the link between cancer and environmental pollution generated by neighboring corporate polluters. The corporate polluters responded by issuing a statement calling this activity "insensitive" and "playing politics with the sentiments of families of the sick"—as though the problem was not the industrial polluters but the people who were calling attention to them.

•We hear reports of famine, but never about their connection to the policies that misdirect food supplies, or to global warming. The "human interest" story of suffering, illness, and injury is rarely accompanied by the ecological story of inexorable environmental degradation.

I know that television stations are owned by large corporate interests and funded by corporate advertising, so they are not going to link the problems we face in daily life to a global economy run by these same corporations. Without an awareness of these causal links between environmental and economic arrangements, how easy it becomes to fall back into pathogenic beliefs about the impossibility of changing anything!

The Destruction of Our Environment

Do you have ecology fatigue? You may have read the catalogue of environmental destruction dozens of times. If you feel all too familiar with it, you may just want to skip this section, but please read the analysis in the following sections. If you want greater detail than I provide here, I urge you to read Thom Hartmann's *The Last Hours of Ancient Sunlight*, Josh Karliner's *The Corporate Planet*, and Edward Goldsmith's *The Way: An Ecological Worldview*. Follow the unfolding story in TIKKUN magazine and in *State of the World* (the annual publication of the Worldwatch Institute), which offers an annual update on the state of the environment. The facts listed below could easily change in the next few years, but the framework of the situation won't change: for every specific reform environmentalists have managed to get through Congress (whether controlled by Democrats or Republicans), a greater number of previously unattended-to problems emerge. The environmentalists run from one area to another, and the public, feeling both powerless to change the basic structure and overwhelmed by all the technical details, loses interest, which gives the reformers even less of a base from which to press for future Band-Aids on the problem.

The basic environmental picture is this: the growth of the human population and the blind human faith in science and technology to provide solutions to our problems and make unlimited "progress" possible have together led to the degradation of the Earth's environment and severe problems that all the world's peoples face together.

• As Lester R. Brown and Christopher Flavin put it in *State of the World, 1999*, "Stratospheric ozone depletion and greenhouse warming have begun altering natural ecosystems in the past two decades, doing particular damage to coral reefs and suspected damage to species ranging from frogs to trees" (p. 7).

• The same gasses that destroy the ozone layer also contribute dramatically to global warming. A United Nations-appointed group of more than twenty-five hundred of the world's leading climate scientists concluded in 1995 that without a substantial reduction in carbon dioxide emissions from the burning of oil, coal, and wood, global warming is almost a certainty. The result will be more frequent and more powerful storms, melting of the polar ice caps, a rise of sea levels, and an increase in the prevalence of floods and drought (Reported by Karliner, ibid.). Human health will be compromised by the spread of disease-bearing insects and pests in response to rising temperatures. Millions of people worldwide will die, and millions of others will become environmental refugees.

• As *The Ecologist* magazine's "Declaration on Climate Change" (Vol. 29, No. 2, March/April 1999) points out, the effects of climate change are already present. We face a real possibility of "releasing billions of tons of carbon into the atmosphere, as rising temperatures trigger a huge die-back of trees, causing billions of acres of South American rain forests to turn into desert before 2050," we then will face "a situation of catastrophic, runaway climatic destabilization."

• Governmental responses have been thoroughly inadequate. The Kyoto agreements on climate agreed to a cut of just 5.2 percent of greenhouse emissions to be achieved between 2008 and 2012, far below the 60 percent reduction below the 1990 levels that the UN's Panel on Climate Change said was necessary.

Worldwatch also draws attention to:

• Fresh water shortages. World water use has tripled since the middle of the twentieth century, and the result is a decline in water tables on every continent. Meanwhile, oceans are increasingly polluted and fish populations are threatened.

• Depletion of forests to supply wood and paper for the industrialized nations. Forests are also destroyed to provide new lands for livestock grazing and intensive crop production.

• Loss of rain forests. In *The Last Hours of Ancient Sunlight*, Thom Hartmann points to a *State of the World, 1996* report that estimates the loss of thirty-eight million acres each year of rain forests, enough to wipe out the entire world's rain forest during our children's lifetime. And that's if the destruction happens at the current rate. But the rate has been increasing.

•Depletion of the world's fish supplies and the possibility that tens of millions of people who depend on fish for income or food will face economic devastation and possible starvation.

•Destruction of plant and animal life. We are facing the greatest decline in plant and animal life in sixty-five million years. As John Tuxill reports in the 1999 Worldwatch issue of *State of the World*, according to a 1997 global analysis of more than two hundred and forty thousand plant species, one of every eight plants is potentially at risk of extinction. This undermines a great source of future medicine.

•Effect on the human life. As in so many of the environmental emergencies, the problems fall disproportionately on those who are the least able to protect themselves. As Tuxill reports, "For the one quarter of humanity which live at or near subsistence levels, plant diversity offers more than just food security and health care—it also provides a roof over their heads, cooks their food, provides eating utensils, and on average meets about 90 percent of their material needs." (The Worldwatch Institute, 1999)

•Environmental degradation. Advances in technology accelerate the rate of environmental degradation. New extractive technologies allow us to take more basic materials from the earth. Advances in transportation and energy allow us to bring a wider range of these materials to market.

Governments provide an infrastructure for the sale of these goods, as in the case of the highway systems constructed for automobiles.

The Role of Corporations

We don't all have equal power to shape the environment around us. There are forty thousand transnational corporations, which are the center of our world economy. As Joshua Karliner points out in *The Corporate Planet*, "These corporations and their 250,000 foreign affiliates account for most of the world's industrial capacity, technological knowledge and international financial transactions. They mine, refine and distribute most of the world's oil, coal, gas, hydroelectric and nuclear power plants. They extract most of the world's minerals from the ground. They manufacture and sell most of the world's automobiles, airplanes, communications satellites, computers, home electronics, chemicals, medicine and biotechnology products. They harvest much of the world's wood and make most of its paper. They grow many of the world's agricultural crops, while processing and distributing much of its foods" (p. 5).

And power is concentrated at the top, both within these corporations (most of the people who work for them can rarely shape their policies) and among them. (The top three hundred firms account for 25 percent of the world's productive assets.)

Corporations and their global power are at the heart of many of the ecological problems we face in the world today. With the collapse of the Communist bloc (which, in its way, was every bit as environmentally irresponsible as anything happening in the capitalist world), corporations have gained increasing power to shape the policies of countries around the world. Even in the democracies of the advanced industrial societies, corporations are increasingly able to dominate governments in a variety of ways:

•They can usually ensure that anticorporate candidates are described by corporate-dominated media in ways that make them look irresponsible and irrational, thus making them unlikely to be elected.

•Corporations can throw their huge financial resources behind candidates who support the corporate agenda; and most important, they can let legislators know that any state or country perceived to be unfriendly will see business interests move their investment dollars elsewhere, causing loss of jobs and actual suffering to the people whose interests the legislator is supposed to serve, thus creating a reason for many otherwise ethical legislators to subordinate ecological concerns to the corporate agenda. Choosing to avoid immediate economic pain for their constituents (as well as possible loss of their own jobs in the legislature), many well-intentioned legislators conclude that it would be irrational and self-destructive to follow policies that antagonize corporate power.

•The Global Climate Coalition, a coalition of fifty U.S. trade associations and private oil, gas, coal, automobile, and chemical companies has put millions of dollars into its campaign to persuade the public and governments that global warming is not a real threat (*The Ecologist*, vol. 29, no. 2). Corporations warn that steps taken to reduce global warming might also reduce employment and raise prices. They mobilize public opinion against international agreements to restrain ecological destruction, warning of a loss of national sovereignty, the potential for economic recession, and the loss of jobs and income for middle-income families.

•Corporations and pro-corporate conservative organizations have established policy institutes to make their stances against environmental protection look as though they come from objective and credible observers. They represent environmentalists as "an interest group" filled with people pursuing "personal agendas" or simply hysterical, overzealous, well-intentioned fools.

•The Heritage Foundation, one of the largest and most influential conservative think tanks in the United States, published a report on the Kyoto agreements entitled: "The Road to Kyoto: How the Global Climate Treaty Fosters Economic Impoverishment and Endangers U.S. Security."[1] It accused the millions of people who were concerned about global warming of being like "Chicken Little" and called the Clinton administration's actions (which actually had substantially weakened what might have been more effective action) an attempt to "pacify a vociferous lobby, which frequently has made unsubstantiated predictions of environmental doom."

The power of these corporations to set the public agenda and to marginalize those who take this crisis seriously is immense. Newspaper

1.   Angela Antonelli, Brett P. Schaeffer, and Alex Annett, *Roe Backgrounder.* No. 114. The Heritage Foundation, October 6, 1997.

columnists who warn of environmental dangers are dismissed as "shrill." Politicians realize that they must tone down any ecological criticisms in order to be deemed "realistic." Even the politicians who actually know something about these issues, even those who find them useful for mobilizing some sector of the voting public, almost always quickly shift to more "realistic" ground after being elected.

But Isn't This the Consumer's Fault?

"Corporations are just in business to make money. If consumers want a given product we produce it. So, if you want to change corporate behavior, change what consumers buy and corporations will change accordingly. The marketplace, after all, is a democratic representation of what people want to do with their money, and it's far more responsive to the wants of the population than governments have ever been." So, at least, say those who seek to blame the ecological crisis solely on the rest of us.

There are two fallacies in this reasoning:

Markets respond to whoever has the cash. But money is unequally distributed. A mere 16 percent of the world's population purchases 80 percent of the world's material. So most of the peoples of the world are left out of the vote when it's one dollar one vote. Even in democratic, industrialized societies, money is concentrated in the wealthiest 30 percent of the population. Their disposable income (over and above food and clothing and shelter) is far more than the disposable income (often none) of those in the poorest 50 percent of income earners. So the market reflects the desires of those with the most money to spend.

Choices of consumption are made within the context of a social order whose basic framework has been disproportionately shaped by corporate power. When General Motors bought up existing rail systems in Los Angeles and dismantled them in the middle of the twentieth century, it ensured that people who wished to get to their jobs would have to buy automobiles. Gas and auto industries spent enormous amounts of money encouraging legislatures to build more superhighways rather than to provide urban reconstruction that would allow people to live close to where they work. If the only house you can afford is very far from the only work you can get, and there is no public transportation, the choice to use a car is not a moral failing but an economic necessity. Keep this in mind even when discussing my call in chapter ten for "voluntary simplicity"—it's only possible if combined with other systemic changes.

Greed Is a Disease of Fear

Some readers may continue to object, "you try to place all the blame for environmental destruction on corporate behavior, but you fail to acknowledge that it's the greed of the *consumers* that is at the bottom of it all."

Well, greed is real all right. But greed is a disease of fear.

To the extent that we have come to believe we can't count on others, we tend to protect ourselves as much as possible by accumulating material goods, money, power, sexual conquests, or something tangible.

Nor is this entirely irrational.

In times of crisis, people have historically pulled together, delaying their personal gratification for the common good. To do that, people need to trust that others will do the same. But what if you live in a society in which corporations pour poisons into food, air, and water because doing so ensures a high level of profits? What if you live in a society in which most people have come to believe that everyone else is going to rip them off unless they do the ripping-off first?

In such a society, urging people to reduce their level of consumption in order to protect people in other parts of the world is whistling in the wind. People will be unwilling to make those choices if they believe they will be the only jerks who pursued a selfless agenda. That's why, even though most people agree with ecologically oriented parties like the Greens or the New Party, they don't vote for those candidates. They are convinced that everyone else will vote according to selfish interests and that they'd better do that as well.

Ecological programs can never succeed unless ordinary citizens are willing to face a reduction in the level of consumption, are willing to pay higher prices for nonreplaceable energy sources, and are willing to support programs for international planning on how to use the world's remaining resources.

Similarly, when asked to support programs that constrain corporate selfishness, many people are reluctant to impose on others an ethos that they don't believe they can follow in their own lives. In my view, the quality of people's lives can dramatically improve if we revamp our whole system for ecologically sustainable production and consumption. But most people mistakenly believe that to be ecological will require immense hardships, and they interpret environmentalism as a demand that they stop using their computers, stop enjoying beautiful furniture, and stop wishing for comfortable homes. Fearful that they must give up their VCRs and compact discs, their Web surfing and their networking, many sensitive people see themselves as "just as bad as the corporations," and thus feel very conflicted about constraining corporate power.

Ecologists often play into this dynamic, blaming ordinary people as the source of the problem. Instead of wagging accusatory fingers, those who wish to transform America need to preach an ethos of compassion—helping people understand that their underlying fears are rational, yet can be overcome. That, of course, is precisely what the rising spiritual energies are all about: legitimating a new way of thinking about our own lives and about the economy.

As we become increasingly aware of the Unity of All Being, we become increasingly connected to the well-being of every human being on the planet and less able to close our eyes when corporations dump toxic wastes in the Third World or when the environmental consequences of past injustices fall disproportionately on others. This same consciousness makes us feel personally involved and hurt when species die out, rain forests are destroyed, natural habitats are undermined, and acres of wilderness are turned into shopping malls. And as we develop our sense of awe and wonder at the universe, we become increasingly unable to view the world as anything more than a disposable "resource" to be used for human consumption and discarded. It is this sense of the miraculous and the sacred that will eventually provide the foundation for saving the planet. Spirit Matters.

Aren't Corporations Recognizing These Problems and Becoming Environmentally Conscious?

Some corporations are environmentally sensitive. Others are taking steps in this direction, if for no other reason than because they imagine that a percentage of their potential consumers will be more interested in them if they show environmental awareness. So, there are environmentally sensitive programs in many corporations. In some there are even attempts to take environmental issues into account when making fundamental investment decisions.

But it's amazing how few these are.

And the reason is simple: corporations are set up to make money, and the corporate boards will honestly explain that they have a "fiduciary responsibility" to their investors to make as much money as possible. They will tell heartrending stories of little old widows who have invested in the corporation and who would be left destitute should corporate profits go down for the sake of ecological responsibility.

The simple reality is that the bottom line for most corporations is maximizing profits, and corporate leadership that failed to do so would quickly be booted out.

So, when someone tells you there's a new spirit of corporate responsibility, ethical awareness, or ecological sensitivity, be sure to ask one question: "What is their bottom line when it comes to corporate decision making?" Similarly, when you hear that corporations are considering double or triple bottom lines that include ecological or moral considerations, ask again: "What happens when the corporation recognizes that it can make more profit in the next twenty to thirty years following Path X but that Path Y will be more environmentally sensitive or ethically congruent with the values of love, caring, and community?"

If you ask these questions seriously, you'll find out that much of what appears to be changing in corporations has more to do with hype and marketing than it does with a fundamental change in values.

There are important exceptions to this reality. There are many corporations that do seek to be environmentally sensitive, and others that are actively engaged in selling products that might actually help offset the negative environmental degradation that I've described. Those corporations deserve our support and encouragement.

The Globalization of Capital Undermines Democratic Attempts at Environmental Sanity

Government policies are heavily influenced by the inordinate influence of money in elections. Many of the most environmentally sensitive candidates know that they have little chance of raising the millions of dollars it takes to run for major office in the United States unless they can sell themselves to the moneyed interests, who, quite often, have inherited or earned their money through investment in environmentally insensitive operations. Some political donors have transcended these kinds of considerations, but many have not, so it's very difficult to raise enough money if you are a serious environmental advocate, and harder still once the corporate media decides you are a threat. No surprise, then, that it is very rare for elected officials to be environmental crusaders. Given this reality, government budgets tend to favor large corporate interests and to supply the infrastructure for an ever-expanding production of goods that are destructive to the environment.

But even the elected officials who would like to take important steps to control corporate power find that the globalization of capital has dramatically reduced their ability to do so. Corporations are able to tell even powerful governments like that of the United States that they will move some or all of their production to other countries if they face serious environmental "costs." The flow of money through electronic markets makes it difficult to trace, much less control, investment decisions on the part of major capital investors, but it's safe to predict that they will invest where they believe their profits are most secure.

Faced with this reality, decent people in government decide that they simply can't face the consequences of the potential economic decline that might accompany serious environmental programs. They water their programs down to make them appear more friendly to "the business community," so that they don't precipitate a "loss of confidence," which would result in corporate disinvestment.

The One Hope: The Globalization of Spirit

What I have described above is a system in which everyone acts according to the narrow criteria of self-interest within a social context that teaches us to maximize our material power and control above all else.

But, as I've written in previous chapters, that system has one major weak link: it doesn't satisfy the fundamental human needs of many of its participants.

"Lefties" used to think that our society didn't satisfy those needs because it didn't deliver enough material goods to enough people. On a global scale this may be true, but in the United States, material well-being is distributed broadly enough that political upsurges around redistribution of wealth can be mostly contained. This was the battle of the 1930s, and the Democrats are still waging it, stuck in a time warp that will not acknowledge the realities that make New Deal visionaries and their New Left allies seem tired and outdated. Though important parts of their program still remain to be implemented, they never will be implemented until the leaders who advocate redistributive politics link that to a higher social vision.

What cannot be contained or outdated is a different kind of struggle: the struggle for a *new* bottom line based on love and caring, on ethical, spiritual, and ecological sensitivity. It cannot be contained because there is a universal need for this kind of society. The deprivation of meaning and Spirit causes pain that even the greatest material rewards cannot adequately offset. As I've shown in chapters two and three, spiritual deprivation permeates our daily lives and gives us a powerful motive to challenge the ethos of selfishness and materialism generated by the competitive market.

Environmental activists often propose workable alternatives to our current boundless consumption. But their strategies cannot gather the necessary support to stop the degradation of the environment. Why not?

Many an environmental activist may respond here by wondering "Why doesn't ecological survival count as equally pressing as spiritual needs? Why don't people from every class rally around a powerful ecological agenda, joining parties like the Greens or environmental movements, or at least voting for candidates who are ecological crusaders?"

Well, let's start with the fact that this is not happening.

Even if the environmental activists respond to this by saying, "It's not happening because the other side has the money, so we can't get our message out, and people would respond if only we could get through to them . . ." we have to follow up by asking, "Well, if that's the case, how are you going to change anything when your approach fails to generate the support it needs?"

But the environmentalists rarely try to understand why it is that their programs do not generate the support they need. The basic reason is that in our spiritually deadened society, people don't allow themselves to hope for change. And that's not too hard to understand either. Our society defines the accumulation of material goods as real. It defines the desire for love and caring as utopian. No wonder many people embrace the pathogenic belief that nothing fundamental can change, because people will always be motivated only by narrow self-interest. So how can they be expected to put aside what is taught to be our most fundamental desire, namely the accumulation of things, for the sake of the long-term well-being of people in the future?

Even many people who care about ecological degradation still end up telling themselves some variant of the following story:

•I am up against a system that seems overwhelmingly powerful.

•Most people are interested in themselves and unwilling to make sacrifices for anything larger than themselves. Even people who support social change are constantly pointing out how screwed up most people are (a pervasive, though sometimes unconscious, theme in lefty magazines like *The Nation* and *Mother Jones*). Deconstructionism (taught in many universities as the contemporary radical critique of society) has led me to conclude that there is no such thing as a shared or general ethical interest but only particular groups seeking power for themselves under the cover of flowery universalistic concepts. So, when I feel I ought to struggle for ecological sanity, I am already convinced that no one else will join me. The momentary upsurges of interest in things like Earth Day only highlight how little follow-through there ever is, and how quickly people return to their narrow self-interest. If I do take risks, I'm likely to find myself isolated and vulnerable.

•The power established interests have to discredit me makes it possible that were I to get seriously involved in struggles that really challenged their power, it would be me, not them, who would end up paying a high price—a price I may have to continue bearing for much of my life.

•The kinds of changes I want to see require people to make major changes in their lifestyle and consumer choices. But most people are more interested in material well-being than anything else. They'll never put the environment above their own interests.

•Environmental degradation still hasn't reached proportions that will destroy my personal life. The environmental harm will affect people in the Third World. It'll affect future generations. But it won't hurt me.

•So, I'd better control the things I actually can control, like my own personal family and community. I can do little things like buying environmentally better products and organic food, but it's better to leave the big issues to others, because I can't really handle them. After all, my own hands are clean because I recycle and buy organic.

Environmentalists with a background in the kind of elitist thinking that permeates liberal and progressive circles often find themselves frustrated by these arguments, because they can't imagine how people will ever change. Some turn toward variants of ecological theory that denounce human beings as an arrogant form of life that needs to be controlled.

The reality is that liberal and progressive thought is unable to meet the ecological challenge. The Left struggles for equality and democracy. But it has no answer to the fact that many of the most democratic and egalitarian societies the world has ever known have some of the most environmentally destructive levels of consumption. To the extent that the Left seems to be primarily concerned with the inclusion of everyone in the benefits of advanced industrial societies and makes its major focus the extension of democracy to economic decision making, the progressive forces have no theoretical foundation on which to build a critique of profligate consumption or environmental irresponsibility. Drowned in the ethos of selfishness and materialism, it is possible for people to democratically decide to consume the resources of the world in ways that might leave future generations without the environmental supports they need to survive on this planet.

The Globalization of Capital
or
The Globalization of Spirit

Only an Emancipatory Spirituality can add the necessary dimension to our societal thinking by teaching us to think about the universe, the planet, and each other not as resources to be used to maximize our own advantage, but as gifts from God or Spirit, for which we have the responsibility to serve as stewards and nurturers, and to which we respond with awe and wonder. Thinking about the world as sacred makes it possible to stand up to the underlying logic of the globalization of capital, a logic the Left can't really counter, because it shares the notion that what people want is more material goods, and that the only challenge is to make sure that everyone has equal opportunity and that decisions are made democratically.

Only those grounded in a spiritual consciousness can bring a more hopeful vision. The perspective I call Emancipatory Spirituality challenges the premise that people care only about themselves and instead provides antidotes to the stultifying dominant cynicism. Spiritual communities frequently teach and model a basic truth denied by the dominant society that: *people are willing to take risks and make sacrifices for causes that go beyond self-interest.* As for the premise that people are never willing to sacrifice their material comforts for the sake of some higher good (like environmental sanity), spiritual communities demonstrate that many of us have spiritual needs that are at least as important to us as our material needs and that we are sometimes willing to act accordingly. Emancipatory spirituality challenges the premise that we won't be concerned about environmental problems if they affect only strangers by fostering within us an appreciation of our common humanity, which transcends class, race, sex, and nationality. It teaches us to see the God, or Spirit, within each human being on the planet. It challenges the assumption that people are concerned only about the moment and are not fundamentally linked to the past and the future.

The new spirituality emerging today is all about overcoming our own individual ego orientation and connecting to the world in a whole different way, a way that focuses on awe, wonder, and a sense of stewardship and caring for all that is. The more it becomes widespread, the weaker the "common sense" rationale we give ourselves that "all people want is material goods" or that people are "never motivated by anything higher than narrow material self-interest" will be.

The way the public debate is currently framed, environmentalists are made to look ridiculous if they call for any reduction in the level of material consumption. "You are being undemocratic. The 'people' actually want and enjoy new consumer goods. You are being elitist by trying to impose your environmental agenda on everyone else."

Daunting as it may seem, that argument can effectively be countered by speaking of a higher set of values that derive from the realm of the Spirit. In our empirical work as therapists, my colleagues and I have demonstrated that people have a set of spiritual needs. If environmentalists were able to frame their concerns in a language that spoke to these highest spiritual values, they could reach millions of "ordinary people" who are unmoved by the current technocratic and "rights" oriented discourse.

Unfortunately, most contemporary leaders of the environmental movement cannot make this change in focus. They either don't yet have enough familiarity with Spirit or are fearful of acknowledging that familiarity in public discourse. Reared in liberal and Left circles, they believe that Spirit should be kept out of public discourse, and they feel more comfortable citing facts that everyone will acknowledge as "scientific" and hence "objective" than appealing to values or perspectives that are "merely" subjective. But only the discourse of the Spirit can respond effectively to the world of capital:

"We humans need more than just money and power; we need more than scientific innovation and technological advance. What we need is a world based on love and caring, awe, wonder, and radical amazement. You say that people only want more goods, but I know that most people want to live in a world in which our response to nature is not limited to what we can get out of it. In fact, the way of thinking about life as little more than an attempt to maximize our own advantage without regard to the well-being of others and without regard to the consequences for the future is precisely what leads to so much pain in our personal lives. We need a whole new way of thinking about ourselves, our planet, and our society—and we environmentalists are part of the growing spiritual transformation that is happening in every sphere of our society and that seeks to bring us back to a reverence and awe for the universe taught by our religious and spiritual communities. So don't tell us that most people just want more material goods, because that perception on your part is what makes most people feel discouraged about their own higher values and makes them feel isolated when, in fact, they are part of a growing new consciousness that will change every aspect of life in the period ahead."

It's only when environmentalists challenge the discourse of selfishness and foster a spiritual culture with a new orientation to nature that they can hope to win. As long as the argument is carried out within the framework of a materialistic orientation to the world, environmentalists will always be on the defensive and will never be able to awaken their own constituencies to the yearning for a different kind of world.

This is why, in the final analysis, Spirit is the indispensable element in countering the globalization of capital. The logic of capital is that people want products, and that globalization is a good way to get more material goods shared by more people. All the globalists are doing, they tell us, is finding effective ways to respond to the desires of the majority of people. What could be more noble than to make money while fulfilling human needs? Those who wish to stand in the way of these desires are totalitarians forcing their value system down the throats of an unwilling public!

Only when environmentalists can understand the logic of spiritual needs, needs that are just as real but that do not manifest in market terms, can they effectively respond to the powerful "free trade" and "let everyone choose whatever they want" arguments of the corporate globalists. Unfortunately, most hard-nosed environmentalists do not yet understand this need for a spiritual framework. They have no idea how to foster an ethos of awe and wonder in society and no idea that this is what they will need to do in order to counter the logic of unlimited consumption accelerating with the globalization of capital. They and their friends in major progressive foundations pour millions of dollars and huge amounts of energy into approaches that can never work because they do not address the underlying structure of our environmental problem. It never occurs to them that the best strategy would be to help the growing spiritual movements understand the ecological aspects of their spirituality and help environmentalists speak to the spiritual crisis in daily life (described in chapters two and three). It is only when our hunger for love and caring and our need to respond to the world with awe and wonder can be linked through Spirit that environmentalism will achieve the social and political power to save the planet. It's only through the fight for new definitions of productivity, efficiency, and rationality that we will develop a majority ready to put environmental consciousness above the expansion of material production.

Many environmental leaders imagine that a purely technocratic solution can be found, and that "if only" they could get the people's attention, everyone would recognize how rational their approach is. Some imagine that an environmentally sensitive president will get elected and manage to sneak some decent legislation through Congress or issue some useful regulations. When that *doesn't* happen, they either withdraw from politics in despair or decide that to accomplish anything they have to be "more realistic" and narrow their focus on what is achievable within the current political context. People who once were environmental visionaries transform themselves into lobbyists fighting for narrow victories that cannot possibly save the planet from ecological destruction because they've given up their dreams and despair of ever obtaining support from the majority of people.

In the course of the next fifty years, more and more environmentalists will come to understand that Spirit Matters. They will make the spiritual transformation of our consciousness the linchpin of their strategy to save the environment. In the meantime, though I've been critical of some of their strategic choices, I do want to encourage us to show lots of support and compassion for those who have chosen to dedicate their lives to protecting our environment. Many of these people are underrecognized and, like all social change activists, underpaid. They are often on the front lines of the struggle, taking personal risks, and doing so for the highest altruistic motives. They deserve our gratitude, as do all who have dedicated their lives to social transformation and healing.

And while I'm on the subject of compassion, let's acknowledge that there are millions of decent individuals involved in corporate life who would be thrilled to be part of a society that served higher goals than corporate profit. They, too, are part of the constituency that will eventually transform our society, and they need to be approached not as "the enemy" but as potential allies. An environmental movement that speaks to a higher spiritual consciousness has much greater chance of reaching the people like Samuel Hughes—corporate people whose lives are in spiritual crisis but who would never link their own needs with those of environmentalists unless there were a progressive movement that could make those links. The way to do that is through the discourse of Emancipatory Spirituality.

Countering Globalization with a New Consciousness

As spiritual consciousness becomes more prominent, it will become easier to take decisive steps to counter the destructive elements of globalization.

The collapse of societies that described themselves as Communist opened the world to what appeared to be unimpeded power of global capital. Globalization seemed almost invincible just a few short years ago. The World Trade Organization, created to facilitate this process, was ready to consider proposals that would increase the power of multinational corporations, giving them the right to sue national governments if they sought to protect their own industries or shield themselves from the onslaught of foreign capital. In the name of free trade, environmental restrictions were challenged and "the right" to sweatshop conditions was protected. Elites of wealth and power in Third World countries even insisted that they were serving the best interests of their own people by rejecting environmental or human rights restrictions. After all, they argued, if multinationals (largely based in the developed world) could be enticed to produce their goods in third world countries without environmental regulations or a minimum wage, that would create jobs, albeit at thirty-five dollars a week.

It seemed that the multinationals had the perfect solution: they could use capital-hungry elites in Third World countries to prevent environmentalists, labor, and human rights activists from pressuring first world governments to demand minimal safeguards in the process of globalization. Since the first world governments and media were primarily responsive to the needs of their corporate funders, it would not be hard for them to shed a few crocodile tears about their desire to be environmentally sensitive and supportive of human rights and living wages, but then argue that they were caught by their equally important commitment to helping poor people in the Third World who would best be served by not imposing "our Western standards" (for environmental safety, labor rights, or human rights) in ways that would limit "free trade" and the benefits it would bring to Third World economies.

Imagine their surprise when, in the very last year of the second millennium, tens of thousands of demonstrators showed up at the World Trade Organization meeting in Seattle to burst the bubble of governmental hypocrisy and insist that globalization without ethics would no longer be acceptable.

The WTO protests brought together groups that had seldom before seen common cause. Protesters carried signs that read "Turtles and Teamsters—Together at Last." But in the coming decades, the momentary ties between labor, environmentalists, and human rights activists will probably be severely strained. These groups have been schooled in the practice of putting their own concerns and interests above the larger struggle, and that practice will almost certainly weaken the kind of alliance that the Seattle demonstrations seemed to portend.

It is possible for that alliance to form again and become a powerful factor in shaping public policy. But that possibility depends in part on the degree to which social change activists are able to articulate their goals in categories that transcend narrow or sectoral concerns and touch on the common needs of the entire society. The more these activists are in touch with a higher spiritual energy and vision, the more they will be able to sustain the kind of political alliance that could actually win each group's goals.

Contemporary social change movements that lack a spiritual foundation have often gone through a kind of "natural history" that includes many of the following steps:

People come together around some specific grievance, then;

They begin to understand that what they really need is some deeper transformation of the world, then;

A period (a few weeks, months, or years) ensues in which people experience the incredible high of hoping for these kinds of fundamental changes, but;

As the full intensity of corporate/media/governmental power is mobilized in defense of the status quo, people begin to realize that their full vision is not going to be won very quickly, possibly not even in their lifetimes. Without the immediate possibility of achieving the full vision, people become more focused on the quality of the movement itself. Their frustration about not being able to achieve their vision makes them feel more critical of each other and they begin to focus more on the ways people around them are disappointing and do not fully embody the goals of the movement. This then leads to;

Growing internal resentments, rivalries, displacement of anger at the larger social world against movement leaders or fellow participants, and incessant bickering over tactics or theories, which in turn leads to;

A narrowing of focus away from the shared vision and toward what can be won in the short run, and a growing despair about the larger vision ever happening. This in turn is followed by;

An even deeper despair about anything changing, because now the movement seems to be just another narrow interest group seeking to move for its own advantage, which finally leads to;

A deepening cynicism, depoliticization, and dissolution of the movement to the point that people feel all alone and unable to act in the world.

The only thing that could stop this process is the development of a spiritual consciousness, which would counter some of these dynamics by:

Helping people stay in touch with their transformative visions even when those visions do not seem immediately winnable;

Helping people develop a practice of compassion for others that would allow them to be less disillusioned when they found that their fellow participants in social change movements were as flawed as we all actually are;

Helping people resist the tendency to settle for the kinds of short-term payoffs that divert attention from longer term goals;

Helping people resist the tendency to restrict their political activity to goals that are practical and realistic, since what is practical and realistic in a society dominated by corporate globalization will be that which is least threatening to the powerful;

Preventing people from demeaning participants in corporate structures, or otherwise engaging in us/them dichotomizing, and instead helping social change activists see the humanity, decency, and spiritual potential even in the people on the opposite side of the table;

Providing activists with a foundational vision that would help them recognize their common goals even as parts of the movement may emphasize more narrow tasks.

Armed with a spiritual consciousness, social change activists have a much easier time acknowledging that there are good aspects of globalization that need not be resisted. As means of communication, the Internet and other forms of global communication encourage the development of shared democratic and pluralistic values that have brought distance learning to people who might otherwise be isolated or confined to homes or hospital rooms. It has facilitated the development of international citizen organizations that may become the foundations for international movements toward social healing and environmental sanity. It's not necessary to deny the benefits of globalization to challenge its seamier sides, or to insist that we create social, economic, and political institutions that are more supportive of our growing sense of awe and wonder at the universe and our desire for ecological sanity, social justice, and a world based on love.

A growing spiritual awareness empowers us to fight the TINA (There Is No Alternative) ideology, powerfully articulated by Thomas Friedman of the *New York Times* and repeated as a mantra by Western political leaders who seek to sanctify corporate globalization with the crown of historical necessity. There *is* an alternative to unrestrained corporate globalization: it is the globalization of Spirit. As more people build their lives around Emancipatory Spirituality, craven bowing to corporate globalization will appear less the march of necessity and become more recognizable as a contemporary form of idolatry. It then becomes possible to ask the relevant spiritual question: how do we shape globalization in a way that maximizes ecological sustainability, enhances our global responsibility to reduce suffering and promote health and ethical well-being, increases our capacity to see our unity with all other human beings and our part in the Unity of All Being, and incorporates a sense of human limitations and humility. Globalization of awe and wonder rather than globalization of our tendency to see the world as something to be used and manipulated, globalization of our sense of the sacred, globalization of our caring and our love for each other and for all life forms, globalization of compassion and generosity—this is what the globalization of Spirit has to offer in response to those who talk about the inevitability of the globalization of capital.

Once they are armed with a spiritual consciousness, social change movements will be able to sustain themselves and resist the internal tendencies toward self-destruction that have almost always undermined social change in the past. To the extent that they embody spiritual consciousness and affirm spiritual visions through some of the methods described in chapter ten, these movements will be in far less peril of self-subversion as they take on important intermediate steps and demands. Imagine, for a moment, a spiritually grounded social change movement that could:

• Seek new measures of the quality of life that supplement traditional Gross National Product/Gross Domestic Product systems of national accounting. The king of Bhutan has recently called for a "gross national happiness" index, (bootan.com 6/21/99). Such accounting would have to value unpaid caring work (for example, parenting or caring for the sick and elderly) and what Inge Kaul, Isabelle Grunberg, and Mark Stern call "public goods" (namely the goods and services needed for global human security, survival, and development—including peace, equity, financial stability, and environmental sustainability).

• Create mechanisms of accountability for multinational corporations. In chapter ten I propose first steps in this direction: the Social Responsibility Amendment to the U.S. Constitution, which would require corporations to obtain a new corporate charter every twenty years, a charter would be granted only if the corporation in question demonstrated a history of social responsibility; and the Social Responsibility Initiative, which would make a priority of awarding public contracts to corporations with the best history of social responsibility.

• Build institutions of civic society on the local, national, and global levels that can operate as counterforces to the market and to global capital's international power base in media, governments, and globalized economic institutions.

• Develop programs to ensure that the earth's resources are shared equitably. Make decisions about production and distribution of goods on a democratic basis. But, as Hazel

Henderson points out in *Beyond Globalization*, "Reshaping the global economy also requires including at all levels the missing feedback from nature, planetary and local ecosystems as well as the human beings also marginalized by the current runaway forms of globalization" (p. 22).

•Create incentives for nations to reduce military spending and to direct resources toward building global economic well-being, adequate housing, education, health care, and ecologically sustainable production. For example, create an international fund that will provide development dollars for countries that significantly reduce military spending. To help reduce conflicts that lead to military conflicts, create a truly effective peace corps. As a step in this direction, groups of social change activists are now developing plans for a volunteer army of nonviolent peacemakers that would work to de-escalate tension in areas where conflict might lead to violence. Committed to a spiritual vision of love and caring, and not tied to the specific interests of any particular side in the conflict, such a team might have more prestige than any force that seemed to be a reflection of political intentions of power-hungry national entities. These kinds of interventions, of course, are effective to the extent that their spiritual integrity is assured. The United Nations has lost much of its potential effectiveness precisely because it is seen as the handmaiden of great power interests rather than as an expression of the highest shared ideals of the human race. To assure spiritual integrity, these interventions must be understood to be an outgrowth of a long-standing commitment to a bottom line of love and caring, not of power politics and self-interested maneuvering. Hence the importance of a corps of people whose commitment to a spiritual vision of love and caring is so transparently obvious that it would take enormous energy to see them as anything but spiritually centered and dedicated activists for peace.

•Move from highly concentrated absentee ownership to stakeholder ownership of a society's productive assets. Each person should have an ownership stake in the assets on which his or her livelihood depends.

•Create a Jubilee in which the international debt of poorer nations is forgiven if they establish democratic regimes with functioning guarantees of free speech and assembly, a free media, jury by peers, workers' rights to organize, living wages, and ecologically sustainable policies governing their economic growth.

•Make the funding of international and local media independent from global capital either directly from advertising (commercial media) or indirectly in the form of corporate sponsorship (the misnamed "public" radio and television, which today is often another extension of the corporate mind-set rather than a serious alternative to it). Such media would give honest accounting of the seriousness of environmental problems and of the most critical strategic alternatives facing the human race as we try to save the planet from further destruction of our life-support system. Such media would see their explicit task as fostering a sense of awe and wonder at the universe, a deepening of our understanding of mutual interconnectedness, and our awareness of the Unity of All Being.

These are a few of the partial measures that could be enacted by a movement that defined the bottom line as love and caring, ethical/spiritual/ecological sensitivity, and the promotion of awe and wonder. Our environmental crisis will only be solved when such a movement develops. Until then, the momentum of the demonstration at the World Trade Organization may recede, criticisms and mutual recriminations may replace solidarity, and narrow reforms may replace a larger vision of a planet saved from moral and ecological degradation. Though it may recede for years or decades, though the bureaucracy of social change may replace passion and vision, it will always be possible for that transformative energy to reemerge. And for reasons that I've argued in the earlier chapters, the pain caused by living in a society without spiritual moorings will make people increasingly hungry for spiritual alternatives. Eventually, that hunger, united with an understanding of the destruction being done to our planet, will generate the kind of movement for Emancipatory Spirituality that can save us from ecological destruction.

five

EMANCIPATORY SPIRITUALITY

We are in the midst of an extraordinary upsurge of interest in the realm of the Spirit. Tens of millions of people in advanced industrial societies live at a level of material well-being that far surpasses the luxuries and comforts available to kings, queens, and nobles just a few hundred years ago. But many of these are in the vanguard of those who seek a new spiritual reality.

Emancipatory Spirituality is emerging on college campuses and in churches; at ashrams, synagogues, and mosques; in poetry and fiction, in movies and books, in community centers, and in zines and websites; and in little acts of loving kindness.

But, and this is a big "but," most of the people involved do not yet recognize themselves as part of some larger movement.

I remember giving a talk about Emancipatory Spirituality at a Methodist church in Kansas. My message was greeted with great enthusiasm, but afterwards many people told me: "We here in Kansas believe that there ought to be a new bottom line, but we know very well from watching television and reading the newspapers that people on the coasts are so selfish and narcissistic they'd never support a more loving world—in fact, they'd just laugh at our foolishness and think of us as country bumpkins for believing in love. So how can we ever believe that anything will change?" Now, I've been in so many rooms with people in New York; Los Angeles; San Francisco; Seattle; Portland; Miami; Boston; Philadelphia; Washington, D.C.; Atlanta; and so many other places—and in each place the people in the room thought they were the only ones who shared all this idealism— because the media has done such a terrific job of making us all invisible to each other. The people on the coasts considered themselves different from the "Middle America" people I met in Kansas. In fact, they have very similar needs and interests. Yet the media makes us invisible to each other.

So, how will we become visible?

There are a wide variety of spiritual projects emerging today that will help in this process. Some of these projects are detailed in books like *Spiritual Politics*, by Corinne McLaughlin and Gordon Davidson; *Conscious Evolution*, by Barbara Marx Hubbard; and in magazines like *Sojourners* (which comes from the Christian Evangelical world), TIKKUN (the magazine I edit), and *Yes* (a journal edited by David Korten). Even this book, *Spirit Matters*, could play some role in making people more visible to each other. Dozens of important books published each year play their part in making it easier for people to "get" that something is happening beyond their own inner lives. Don't underestimate the power of putting this and other books in the hands of people you care about—or the impact of people getting a spiritually oriented magazine on a regular basis. These little concrete manifestations of spiritual interest can provide a massive dose of hopefulness for people who thought they already knew all the idealistic people in the world, and that there weren't very many of them.

But it will take a lot more than books or magazines. We need a social movement committed to spiritual transformation that can publicly champion a new bottom line of love and caring. As such a movement grows, it can shake us loose from our depressive resignation about the impossibility of what we yearn for.

Such a movement is already developing, though it has not yet reached a level of public visibility that can protect it from being dismissed as flaky, naive, or irrelevant. It will take many years, perhaps even decades, before it reaches a "critical mass" and its ideas are allowed serious consideration by the gatekeepers of public discourse.

We will reach that critical mass as more people begin to struggle for a new bottom line in society. In our economy, our legal structures, our medical system, our education, and in every other sphere of our lives people will increasingly challenge the ethos of selfishness and materialism in the name of what I call Emancipatory Spirituality.

That transformation will be aided as more and more people engage in a regular daily spiritual practice. The deeper the spiritual practice, the less they will be willing to tolerate a society that functions on the assumptions of competitiveness and looking out for number one.

Eventually, the millions of people who already desire a new bottom line will become more visible to each other. The more they realize that they are not alone, the more they will feel empowered to publicly assert their commitment to an Emancipatory Spirituality.

It will happen as more and more people engage in acts of loving kindness toward each other and in joyful celebration of the grandeur of the universe. The more love and celebration around us, the more awe and wonder, the harder it will be to sustain the old ways of being that are considered "common sense" today.

What Is Emancipatory Spirituality?

Some of what is central to Emancipatory Spirituality links it to older forms of spiritual life, while other aspects are quite new and unique. Here is my description of this emerging spiritual orientation and practice:

1. Emancipatory Spirituality means a celebration of the wonder of the universe—and the cultivation of our capacities for awe and radical amazement at all that is. It involves a deep recognition of the Unity of All Being and a humble recognition of ourselves as one small but valuable part of the totality, and an ability to see our endeavors from the perspective of the totality.

This way of seeing is not the same as a detached aesthetic appreciation of the universe. Awe and radical amazement elicit a complete involvement of one's whole self, moments of being overwhelmed, having one's breath taken away, being captivated and excited by the marvel of all that is.

To see in this way is to recognize other human beings, the earth, and the entire universe as sacred. We do not orient toward them primarily in terms of how they can be of use to our purposes, but in terms of their intrinsic value and our responsibility toward them. We feel ourselves drawn to them, concerned about their well-being, desiring to promote their best interests, and grateful for the ways we receive nurturance from them. We do not see ourselves as dominating them, but as in relationship to them, involved in their well-being, and a beneficiary of their goodness.

2. Emancipatory Spirituality means cultivating our capacity to see each other as ends, not means to some other end. Every single person on the planet is to be treated as valuable and deserving of love, respect, and solidarity (in secular language) or as created in the image of God (in religious language).

This is not merely a matter of holding the correct opinion. Emancipatory Spirituality encourages an inner spiritual practice aimed at shaping our inner selves to respond to others with empathy, compassion, great feelings of love, and an unmediated desire to enhance their well-being and to ensure that they are fully able to actualize their capacities as loving, free, self-defining, creative, intelligent, and joyous beings.

If we have these feelings, we will also feel a passionate commitment to democratic forms of government and democratic economic decision making, as well as to the separate development of each individual. We will support free speech, freedom of assembly, tolerance, and respect for difference and we will resist every attempt to coercively impose a single right way to be, whether that comes from government, from the pressures of the market and advertising, or from communities of the self-righteous. There may be many different forms for achieving substantive democracy, but they must all function in ways that affirm the sanctity of each individual.

3. Emancipatory Spirituality affirms the equal worth of every human being, regardless of race, gender, sexual orientation, nationality, religion, cultural ties, or anything else that has been used to deny equality of respect.

4. Emancipatory Spirituality seeks the healing and transformation of the world, so that all of our public institutions cooperate to enhance peace, tolerance, cooperation, mutual respect, ecological sanity, social justice, and celebration of the grandeur of the universe.

To achieve and sustain this transformation, Emancipatory Spirituality encourages people to work together in social and political movements, and to fill those movements with a powerful spiritual practice that includes meditation, celebration of the universe, loving care for each other, love for those who do not share the movement's particular philosophy or transformative strategy, and a genuine recognition that its goals cannot be achieved by means that are not as holy as its ends. It is committed to non-violence as a strategy and as a way of life.

5. Emancipatory Spirituality means cultivating our capacity to transcend our individual egos so that we can experience connection to the Oneness of All Being.

To transcend the ego does not mean to permanently eliminate it, but rather to put ego concerns in balance. It takes a strong ego to be able to transcend ego without allowing one's own intellect or good judgment to be subordinated to that of a guru or a charismatic leader. People with strong egos can follow a teacher or leader without losing their own integrity and freedom, because they retain their own independent judgment and freely decide to follow a particular path. Those with weaker egos will sometimes find themselves giving up too much of themselves, feeling resentful, and ultimately engaging in a dialectic of antileadership that can be destructive to spiritual communities. So, Emancipatory Spirituality supports the development of strong egos and the spiritual practice of transcending those egos.

6. Emancipatory Spirituality means developing mindfulness, a form of alert attention to each act and experience, so that we are alive to everything we encounter in ourselves, in each other and in the world—and so we can experience the potential sanctity of every aspect of our lives. This mindfulness requires a deep openness to the truth of what is and a capacity to see the potential for transformation in all that is.

7. Emancipatory Spirituality encourages us to develop rich inner lives connected to Spirit and to sustain that connection even through periods of adversity and pain. It is not a "feel

good" spirituality that calls attention only to that which is pleasing in the world, but rather a spirituality that asks us to attend to all that is, to be conscious of the pain and suffering of humanity, and to overcome our tendencies to "space out" when something seems disagreeable or frightening. There is great suffering in life, and a grounded spiritual practice does not seek to deny the reality of suffering but to help us be with it, to distinguish the parts that are changeable from those that are not. While acting to change what we can, we also learn to accept what we cannot change without denial, without fleeing into pseudo-consolations or partial distractions, without closing our minds or our hearts.

Only through fully experiencing our own emotions can we free ourselves from our fears enough to be truly conscious of the needs of others. And it is through this alert attentiveness that we can begin to recognize our own ego distortions and connect to the totality and unity of all.

To achieve this ability to be present to our own experience, we need to overcome blocks from the past, including anger and resentments against parents. Spiritual life requires cultivating a capacity to forgive those who have hurt us in the past, starting with compassion for our own parents.

8. Emancipatory Spirituality means enhancing our capacity to play, to experience joy and pleasure, to honor our emotions and the emotions of others, to educate the next generation with love and compassion, and to experience solitude and silence. It means building communities and social practices that encourage and foster these capacities.

9. Emancipatory Spirituality encourages non-goal-directed aesthetic creativity in music, dance, painting, poetry, theater, fiction, video, and in any other form of human artistic expression.

Rejecting censorship, Emancipatory Spirituality embraces the notion of "all power to the imagination" and integrates that understanding into the framework of a loving, respectful, and awe-filled universe.

10. Affirming pleasure and sexuality while rejecting all attempts to separate Spirit from its embeddedness in body, Emancipatory Spirituality promotes a sexuality that is integrated with a sense of sanctity and reverence for others, a sexuality that permeates and rejuvenates us, a sexuality that enhances loving commitments and trust between people.

To fully experience pleasure and joy, we must also be open to our anger and our hurt. Emancipatory Spirituality rejects a kind of airy-headed spirituality that encourages people to see everything as happy-making and wonderful, and to avoid anger and confrontation with evil and suffering in the world. There is an ongoing function for righteous indignation and rage at injustice and these feelings are an important element in Emancipatory Spirituality to the extent that they lead to active involvement in healing and transforming the world.

11. Emancipatory Spirituality means encouraging an overwhelming feeling of love toward others and a respectful caring for their needs, without forgetting our own needs.

Loving others involves, in part, a desire to help each other leave the goal-directed consciousness required by the struggle for survival and to encourage each other to spend more energy in the world of playfulness and joyful celebration. It means encouraging others to take pleasure in some of life's greatest joys: (a) connecting with others and fully recognizing them in all their complexity, (b) deepening our understanding of the complicated and multilayered nature of reality, (c) sharing love without fear that there won't be enough to go around, (d) rejoicing in the well-being of others, (e) generously sharing our talents and our material resources with others (f) sharing responsibility for the raising of children and the care of elders in ways that affirm their self-worth and preciousness, (g) respecting individual differences and alternative life paths, (h) respecting privacy and the desire of people to not always be part of the group and to not always participate in whatever others are doing.

Emancipatory Spirituality also supports healing that enables us to be fully loving, caring, trusting, trustworthy, gentle, creative, attentive, intellectually developed, and bursting with erotic life-energy, curiosity, compassion, wisdom, and joy. So, it encourages every form of spiritual counseling, spiritually sensitive psychotherapy, and family counseling as well as any transformative process that actually leads to this kind of spiritual and emotional healing.

12. Emancipatory Spirituality promotes respect and care for the well-being of the entire universe, a desire to live ecologically sustainable lives and to create human societies that are environmentally sustainable and that embody respect for all other life forms. (This respect does not mean accepting every life form as equally valuable. For example, it must allow us to engage in research to prevent or combat cancer or heart disease, no matter how "natural" they may be.)

Emancipatory Spirituality encourages us to support cooperation and morally sound, ecologically sustainable planning on a global, national, regional, and local basis. We need to steward the universe's resources, and to do so with humility and reverence for all creation.

13. Emancipatory Spirituality supports the deepening of our intellectual capacities so they can be directed toward ensuring the survival and spiritual flourishing of the human race and our integration into the universe with humility, ecological sensitivity, and a realistic understanding of the limits of our knowledge and our wisdom.

Emancipatory Spirituality acknowledges the importance of science and technology, and of the kind of rational thinking associated with Western philosophies and systems of logic and mathematics. It honors these.

But Emancipatory Spirituality also sees the limits of science and recognizes other forms of knowledge. It treasures the wisdom that emerges from the mystical, religious, aesthetic, and moral traditions of the human race, as well as the wisdom that comes to us in intuitive and inner ways. It recognizes the wisdom of women. It acknowledges that there are many levels of reality that we as humans only dimly understand, and it encourages us both to respect our limitations and to seek ways to expand our capacities to receive information from the universe and to be open to God's voice in whatever ways it can be received.

Emancipatory Spirituality reveres learning and discourse

as sources of pleasure and joy and as activities that can be playful and rewarding for their own sake, not only to achieve some higher individual or communal goal.

14. Emancipatory Spirituality seeks an integration of our many capacities and strengths, both on the individual and global levels, without insisting that our unique traditions be subservient to some new universal view of "the single right way." Integrating the different forms of wisdom is not a call to abandon uniqueness, but to share and integrate what we each have to contribute with the wisdom of others.

15. Emancipatory Spirituality supports "changing the bottom line" of society from an ethos of selfishness and materialism to an ethos of love and caring. Emancipatory Spirituality seeks a fundamental redefinition of concepts like rationality, productivity, and efficiency so that they include love, solidarity with others, awe and wonder at the universe, and ethical, spiritual, and ecological sensitivity.

If any economic, political, or social system cannot accommodate to this "new bottom line," it needs to be transformed in ways that make this set of concerns seem realistic rather than utopian. That the world can be based on love and awe—not just in our private lives but in the way we interact with each other and build our economic and social institutions—is a central tenet of Emancipatory Spirituality.

16. Emancipatory Spirituality encourages the spiritual evolution of the human race toward higher forms of knowing, loving, sharing, and rejoicing. This openness to evolving higher levels of consciousness and connection to the Unity of All Being involves a willingness to let go of old ways of thinking and organizing our lives so that we can further evolve as conscious and loving beings. It encourages us to move beyond the smallness of our vision and to allow ourselves to be guided by Spirit, approaching our world with openheartedness, rejoicing in serving God's plan, radiating blessings and health to all whom we encounter, and allowing ourselves to sink into a paradoxical state of relaxed trust and animated engagement, a sense of surrender into a greater awareness, and basking in the luminous lovelight of the One.

The Danger of Reactionary Spirituality

Reactionary spirituality can be easily identified by three characteristics:

It usually asserts that one group has the authoritative account of truth. For example, a group can claim that it received God's revelation first and that it therefore has the exclusive ability to correctly interpret God's will. Or it can claim that it has some special current tie to God or to Spirit that makes its understanding superior to that of everyone else. Or it can claim that people of a certain kind (men, women, white people, people who share some physical or emotional attribute) are innately more attuned to spiritual truth than others.

However, the countercultural view, now sometimes finding support in New Age spiritual circles, that equality requires that we give equal value to the ideas of every human being, is deeply mistaken. There is nothing elitist or harmful in believing that some ideas are better than other ideas. Nor is it intrinsically elitist or hurtful to assert that some people came to those ideas first and deserve to be honored for having played a vanguard role in delivering good ideas to the rest of the human race.

What becomes elitist is the belief that certain truths can *only* come through some privileged group of people, or that one group has an exclusive right to interpret sacred ideas or has an exclusive access to Spirit.

I have no trouble thinking that certain people are more highly developed in their aesthetic capacities, physical prowess, sexual aliveness, intellectual sophistication, emotional sensitivity, spiritual development, or any other valued traits—and believing that I can learn more from them in their field than I could from others. What I do find offensive is when these same capacities are attributed to a subgroup, be they priests, gurus, teachers, or whatever, without regard to each practitioner's personal development or message. So, when someone tells me that a given person is spiritually elevated because he or she was born into a particular family, group, or social status, or because she or he has been designated a teacher of a particular tradition, I want to know more about the individual person before I'm willing to accept such claims.

Reactionary spirituality rejects the claims of science and rational inquiry, rather than recognizing some legitimate sphere in which science and rational inquiry should have a definitive say.

Reactionary spirituality may critique the values of capital or those of the ruling elites of a given society, but it is *not* willing to support the democratization of the society, the economy, or the political order. Usually it finds itself backing other elites who are no more democratic than the ones it initially opposed. It talks about social justice, but it is unwilling to struggle for transformation of our economic and political system in ways that would promote that social justice. It conforms to the values of the societies in which it operates rather than actually seeking to build social and economic institutions that value love and caring above money and power.

The usual outcome of this combination of characteristics is this: to glorify some particular part of the human race and to denigrate some "other." It is this disdain for the Other that is the most unacceptable element in reactionary forms of spirituality.

Demeaning the Other runs counter to the highest goal of Spirit. It undermines the belief in the Unity of All Being and the possibility of recognizing every other human being as equally created in the image of God. For that reason, any alliance with reactionary spiritual circles must be seen as merely temporary and as morally problematic.

Religious Nationalism and Fundamentalism as Flawed but Real Constraints on the Globalization of Capital

The fundamental tension of the next few centuries will be between reactionary and emancipatory forms of spirituality. I hope that this book will be part of a process that encourages people to develop an emancipatory consciousness.

But the difficult truth is this: at certain moments, reactionary forms of spirituality *do* play a positive role in the struggle against the globalization of selfishness.

A handful of multinational corporations control a sizable portion of the world's wealth and are more powerful than most countries.

These corporate entities routinely bypass democratically established regulations intended to protect fragile ecosystems, workers' rights, or human health.

Labor movements have been marginalized by the tremendous power of these corporations. They lack the power and resources to significantly limit the way capital takes advantage of differentials in wages and profits around the world (for example, by threatening countries that seek to put constraints on corporate power that the corporations will simply move to another country and cause job loss). The result has been a widening income inequality both among and within nations.

Even in the United States, states often find themselves at the mercy of capital. They feel that in order to provide jobs to their people, they must attract and retain investment. But to do so they must accede to capital's demands: limit ecological regulations, lower taxes, and make less money available for welfare, health care, child care, or education.

Yet in an "every man for himself world," even the people who are most harmed find it impossible to organize to do battle. To organize would presuppose the possibility of suspending narrow self-interest for the sake of common interests. That, in turn, would require a level of trust that the entire system so powerfully undermines.

It is precisely here that religious fundamentalism and nationalism raise the possibility of temporarily constraining capital.

Religious communities offer a counterlogic to the logic of capitalism. The realm of Spirit does not subordinate human needs to the needs of "progress."

Religion inherently values human beings as embodiments of the sacred, and this puts a restraint on the way capital sees human beings as means to an end.

Religions often tell historical stories. The nurturing of historical consciousness itself is subversive to the extent that it reminds people that the social world is not fixed, that it once was different, and that it might be different again in the future.

Religions offer a language of solidarity that transcends the individualism of the competitive marketplace and the broader but still limiting self-interest of class politics.

Religion offers a sense of sacred time that cannot be colonized by the work ethic of the capitalist world. It offers a sense of the sacred, of beauty, of goodness, and of responsibility to others—all of which are untranslatable in the language of capitalist development.

It's no wonder, then, that so many people turn to religious communities to find solace and escape from the logic of the marketplace.

The people who feel most attracted to reactionary spiritual or fundamentalist communities are often those who have come to believe that they will not "make it" in the capitalist market. In the religious world they are considered valuable not according to what they can do or accumulate, but because they *are*. Their very being is seen as intrinsically worthwhile.

Our establishment media always portray people who choose fundamentalist communities as the embodiment of irrationality. The only question the media shapes for us is how to contain or offset this craziness that, they imagine, threatens to swallow the world. It never occurs to them to ask: "Why, if the world of materialism and selfishness is so terrific, do reasonable people find themselves gravitating to or attracted to forms of religious nationalism or fundamentalism that are so at variance with our understanding of rationality?" The only answer they offer is because these people are either evil or stupid.

If we move beyond elitist explanations and seek a reasonable core to people's attraction to fundamentalist religions, we immediately find ourselves trying to figure out how that reasonable core could be associated with sexist, homophobic, or reactionary nationalist components that often accompany fundamentalist spirituality.

But why is it so hard to imagine that a single vision or a single community could have contradictory elements? Are *we* so far above this? Certainly the liberals and progressives who usually shout loudest about the distortions in the fundamentalist world might remember how the peace movement of the 1960s nurtured groups like the Weathermen, who advocated armed struggle and glorified bombing attacks on office buildings only distantly connected to the war effort. Nor is the fundamentalist distortion harder to understand than how a progressive movement could have glorified a "sexual revolution" that too often was merely a cover for male exploitation of women in the movement. Nor harder than to understand how Black Liberation could give a place at its table to overtly anti-Semitic and homophobic elements like those around Louis Farrakhan's branch of the Black Muslim movement.

No matter what happened in our own corner, we were always able to come up with sophisticated explanations for how the distortions did not undermine the moral content of these movements. An equally charitable approach could help us separate the positive and reasonable impulses that lead people to fundamentalist religions from the more distorted elements in these communities.

I can imagine someone reading these lines and taking them out of context to imply that I'm advocating fundamentalist religious traditions. But that is *not* what I'm arguing for.

What I am arguing is that fundamentalist religions will, for some short period of time, be one part of the movement of Spirit against the globalization of capital. To the extent that they provide alternatives and restrain the march of capitalist progress, they can, at times, be allies in the struggle for a more humane world.

I'm envisioning an alliance like the one amassed to stop Hitler. Each of those allies had their problems. The United States, Britain, and France each had imperialistic agendas they hoped to advance through the defeat of the Axis Powers. The Soviet Union was a totalitarian dictatorship run by none other than Josef Stalin, who killed millions of people in his ruthless opposition to the idealists and internationalists who remained loyal to progressive politics. Nevertheless, I'm glad these forces allied to stop Hitler. In this very limited sense, I see reactionary forms of religious and spiritual life as having the potential to be, at specific times and places, momentary allies in the struggle against the globalization of selfishness and materialism.

When *New York Times* columnist Thomas Friedman argues in *The Lexus and the Olive Tree,* that "There Is No Alternative" (TINA), that nothing can stop the globalization of capital, that nothing can keep the world from becoming one big consumer and media market, spiritual people, including religious fundamentalists, are trying to shout at the top of their lungs "We will not go silent into that dark night of the soul—we don't want a world governed by Hollywood and Wall Street, McDonald's, and Wal-Mart." Thus, as in the alliance with Stalin in World War II, we may sometimes need to align with reactionary forms of spirituality. However, although aligning with Stalin was a momentary necessity, but it should not have involved any romanticization of that moral monster. Similarly, a moment of joining religious fundamentalists in the struggle against the globalization of capital must not lead to the romanticization of reactionary spirituality.

For example, if I were living in Iran, Afghanistan, or other Islamic fundamentalist countries today, I would be opposing the Islamic Republic and seeking a society that incorporated freedom of religion, freedom of speech and assembly, and an end to the oppression of women. But at the same time, I can see how ordinary Iranians and other Islamic fundamentalists might support their current system, hoping it will stop what they must perceive as the inexorable spread of global capitalism.

Emancipatory Spirituality as a Loving Alternative to Reactionary Spirituality

Rather than romanticize reactionary spirituality, those involved in developing Emancipatory Spirituality will fight alongside it in resisting the globalization of capital and the ethos of selfishness and materialism, but this fight will be in the name of a deeper way to serve God that rejects the distortion of demeaning the Other.

When I talk about "struggle," I'm not referring to armed struggle or competition. I'm referring to a movement in consciousness, a change of orientation, a new way to think about ourselves and the universe.

The most recent example of this kind of spiritual struggle was the transformation of women's consciousness in the last three decades of the twentieth century. The struggle was not only against external institutions that upheld sexist assumptions and practices, but also an internal struggle in which women gave up certain conventional ways of thinking about themselves and began to adopt a new understanding that they were fully entitled to respect and power in the world.

Although the women's struggle involved changes in legislation and reallocations of economic and political power, its primary focus was on the way people thought about themselves and each other. With those changes in consciousness came changes in the way women spoke and acted in the world, what kinds of behavior they would or would not accept from others, and what kind of treatment they demanded from the institutions where they worked and played.

Along the way, many of those women faced severe opposition, both from the men in their lives, and from women who did not yet share their perspective. But the deepest level of struggle was internal—a struggle to overcome the remnants of patriarchal thinking that had been deeply internalized and that made women feel they deserved to be treated unequally. It was that inner work, facilitated by consciousness-raising groups, that served as the indispensable step from which all other changes flowed.

In this context, "struggle" often meant the difficult task of challenging others in what they said or assumed. But it also meant struggling with one's own doubts and fears. It did *not* mean physical combat, competition, or aggressiveness, but rather a firm determination to live life in a whole new way, with new confidence in one's own consciousness.

That's the kind of struggle that is increasingly taking place between Emancipatory Spirituality, reactionary spirituality, and market consciousness.

However, both emancipatory and reactionary spirituality will combat the ethos of selfishness and materialism. Simultaneously Emancipatory Spirituality will challenge reactionary spirituality in a variety of spheres.

Let me highlight some significant aspects of the way that these two forms of spirituality may clash.

Reactionary forms of spirituality often give expression to impulses to contain or control female sexuality and to reaffirm male dominance. Reactionary spirituality sees women's sexuality as threatening or overwhelming unless carefully tamed. Some of these assumptions are little more than masks for old-fashioned male privilege. Many men felt that a world where women have more power would mean that men had less. Many working class or working poor men came to feel that their power in relationship to women is the only power they have.

In her 1999 book, *Stiffed, The Betrayal of the American Man,* Susan Faludi shows that, in fact, many men did experience a decline in power. The remedy for that, of course, would be to redistribute economic power equitably to both men and women, but since most men believe this kind of redistribution will never happen, they see women's power as a net loss for themselves and end up being fearful and threatened by women's equality. And, as Faludi and others have reported, they are not entirely wrong: as the women's movement has made important gains, these men often do lose the minimal power they had. So it's not surprising that some men are attracted to reactionary spirituality as a way to hold on to power that would be seen as mere chauvinism in secular contexts but is sanctioned in some religious communities.

But there's often something more going on that helps explain why the resistance to women's liberation has taken a specifically sexual quality among some forms of reactionary spirituality.

Consider, for example, the remasking of the female body in a veil or in clothes aimed at modesty—an approach popular in many variants of contemporary religious fundamentalism. This move has another meaning: it rejects the exploitation of female sexuality by the capitalist marketplace. As Roger Friedland puts it in "When God Walks in History" (TIKKUN, May/June 1999), "When the sensuous female body has become the prime commodity of fetish and when women can decreasingly count on the vows of marriage, then the embedding of the division of gender in the sacred unity of marriage offers many women a refuge and an alternative substance of love. The swathed and separated body of woman, out of sight and beyond reach, registers for many fundamentalist women as valuation, not degradation."

In fact, I've known women whose experience in the marketplace of relationships was one of going from one man after another, over and over again encountering men who were unable to make a commitment but who were all too willing to enjoy the easily available sexuality encouraged by the market ethos of "looking out for number one." Many of these women felt emotionally exploited—and this has led some to join fundamentalist religious communities in which sexual restrictions were experienced as protection and as a way of honoring the female. The same was true for many women who didn't feel that they had the qualities the competitive marketplace valued—a slim body, a beautiful face, and a sexuality easily separated from feelings and commitment—for many, the protection of a community of "traditional values" actually provided sexual freedom by removing the competitive pressures of the "meat market."

Emancipatory Spirituality acknowledges the ways that sexuality has been distorted by the marketplace and the way that women's bodies have become objects and subjects of consumption. But the response it offers is not a symbolic withdrawal from the public sphere, but rather an active confrontation with the market's bottom line. And this is precisely what reactionary spirituality does not do—it does not propose a new bottom line, it does not challenge the market. It leaves all that intact and seeks to set aside some pure spiritual space elsewhere, untouched by the dirtiness of the market. The media can have a cynical heyday whenever it explores these spiritual spaces and finds people or practices that actually manifest the same distortions one finds in the larger marketplace (a guru who is a sexual or economic exploiter, for example, or a preacher who seeks to amass power and fame). From the standpoint of Emancipatory Spirituality, no corner of the world can be protected from the distorting impact of the competitive market until we create a whole new way of evaluating productivity and efficiency, a way that rewards love and caring.

Rather than "protect" women with the veil or demanding modesty, Emancipatory Spirituality seeks to challenge the way the media and market function to manipulate us in order to sell products. Rather than resubordinate women, Emancipatory Spirituality affirms the full equality of women as equal partners in the struggle to build a world of love, kindness, and justice. It affirms equality not merely to give women "equal opportunity" to compete in the competitive market, as so many liberal and progressive movements do, but so women's creativity and brilliance can be fully liberated to provide leadership in the struggle to build a new kind of world.

It's easy to see why people within a patriarchal framework would experience disempowerment as "emasculation." But there is nothing inherently weak or submissive about femininity, and no strength is gained by reinscribing the discourse of male power. On the contrary, the imagery of the powerful warrior is quickly absorbed into the fantasies of the lone and powerful individual standing on his own against the world, and this individualism is the linchpin of capitalist expansion. So let's not accept as liberating those versions of Jungian psychology or New Agey spirituality that actually glorify the individualism that is a dominant motif of contemporary narcissistic societies.

Counter to all this, Emancipatory Spirituality affirms new sources of power: the power of love, interconnection, interdependency, mutual vulnerability, and mutual solidarity. Emancipatory Spirituality thus embraces aspects of the human experience that have been relegated to "the feminine" in many patriarchal societies, and insists on making these female qualities universal aspects of the human experience. So, Emancipatory Spirituality does not seek a feminization of the human race, but rather a reclaiming and reintegration of the strengths, experiences, and talents of women.

In the final analysis, love is not "a woman's thing" (as some sociobiologists seem to suggest) but rather an aspect of human life and reality that has always been present, a gift of the universe that sustains and nourishes us, but one that has not always been acknowledged or valued.

Emancipatory Spirituality takes love out of the closet and places it at the center of the human experience. It challenges the cynical voices around us and inside us that have taught us to see love as less real, less hard (in male terms), less solid, "merely" an emotion, not something like money or power around which one can build a solid future.

One might argue that the goal of reactionary spirituality is to create a safe space so decent values can flourish. Thus, the woman hidden away in private space, kept from the assaults of the marketplace, her skin and face shielded by the vigilance of male power, becomes the symbol of a spirituality that must be protected in private space even as the forces of evil and corruption may rule in the larger society.

Emancipatory Spirituality takes a very different approach. It does not seek to create a private space, but to reshape public space in ways that will make it safe for love, caring, awe, and wonder. Emancipatory Spirituality does not reconcile us to a world of oppression by focusing our attention on the sanctuaries of some other world. Instead, it seeks to rebuild *this* world in accord with spiritual principles. As such, it flows from the spirit of the Bible—and of many other ancient spiritual traditions whose original goals were revolutionary. The ancient Jewish prayer, Aleynu, was a call "to transform the world so that it might be governed by God." This does not mean a new kind of subordination to an authoritarian monarch, but rather a recognition that our lives are bound to the Totality of Being in love and mutual dependence, and that the world can be rebuilt on that principle. This kind of healing will be the next quantum leap in the evolution of the consciousness of the universe.

We have already begun to take that quantum leap. But it may take decades or even centuries for it to be completed. From the standpoint of the evolution of human beings, this is just a few moments, but from our standpoint (those of us who are alive at this particular moment), we'd probably like to see the process accelerated.

Why Progressive Struggles for Rights— and Their Communitarian Critics— Miss the Mark

At this point you might be thinking, "Fine, we need a new societal ethos, but why look to Spirit as the way to create that new ethos? Wouldn't it be more useful to put our energies into liberal, progressive, or communitarian politics? After all, they too wish to constrain irresponsible corporate power and save the environment."

I often do feel sympathetic to the issues these movements raise. But they are fundamentally misguided. Over and over, they formulate their struggles in precisely the wrong terms: the "inclusion" of those who have been left out in the material benefits that others have already won. Please don't misunderstand. I'm in favor of everyone having equal access to those benefits, yet the exclusive focus on these issues by most liberal and progressive movements communicates the message that if only people had equal opportunity to compete for material well-being, all would be well in our world. No wonder the Right is so successful at portraying the Left as spiritually obtuse.

Nor does it help that the only other important focus of liberal and progressive struggles has been the focus on winning more and more "rights" for individuals and groups.

When "rights" were part of a larger spiritual vision of a society based on love and justice, as when Martin Luther King Jr. rooted the movement in Biblical aspirations, the struggle for rights was merely one part of a transformative spiritual mission. But when the struggle becomes secularized and divorced from Spirit, it has a disempowering and individualizing impact. The more people come to see themselves as individuals set apart from each other and holding "rights" that need to be enforced by government, lawyers, or politicians, the less they feel themselves part of anything at all. "Rights" then are reduced to accumulating more benefits and goodies—not ways to connect to others. Ironically, the secular liberal formulations of the struggle do more to strengthen the hold of the existing society than any reform might do to change it.

The outcome of the rights strategy is that most people feel grateful to the liberals who win them their rights, yet still feel distrustful and disconnected from people around them. In fact, the focus on rights fits all too well into the selfishness and "looking out for number one" that leads to political conservatism. "I have my rights" may lead previously excluded groups to embrace the dominant ethos once they've been "included": "now it's our turn to get for ourselves, and screw everyone else." I can't tell you how heartbreaking it is for me when I occasionally meet Holocaust survivors who feel that way about non-Jews or Palestinians, African Americans who feel that way about whites, women who feel that way about men, gays who feel that way about straights. Yet this is the consciousness that tends to emerge from the way many liberal and progressive struggles get formulated. Imagine their surprise when the beneficiaries of past struggles for inclusion end up being their worst enemies, supporting exclusion of others now that the formerly excluded have gotten some degree of economic security.

It's only when a Martin Luther King Jr. comes forward with a religious message, helping people see their common interest in a world of justice and love, that people are willing to sacrifice for a higher good. But liberal and progressive politics have largely abandoned the categories and visions of King and of the spiritual foundations that nourished him and are stuck in a narrowly economistic vision that reflects the dominant society rather than posing an alternative to it.

Actually, most people don't feel very happy with our political system. But they help keep it in place by continuing to vote for "lesser evil" candidates, fearing otherwise to "throw away their vote" because they are sure others will not act similarly. Yet the mediocrity that dominates in politics is usually a product of this fear. It can only be overcome by a new spiritual sensitivity that takes us beyond the old Left-Right distinctions.

In recent years, a communitarian movement has emerged with the good sense to try to move beyond narrow self-interested politics. But communitarians often miss the mark with their emphasis on socially imposed responsibilities. The model of reality is still the same: greedy and self-seeking individuals needing to be constrained by laws or communal norms that impose upon them some sense of decency and limits. The communitarians seek to impose some basic ground rules to keep these otherwise avaricious people within bounds.

Such a worldview will only recreate the reality it is trying to change: a world in which people believe everyone else is narrowly self-interested.

The only way this can be overcome is through a whole new way of thinking about reality—one that emphasizes our fundamental interdependence and interconnectedness. Even then, however, communitarianism needs to move beyond being a movement about ideas and become a movement embedded in a spiritual practice. I know too many people who spend their lives theorizing about community but who wouldn't dream of living communitarian realities in their daily lives.

The underlying principle of that way of seeing is the world of Spirit. When communitarian politics grounds itself in Spirit both theoretically and in an actual spiritual practice, it will become a version of Emancipatory Spirituality.

The Legacy of the Twentieth Century's Brutality and Evil

Looking at the extraordinary brutality and cruelty that shattered utopian hopes for the twentieth century, some intellectuals were so overwhelmed that they began to imagine that "evil" was a fundamental reality of human life, and that anyone who ignored this "shadow" side of reality was simply shallow and dangerously naive. Anyone who lived through the mass murders of Hitler's fascism or through Stalinist oppression could understandably see the future of the human race as clouded by human cruelty.

Yet there is a corresponding danger to which many of these intellectuals have succumbed: allowing the distortions and evil of the past to prevent us from addressing the distortions and evil of the present. Convinced that visionary and transformative political action will inevitably lead to the same distortions that generated the evils of the twentieth century, these intellectuals caution us to do little more than tinker with the current economic and political system.

The United States, with 5 percent of the world's population, regularly consumes 40 percent of the world's yearly production. Supposedly liberal or progressive political leaders focus their programs on ensuring that all American children, not only the offspring of the wealthy, receive "the best" education in order to compete more effectively in the world market and to continue to dominate the world's economic life.

But the consequence of this domination is that much of the world is left without adequate resources. Malnutrition and the diseases it produces in Third World countries are the major factor in the deaths of tens of millions of children and adults each year. The numbers of this "Invisible Holocaust" rival those caused by World Wars, genocide, and Communist gulags of the twentieth century. But because they are consequences of the "free market," and not of some policy consciously pursued by demented Communist or fascist thugs, we are encouraged to avert our gaze and see contemporary suffering as little more than "the cost of doing business." Enmeshed in celebrating its own material successes, American society has become as oblivious to the suffering it causes other human beings as it has to the destructive ecological consequences of its profligate consumption. Yet future generations may look back on this period as one in which the wealthiest parts of the world became "silent executioners" by willfully shutting our eyes to the pain of others and to the ecological destruction our economic system generates.

In face of all this, it is encouraging to see millions of people taking steps in their own lives to create a different kind of reality. Some are engaged in acts of charity and kindness in their own neighborhoods. Others are involved in ecological organizations that at once seek to repair some of the damage inflicted on our environment while agitating for policy changes at the global and local levels. Still others have become involved in global peacekeeping and healing efforts.

There are increasing opportunities to be involved with groups like Doctors Without Borders: its caring for the suffering of others transcends national boundaries and provides care and nurturing to those who have been hurt by violent struggles or by the "normal" operations of the global market. Recognizing philosopher Emanuel Levinas' shrewd observation that "justifying the pain of my neighbor is the source of all immorality," more and more people are allowing themselves to identify with the suffering of those who are physically distant.

As Alain Finkelkraut puts it in *In the Name of Humanity*, "We are not afraid to dirty our hands. Overcoming our revulsion, we plunge them right into the excrement and blood, in order to put lives crushed by history back together again and prevent further destruction. We no longer divide the wounded into those on the right and those on the left."

Finkelkraut warns that the practice of obliterating differences and seeing everyone as victims also obliterates our ability to recognize the uniqueness of each person's situation and may lead to a condescending solicitude and indifference to the causes of suffering. Humanitarian gestures can become a substitute for true caring, which would be manifested not only in healing the wounds of those who suffer but also in uprooting the causes of suffering. It may be far easier to declare our desire to assist those in pain than to engage in the frustrating work of trying to change the larger social realities that caused the problems in the first place. Fearful that we may stumble into yet another misguided ideology like those that led to the crimes of the twentieth century, many people find it easier to feel than to think, to respond to pain rather than to develop strategies to change powerful social systems. Fear that we will merely approach everything from the limited perspective of "Westerners" or "whites," many people allow multicultural humility or moral relativism to prevent them from making the kinds of judgments we need to mobilize movements for greater social change. Thus we sink into a practice of healing that flows only from the heart and avoids the difficult thinking we need to do together. The spirituality we need must enable us to integrate mind and feeling as we work toward social transformation.

Of course, it's equally possible that the reaction against the distortions of nationalism, racism, and sexism of the past will lead to a celebration of the new internationalism of the global market and of the rootlessness of virtual reality. A new global consumer society obsessed with avoiding commitments and entanglements and focused on individual pleasure—this may be the ultimate beneficiary of our desire to transcend our particular roots. Detached from everything that roots us to place and time, we can then endlessly surf the Web, isolated tourists in a world of virtual experiences. Our emancipation from the weight of the past creates an unbearable lightness in the present: we become tourists to our own inner beings and tourists to others, never staying long enough to risk getting involved.

But there is yet another possibility: a deeply rooted spirituality that will facilitate a willingness to stay present in the present, to deepen our connection to ourselves, to others, to the universe, to the totality of all. That spiritual possibility is offered us in the Emancipatory Spirituality that is capturing the attention of millions of people around the world.

Stages of Spiritual Development

Another way to understand Emancipatory Spirituality is to see it as a higher stage in spiritual development and as an attempt to work out the basic spiritual intuition that our task is to honor and actualize Spirit in the world.

Ken Wilber's important work on the stages in development of consciousness provides a sophisticated and powerful map of the human mind and of what we need to go through in order to get to the next phases in the development of the human race. I highly recommend his books, *Sex, Ecology, Spirit; A Brief History of Everything*; and *The Marriage of Sense and Soul: Integrating Science and Religion*. Frankly, I think his presentation is far superior to my summary of it, so you might want to skip this and just actually read his books, which are quite exciting.

Wilber persuasively argues that at each stage or level of development, people are doing their best to honor and actualize Spirit, only we do this in different ways at each stage because we acquire different understandings at each level of self, other, and the external world as we spiritually mature.

In a recent and popularly formulated version of the stages of development, which appeared in his article "Boomeritis versus Spirituality in the New Millennium" (TIKKUN, November/December 1999), Wilber distinguishes the following:

> Stage One. Archaic Individual. This is the level of basic survival, in which consciousness is primarily focused on food, water, warmth, sex, and safety. At this stage of development, the individual is scarcely aware of its own separate existence,

because his or her entire attention is directed at fulfilling these immediate survival needs.

Stage Two. Magical-Animistic. Magical spirits seem to control everything. People form ethnic tribes and kinship bonds become central. Spirits exist in everything, and may unite the tribe, but there is little sense of the unity of all these spirits, so we have an atomistic rather than a holistic spiritual understanding.

Stage Three. Power Gods. Here we have the emergence of a self distinct from the tribe, and the emergence of powerful or heroic individuals who are impulsive and egocentric. The quintessence is the feudal lord who protects underlings in exchange for obedience and labor. The world is seen as a jungle full of threats and predators.

Stage Four. Conformist Rule. Life has meaning, direction, and purpose. The outcome is determined by some powerful Other, or Order. The righteous Order enforces a code of conduct based on absolutist and unvarying principles of "right" and "wrong." Violating the rules or code has severe, perhaps everlasting repercussions. There are rigid social hierarchies and one right way to think about everything. Law and order are key, fundamentalist beliefs abound, although one can be secular or atheistic and still be in this consciousness.

Stage Five. Scientific Achievement. At this level, the self moves beyond a herd mentality and seeks truth and meaning in individualistic terms, finding solace in the notion of a rational world with natural laws that can be learned, mastered, and manipulated for one's own purposes. A high level of individualism and the pursuit of material well-being underlie this "achievement society." The world is seen as a resource for one's strategic gains and corporations are created to maximize advantage.

Stage Six. The Sensitive Self. People are communitarian and put lots of emphasis on bonding, networking, and ecological sensitivity. There is a genuine cherishing of the earth and caring supersedes cold rationality. This stage of development is strongly egalitarian and antihierarchical, pluralistic in values, emphasizing diversity, multiculturalism, relativistic value systems, and subjective, nonlinear thinking.

Stage Seven. Integrative. Egalitarianism is integrated with a recognition that there are natural degrees of excellence. Hierarchy is no longer dismissed as fundamentally evil but instead acknowledged as appropriate under certain circumstances. Similarly, ethical judgments are no longer dismissed as merely subjective. Flexibility, spontaneity, and functionality are given the highest priority.

Stage Eight. Holistic. A universal holistic system unites feelings with knowledge. There is a universal order, not based on external rules but on a living and continually expanding consciousness. There may be a form of spirituality that meshes all of existence and embodies a unified vision of the totality of all that is.

Wilber goes on beyond the holistic level to describe states of advanced spiritual development that have been tasted by some of the world's great mystics. These levels reach a transpersonal and spiritual realm that transcends all and includes all. In my own life, I've had moments of experience in these realms, and though they are difficult to describe, they do provide an important part of the motivation for my wanting to share this path with you.

What I particularly like about Wilber's developmental thinking is the way it promotes tolerance of people at each stage of development. Once you think of people as working out different problems at different developmental stages, you see how futile it can be for people at one developmental stage to attack or negate those at another level. Until people are ready to move to a different level of consciousness, no amount of argument or coercion is going to make them change the way they see their world.

Wilber notes that each stage of development transcends and includes earlier levels, but that people at each stage find it difficult to appreciate the other levels.

Wilber is particularly acute in his analysis of the boomers (or people in the "sensitive self" stage of development) and how their consciousness, certainly a developmental advance over the scientific/materialist consciousness of the dominant society, may also present obstacles to the next stage of development. Boomer (stage six) consciousness was developed in reaction to stage five. It is deeply wedded to a pervasive subjectivism that negates the possibility of universal claims for knowledge, truth, or ethics. The boomers are so concerned with ensuring that no one will constrain them that they only feel secure if each person is free from the constraints of rational thinking or moral obligation.

Wilber captures the taste of boomer culture when he describes their meetings: "Everybody is allowed to express his or her feelings, which often takes hours; there is an almost interminable processing of opinions, often reaching no decision or course of action, since a specific course of action would likely exclude somebody. The meeting is considered a success not if a conclusion is reached but if everybody has a chance to share their feelings."

The greatest downside of this inability to formulate decisions is that "pluralism becomes a supermagnet for endless varieties of egocentric self-display" and an unwitting home for the culture of narcissism. In their enthusiasm to move beyond anything that seems a manifestation of the conventions of stages four and five, the boomers sometimes find themselves embracing anything unconventional, even if it includes some of the most regressive aspects of preconventional thinking.

Wilber emphasizes a point that I think is central to Emancipatory Spirituality: it is not a return to earlier stages of spiritual development, though it seeks to renew some aspects of earlier spiritual consciousness. Instead, it involves the incorporation of all that has transpired since—not a rejection of science and rationality, but an incorporation and transcendence of them. For that reason, Emancipatory Spirituality will not feel like pre-Enlightenment spirituality. Though the music, rhythms, poetry, and rituals of pre-Enlightenment spirituality can often be powerful stimuli for connecting us with the spirituality we have abandoned during the Scientific Achievement period, that recognition will ultimately bring us to a higher stage of spiritual development, not a regression to the Magic-Animistic or the Power Gods stage.

Wilber also recognizes that the impediment to developing an integrated spiritual consciousness in today's reality is not only the materialism and selfishness of stage five, but the mushy subjectivism and narcissistic self-indulgence of stage six. Emancipatory Spirituality will, as Wilber suggests in his developmental language, include and transcend level six.

I've avoided the language of developmental stages in most of my work because I think that it may lend themselves to a certain passivity (not at all intended by Wilber, but sometimes adopted by some of those who use his language). I see the boomer stage less as an inevitable development of consciousness than as a historical outcome of the defeat of the more communal and social justice-oriented movements of the twentieth century.

Many people feel far more comfortable in boomer spirituality than in Emancipatory Spirituality precisely because the latter evokes memories of a time when there was a "we" that felt the possibility of social transformation and then failed to accomplish its highest ideals. A powerful establishment media rushed in to convince this huge generation of people they had failed because they were all too narcissistic, because their ideals had been unrealistic or flawed, because everyone is selfish, and because truly it's impossible to do anything other than look out for one's own narrowly defined self-interest.

The moments of transcendence people experienced when they belonged to social movements were represented as moments of adolescent rebellion and irresponsible self-seeking. Having suffered the perceived defeat of their youthful ideals, the boomer generation reacted with shame—and with an unwillingness to risk being shamed again. Boomer consciousness is fiercely protective of the self and resistant to any "we," precisely because of the boomer's previous experiences of hurt and humiliation when they tried to be a "we." Indeed, there is a danger that most boomers will go to their graves with unresolved shame that they abandoned their highest values after they tried and failed to build a different kind of world—though if they can overcome this shame in their retirement years, they might yet play a powerful role in reshaping the world.

What Emancipatory Spirituality offers to boomer consciousness is an element of hope rooted in precisely what was missing in the social movements of the past: a spiritual vision and a spiritual practice. With a spiritual vision, boomers can see that their youthful idealism was really valuable and not to be dismissed because it was also mixed with personal flaws and conflicting motives. As they become seniors, many may return their attention to a search for meaning and may open themselves with renewed vigor to challenging American selfishness and materialism. If they do so, they may find that the very attempt to build

Emancipatory Spirituality gives them a new sense of meaning and purpose and a revitalized energy that may prolong and enrichen their lives.

There is nothing inevitable about the speed at which Emancipatory Spirituality will be adopted. There are tens of millions of people already yearning for this in their personal lives, but often not fully willing to consciously acknowledge their desire. So it could take several generations before a critical mass of people can make it seem a viable option. Or it could happen in the next twenty or thirty years, as the people who are already moving in this direction begin to recognize themselves as part of a larger social movement.

In the last chapter of this book I give some more specific ideas of what we might do to accelerate the process: basically through developing our own individual spiritual practice, building spiritual communities, organizing for a new bottom line in our workplaces, and acting together to build a spiritually sensitive economy. But before doing that, I want to turn to some vision of what the world could be like if Spirit were to triumph.

A Spiritual Exercise

Write a short autobiography of your own spiritual evolution—include where you are now in your own spiritual path and where you wish to be a year from now. Look at your own life as a totality and see what have been the major spiritual lessons you've learned and what are the lessons you yet wish to learn. What has life taught you that you wish you could have learned an easier way? What are the major spiritual challenges you face? Who have been your best spiritual teachers? Who else might you seek out as a teacher or guide? What have been the books, movies, poems, stories, and teachings that moved you most? What are you currently doing in your life, or what might you be willing to do to live a more centered spiritual existence?

If you have trouble writing, get together with a friend, or a group of people who are open to sharing a spiritual experience, and discuss these questions together.

six

The Respiritualization of Our Work and Our Professions

The spiritual transformation of work and professional life is a central challenge for those of us who wish to build an Emancipatory Spirituality in daily life.

Most people spend most of their waking hours at work and preparing for work. Through the stories of Joan Sharpen, Louise Glenn, Samuel Hughes, and Jennifer Cantor, I've tried to show how powerfully what happens to us at work shapes our personal lives.

The fundamental change we need is simply this: we need a new bottom line, a new way of calculating what is productive and efficient. Lesser reforms are unlikely to have significant impact. It's only this dramatic shift in focus that could actually change the way our economy functions.

If you turn to most economic textbooks, you'll find they tend to assume a certain notion of productivity and efficiency, one concerned with the wealth of society or the wealth of the particular institution being assessed.

To make this focus seem more plausible, they refer to the need for certain basic essentials like food, clothing, and shelter. Isn't it obvious that a society is more efficient and productive if it produces more food, clothing, and shelter? So, obviously, productivity in general must be about producing more.

But this logic is weak.

No, it's not obvious that producing more is better.

We need to know whether the society distributes the food, clothing, and shelter broadly to those who need it or primarily to those who can *afford* it.

Traditional economists might respond that distribution is a political, not an economic, question. Well, they are entitled to advocate that view, but I am entitled to say the opposite: there's nothing intrinsically productive or efficient about producing more of anything.

What we need to know before judging whether a particular way of organizing a society is productive or efficient is this: What kind of human beings and human values does it produce?

The very notion of separating the production of goods from their distribution points to a world in which human needs are satisfied for some people but not for others. If we don't want that kind of world, then we don't want that kind of economic theory.

My basic point here is that deciding something is efficient or productive is a value judgment, not a value-neutral description. Whenever you get into an argument with people on these questions, insist on knowing their definition of productivity, efficiency, and rationality—because it's at that point that they covertly build in their value judgments and present them as scientific facts.

From my standpoint, there's a much better way to define productivity than the way that predominates in business schools and popular economic discourse. Institutions are efficient only if they support the development of human beings who are loving and caring; capable of awe and wonder; ethically, spiritually, and ecologically sensitive; and aware.

This definition will increasingly take hold as Emancipatory Spirituality challenges the religion of global materialism.

Sometimes the high priests (economists, journalists, politicians, and social scientists) of the religion of global materialism say it's obvious most people want more money and more power, so anything that maximizes this *must be* efficient or productive.

There are two answers: first, it's not obvious that this is what "most people" want. If you want to know what most people on the planet want, you had better ask them. If you do, you'll find that many people want other things beyond money or power.

But surely people want food, clothing, and shelter. True. But, they don't just want there to be more food or clothing or shelter buried in a vault somewhere. Instead, they might easily say institutions are productive when they produce goods that are available to those who need them, and unproductive when they don't.

Second, people *do* want other things—like love, caring, and connection. They want a world in which their highest values have a better chance of being realized and a world that is ecologically sustainable. So, if you simply ask the six billion people alive today what they want, and attend to their actual family and religious lives, you'll come up with a much broader and more spiritually oriented definition of productivity and efficiency.

Sacred Work and Sacred Professions

When work is experienced as little more than a necessary evil endured solely to earn a livelihood, it becomes a monumental burden and drag. Many people dread going to work each day and, once home from it, do their best to forget about it. This is the situation facing the overwhelming majority of working people in American society.

Yet there are others, an elite of professionals, who find work deeply engaging and at times even exhilarating. There are members of the professional elite who imagine they are on the cutting edge of technology and power, and that if they can just maintain their competitive position, they will be able to experience this high throughout their lives.

Maintaining their positions, however, has required a transformation in the conception of professional work. Traditional ties to community and an ethos of professional service have been displaced. As William Sullivan put it in TIKKUN (January/February 1996), for the young urban professional "status flows from hard work per se, with little corresponding sense of gratitude, few overarching loyalties, faint responsibility to others. Even when they have altruistic urges, entrants into these high-flying careers quickly discover that relentless pressure for more productivity greatly limits the possibility for more than token *pro bono* work or other civic involvements. The very intensity of their work world, accentuated for many by the increasingly international scope of competition, focuses attention on staying viable, leaving little psychic energy for considering the long-term or larger significance of day-to-day decisions."

Who has time for values discussions when there is so much pressing business awaiting us with our unanswered e-mails? So many web sites to check out, so many new investment options to consider, so much new technology to master. This is what is considered real; the talk about values and ultimate goals is seen as abstract philosophy or theology, not the kind of thing we have time for in daily life. No wonder we have seen a precipitous decline in a civic culture that situates one's work in relationship to the needs of the community. From the standpoint of many young professionals, there's no need to worry about the community impact or value of what they are doing with their time—it's all validated by the growth in the value of their stocks. If the market wants what they are producing, it must be valuable.

But when the Bible says, "six days shalt thou do thy labor," it was referring to a labor that sustains the well-being of the community.

Work takes on a whole different character when we feel it to be part of a sacred contribution to the highest values of the community.

I used to think this idea was utopian nonsense until I spent a few months working on a kibbutz. I found many people there who were very smart and yet felt good about doing what I had been taught to think of as "menial" or "demeaning" tasks. People assured me they had plenty of time to engage in creative activity the rest of the day. While they were at work, they felt very good because they knew they were contributing to the well-being of the kibbutz. And they rested without any feeling that they ought to be doing more work. Our conception of work as competitive success makes it impossible for work to be self-limiting. It consumes day, night, and weekend and undermines our connection to family and friends.

Almost everyone I spoke to on the kibbutz shared the perception that the menial tasks were no lower than any other work. It was only after kibbutz life became infected by the values propagated from the market ethos of the larger Israeli society that this spirit was undermined. The larger society worked its way into the consciousness of the children by ridiculing the idealism of kibbutz. After a few decades of this, a new generation of "realists" triumphed over the idealists in the kibbutz movement. The kibbutzim started to amass debts to "modernize" their way of life. Kibbutzim thus put their fates in the hands of the capitalist market not because of their socialist idealism, but because of their abandonment of that idealism. And when an inevitable market downturn occurred, it became impossible to pay back many of the loans, particularly since government leaders were more concerned about defending West Bank settlements and less interested in protecting the Israeli experiment in socialism.

The well-reported failure of kibbutzim was actually a failure to inculcate the idealistic values in their children that could help them resist the heavy influence of television and the worship of the competitive market. Once the kibbutz became integrated into the larger market economy of Israel, the entire kibbutz enterprise became economically impossible. It was the ethos of selfishness, not the ethos of contributing to the common good, that proved to be unrealistic.

This is the ironic lesson of those who decide to be "realistic." For every person who succeeds at this, there are eight others who don't quite "make it." Yet, instead of interpreting their situation as a reflection of a failure of the system, they tend to blame it on themselves and draw the lesson that they were not tough enough, ruthless enough, or "realistic enough" to succeed.

What the kibbutz lacked was a spiritual framework within which it could interpret its own experience. Early on it had been overly influenced by a vulgar Marxism that saw progress in terms of material success. True, the material success in the kibbutz was not just about each individual's success—it looked at material success communally, and it was heavily committed to an egalitarian ethos. Yet, it still held to the same capitalist market "bottom line." So it had no ideological foundation to sustain itself in economic adversity.

At the beginning of the kibbutz movement, there were those who argued that more energy should be given to making accommodations with the Palestinians, integrating Jewish refugees from North Africa, and challenging the selfishness and materialism that were spreading through Israeli society. But the "realists" said that it was more important to build "socialism on one kibbutz," and that the way to do that was to focus on building the economic foundation of the kibbutz itself, rather than on these larger issues. But as it focused inward, the kibbutz never focused on the *inner* lives of its own members, but rather on their productive capacities. All that stuff about ideals and visions and spirituality were dismissed as "empty talk" in a society that valued "deeds" above all. They never understood the wisdom of the spiritual advice: "Don't just do something; sit there."

But what I learned working on a kibbutz was this: to the extent that people could see themselves as involved in serving the common good, work took on a new sense of meaning and purpose.

That's exactly what we will see in the work world of the future. In a spiritually oriented society, everyone will be engaged in activity that contributes to the common good. There will be no incentive to do work that maximizes self-interest at the expense of others. In such a society, all the work will feel valued. And because of that, people will look forward to periodic rotating of job assignments and "careers" (along with the relevant education) every seven years (the sabbatical year, which I'll describe in chapter ten).

It was this notion of service to the common good that originally gave professionals their special honor and entitlement—their professionalism. They were seen as responding to a sacred calling and service to God. Feeling certain that people with this calling could be trusted, the community empowered them to supervise themselves and to develop appropriate standards of behavior. Restoring this sense of mission and sanctity to the world of work should no longer be restricted to people who were previously designated professionals. It should be the goal for all work for everyone.

Having Enough Time

Not having enough time is the shared condition of most working people today. Those who have lower-paying jobs often have to work two shifts a day, and the shifts often do not mesh with those of their spouses. Those in higher-paid, or professional work often feel a pressure, to work long hours and to bring home lots of work.

Labor-saving devices have not helped this in the slightest. The fax, phone, computer, and Internet have all contributed to the acceleration of the pace of life, not to enjoyment and leisure. That people can do more in less time has only raised the bar of expected work output.

The frenetic pace of most of our lives leads to an inability to "find time" to do all the things we profess to believe in. We have less time to play, less time to give to community activities or charities, less time to read and develop our minds, less time to be active in fighting for the causes we believe in, and less time to meditate, relax, or celebrate the glory of the universe.

In a spiritually oriented society, time will be seen as precious. Not only will spiritual time be built into the workday (time at the workplace itself to stop and meditate or pray), but people will have shorter workdays and more free time.

The central refocusing of time will come through the reintroduction of Shabbat—the Sabbath—as a central spiritual practice. I'll describe it in chapter ten.

To get to this kind of reconstituted work world, we need to organize ourselves and begin to mobilize around this vision.

What do we do first?

Revision work.

Revisioning Work: A Spiritual Practice

Get together with four to six fellow workers at your workplace, or with people in the same profession or line of work, and spend an afternoon or evening on the following topic: What could this workplace, profession, or type of work look like if we had a new bottom line? Imagine if our bosses, supervisors, and colleagues all agreed that we were going to be judged efficient or productive to the extent that our office practices, the products we produced, the services we offered, and the way we promoted our services and products created or helped promote love and caring, awe and wonder, ethical and spiritual sensitivity, and ecological responsibility.

The hardest part of this discussion is getting rid of what I call "the reality police"—all those voices in our own heads that tell us that "they" won't let us make these changes and that therefore we are wasting our time even thinking about all this. As long as people allow the reality police to hold them back, the discussions will remain stunted and uninspired.

When people allow themselves to truly engage in this discussion, they end up with amazingly creative and inspiring ideas. I witnessed this in government agencies where members of our groups actually worked. For example, in several groups with government workers, I found people getting very excited as they reconnected to the idealism that had led them to enter government service in the first place, ideals that they had been forced to abandon as they became socialized into a bureaucracy that frowned on idealism and creativity. In another set of groups with machinists and workers at an electronics factory, people were filled with creative ideas about how to make their workplaces more financially successful by producing goods people actually needed rather than goods people had to be convinced to need. In groups like these, people continually surprise themselves with exciting ideas about their profession or work—ideas they do not know they have until they begin to engage in these conversations.

Once the floodgates are opened, it is far easier to engage others in a movement for Emancipatory Spirituality. Our attitudes change dramatically once we get involved in thinking in detail about what our own lives might look like in a different kind of world.

The discussion of how to change your own work world or profession can lead to a new kind of "consciousness-raising group" that broadens the question from the world of work to our whole lives: "What would be different in our *lives* if we lived in a world with Emancipatory Spirituality as its bottom line?" We start with this question in the world of work, but quickly the discussion broadens to our family lives, our relationships with neighbors and friends, the kind of media to which our children are exposed, the kinds of social pressures we face, the kinds of products we consume, the degree of safety we feel in our streets, the problems we face building loving relationships.

The more we allow ourselves to enter into this "fantasy," the more we become aware of how very distorted our lives are in our contemporary "reality."

Part of the way Emancipatory Spirituality will eventually come to be the central transformative movement of this millennium is simply that people will allow themselves to ask the questions we are raising. As they begin to think these thoughts, they will begin to ask for fundamental changes in every aspect of their lives.

So one part of the strategy for those of us who wish to support the development of Emancipatory Spirituality is simple: we can encourage people to engage in this conversation, to foster groups in which these questions are explored in depth in every workplace and profession. We can encourage people to demand that the real world correspond to their highest ideals and visions of what could and should be.

In the following three chapters, I'm going to give a few examples of how a spiritual orientation might reshape medicine, law, and education. The main thing you can learn from these chapters is this: allow yourself to dream and don't be constrained by the way things are now. Your work could become a spiritual adventure.

You might wonder what's the point of jumping so far ahead of the present reality? There are two reasons why it's important to do this.

Some people believe spirituality is merely a side show, something we do for our own personal lives, but without much consequence for our lives together as citizens and as part of a larger community. In the following chapters, I will show you how very different our lives together could be if we took spiritual life seriously and sought to rebuild our world in accord with the vision of an Emancipatory Spirituality. Spirit Matters—and I will show how very deeply it could matter were we to allow ourselves to really move in that direction.

Part of the point of drawing a detailed picture of what a transformed spiritual world could be like is that it helps sustain us as we face hard knocks in the early stages of the campaign for a new bottom line. The temptation to get so involved in these first steps that we lose our sense of where everything could eventually lead is one of the certain pitfalls of political struggle. Keeping our vision clear and returning to it on a daily basis to remind ourselves of where we are going are contributions that spiritual practice can make to social healing.

seven

The Soul of Medicine

Medicine and Health Care

There are two dimensions of medicine and health care that will be transformed by an Emancipatory Spirituality: how they are distributed, and what they will *be* (that is, how we sustain and repair health).

The Distribution of Health Care

Only a society with deep moral distortions would allocate health care on the basis of how much money the ill person has. Yet this is exactly the case in the United States, and to a lesser but nonetheless real extent in many other societies. There is no moral reason why people born into poverty should have less of an opportunity to have their basic health needs met than someone born into wealth.

One of the early goals of Emancipatory Spirituality will be to create a worldwide system of universal health care. The underlying principle: everyone equally deserves first-class health care because everyone is equally valuable and deserving of respect. The central value: human beings participate in God's holiness, and those who work in delivering health care, creating medicines, and medical technologies are engaged in sacred work. I'll consider the implications of these principles on distribution in this section and on *what* we are distributing in the next section.

It's not hard to visualize how a sense of human sanctity might shape our system of distributing health care. Simply divert a substantial portion of the world's military budget to providing food, clothing, and shelter to the hundreds of millions who do not have enough, and then pay for the training and salaries for doctors, nurses, public health experts, and the construction and provision of hospitals and community health-care centers. Provide health education, including a focus on diet, exercise, meditation, prevention, and health maintenance. Make sure all people can get health care when they need it and that they are not faced with financial burdens when they need special care for complicated health problems.

Hasn't universal health care been tried and failed in other countries?

No.

What does fail is when one tries to implement universal health care without giving it the full backing of the society's resources. In that case, the failure is political. The typical scenario becomes something like this: Inadequate resources translate into inadequate health care being available to everyone equally. People end up having to wait a long time for needed services or are denied some specialized services. Everyone grumbles. Then the wealthy manage to pay doctors to offer private medical services, or they cross national boundaries to seek those services elsewhere. The remaining population grumbles even more. Then doctors start to grumble that they aren't getting paid as much as they would in a free market system, pharmaceutical companies stop developing new products because they can't make as much money as they might in a free market system, and the political conservatives who wanted to prove that collective action through government would always fail start to advance the idea of privatization, which is enthusiastically backed by those who control the media and by sectors of the upper and the upper-middle classes, who feel that they'd probably get a better deal (more health care at a price *they* can afford) if the system were privatized. And since they have the power to have their voices heard, they often manage to dominate the public debate.

Yet none of this shows that universal health care doesn't work, only that an underfunded system creates political opportunities for discontent.

There is nothing inevitable about this. If your own family had a medical problem and only enough resources for everyone to afford to see a doctor once every two years, I doubt very much that you'd decide that the highest-paid member of the family got to see a doctor every year, while others were allowed a doctor visit only once every ten years. You wouldn't go to that solution because you care too much about the members of your family. So, you'd either try to struggle to get adequate resources or you'd share the resources according to medical need. It's only because we have not yet gotten to the point where we can truly feel our connection to all other human beings that we tolerate the current health-care system.

Of course, if you assume that the bottom line of Western societies and its logic of "looking out for Number One" without regard to others is unchangeable, then *any* changes will seem utopian.

In the current system, it's not surprising that people who originally went into medical professions to care for others eventually get subverted into thinking of themselves as medical entrepreneurs who have skills to sell to the highest bidder and who invest their profits in hospitals, group practices, or insurance company schemes designed to maximize their wealth. It's no surprise, in such a system, that the most "creative" (if we can use that word for people whose talents do not extend to moral sensitivity) medical professionals, biochemists, and pharmaceutical companies will tend to flow to the countries and markets where they can best maximize their own personal advantage. That's how it is in a world with the bottom line unchanged.

But there's every reason to believe that most of this would change in a society that actually valued the holiness of every individual and the sacred mission of medicine. In that society, people would be recruited into the medical and health care professions because of their overflowing loving kindness and desire to help others. There would not be any particular financial incentive—doctors would be paid enough to lead a comfortable life, as would everyone else. The special benefits accruing to them would come from the inner reward of getting to do this work. Medical technologies and pharmaceuticals would continue to benefit from innovation, because the scientists and technicians would be joyful in the opportunity to do such creative work.

There is nothing far-fetched about envisioning that motivation. The truth is, most people who enter health care and medical professions today originally approach this work from that motivation—it doesn't have to be socially engineered into people. On the contrary, it takes a huge amount of training and indoctrination (sometimes even more than the entirety of medical school) to drum this idealism and desire to serve *out* of health-care people, and even then it pops up residually at various moments in the lives of most doctors, nurses, and other health-care workers. Imagine how much more that would be the case in a world where these feelings were encouraged, not only in the medical profession, but in every corner of the society!

Fine, you might say, that is what it could look like, but how can we ever get there from here?

Well, one early step may be this: the creation of an international corps of medical-care personnel who live according to these values, who donate their services to those in need of care, and who are paid by an international health organization. We could take that step right now. In fact, there are organizations like Doctors Without Borders that are already engaged in this very activity.

But on a social scale, shouldn't we put our energies into a more "realistic" attempt to reform health care, like the kind liberal Democrats are introducing piecemeal into Congress?

I don't think so. I don't oppose those measures, but I do think they tend to give the wrong message: that our health-care system will be made "okay" if a few more benefits are granted. The whole model is wrong: it assumes that the existing system of health care for profit can be "made to work" by kindly reforms. But from my standpoint, the system is fundamentally misguided—its bottom line ensures that decisions about allocation will always be made on the basis of profit rather than in terms of loving our fellow human beings.

The existing system of medical distribution helps instill the values that keep our society misguided. I watched this up close when I was connected to the Clintons in the mid-1990s as they attempted to build a system that would preserve the wealth of the medical profiteers while allowing greater access for all. The outcome was a monstrosity. Moreover, when this monstrosity was nevertheless still opposed by the profiteers, and then failed, the whole country was encouraged to draw the wrong conclusion: that the Clintons had been "too radical," when in fact their problem was not being radical (that is, oriented toward the root problem) enough. They fought for a compromised goal, and they did not even win that—in part because people always find it harder to rally around a compromised goal.

The large health-care insurers and profiteers have fought every attempt at minimal health-care distribution reforms by buying television ads purporting to show ordinary citizens talking to each other about how misguided these reforms are—as though the companies are really trying to champion the interests of ordinary citizens. Ironically, they put as much energy into fighting every little reform as they would into fighting a serious ethical transformation of the system. But this should teach us an important lesson: it will take almost as much energy to achieve minimal reforms as it will to achieve a rational and moral system of distribution, so it makes more sense to fight for the greater cause than for the lesser. The first step is not to fight for the minimal programs of the liberal Democrats, but to fight for a new way of thinking about health care that places the sanctity of human beings at the center of the debate.

Holy and Holistic Care

Once you understand that human beings are fully integrated into a mind/body/psychological/spiritual/communal totality, you begin to see that it's not just the way we deliver health care, but *what* we deliver that needs to change. If each of us is all these interacting dimensions, mind as well as body, spirit as well as emotions, then when we get sick, every aspect of us needs healing.

The dominant model in health care today is one that focuses on the bodily level and works on it as though it could be understood separately from the well-being of the whole.

Even "holistic" health approaches tend to add just one or two more levels, but avoid working on all levels in an integrated manner.

This is a deep mistake. I've met holistic healers who work on the body as a holistic system, but who know little about the emotional reality of the person with whom they are working. I've met talented people who talk about the energy fields around their clients, but seek no information about the family life or communities in which these people live. I've known Reichian therapists who focus on the way feelings get embedded in the bodily tissues of their clients but who are unaware of other aspects of bodily functioning and unaware of the inner spiritual lives of their clients. I've met spiritual healers who don't know much about the emotional lives or social realities facing their patients.

A holy approach to medicine and health care will be holistic in the widest possible sense. It will seek to understand, diagnose, and intervene on all levels of our being at the same time. People will be seen by practitioners who have multiple levels of knowledge, and by teams of health-care workers who together bring a broad interdisciplinary approach to the process of diagnosis and treatment.

The Healthy Environment

What we take in, through our stomachs, through our lungs, and through our pores, has a powerful impact on our health. It's no news today that environmental conditions are central to our health. The air we breathe, the water we drink, the clothes we wear, the products we use to clean our bodies, our hair, and our teeth, and the food we eat have become so filled with carcinogens and other poisons that we are constantly at risk.

The people who perpetrate this are not evil people—they just are living according to the bottom line of contemporary society. If they changed their minds, they would be fired and someone else would be hired to take their place. Only a new bottom line will change this.

Health care must address all these issues, not split them off into realms remote from the everyday practice of medicine.

There's also the responsibility of the consumer to buy healthy products once they become available. But don't blame consumers who don't have that option, or who have it only if they are willing to pay more for a healthful tomato than they could reasonably afford. Responsibility begins when the options are made available. When healthy food costs twice or three times as much as unsafe food, those who cannot afford to buy the better food don't deserve to be disdained. Some upper-middle-class people tend to perceive themselves as saner than the rest of the population in what they eat, whereas in fact they are only richer.

Yet there are also consumption habits that need to be healed.

Many people overeat and do so to offset the emotional, ethical, and spiritual distress in their lives.

Many people frenetically engage in buying consumer goods, and then updating them whenever a new model becomes available. They find momentary consolation in buying.

But it never lasts very long.

You can never eat enough to feed a hungry soul.

So the solution is to address the spiritual hunger. Instead of taking dangerous diet pills or quick fixes, we need to provide the emotional, ethical, and spiritual nurturing people need—so that they don't take their pain out on their bodies.

A healthy environment will be one in which people have meaningful work and live in families and communities suffused with love and solidarity that nonetheless allow for privacy and for each individual to choose his or her own path. It will be an environment in which people rejoice in each other's being and support each other's emotional well-being, spiritual growth, and intellectual depth.

The healthy environment will have healthy foods, and unpolluted air and water, and it will have repaired the sources of global warming. It will have mass transportation and a careful use of the planet's energy and resources.

The healthy environment will give people many opportunities each day to exercise, to meditate, to sing and dance, to engage in aesthetic creativity, to do physical labor as well as mental labor, to be with others in community, and to be alone in moments of quiet, to celebrate the universe in community, and to connect with God in privacy.

A health-care professional will be involved in addressing all these issue, and will always understand the integral nature of health.

The Holy Hospital

Imagine a hospital as a holy place in which all we've learned about the integrated nature of body, soul, mind, and emotions is brought to focus on healing people who are in need of healing. In such a context, doctors and nurses mix with spiritual and emotional healers, with community organizers and family therapists—all dedicated to bringing the most sophisticated understanding to bear in the service of restoring health. Which professional would take leadership in shaping the particular team of healers to fit the needs of the client would depend on the particular case. There would be no hierarchy of pay or professional status, because all would be recognized as making equally important contributions to the well-being of the client.

Now imagine a hospital work shift. All of the healers might assemble for a quarter hour of meditation and prayer in which they recommitted themselves to their holy function. The pressures of work can easily distract health care practitioners from remembering the tremendously important spiritual task they face, so these moments of reconnecting to one's highest spiritual insights would help shape the dynamics in the coming work period.

Patients would understand that they were in a sacred space populated by professionals and lay people who chose to enter these professions in large part because of their combination of talents, spiritual centeredness, and ethical dedication. I do not necessarily have in mind, though, that it would feel like a traditional church or synagogue, with hushed and respectful tones (in fact, I'm not sure a church or synagogue should feel that way either), because part of a healing environment is music, humor, and entertainment (yes, the hospital would have dramatic presentations, live music, poetry and fiction readings, art, etc.—all supplied by the surrounding communities, whose volunteer efforts would pour into schools and hospitals) as well as religious services, meditation rooms, and other aids to spiritual healing.

While many patients need peace and quiet and have no interest in connecting to these activities, others will be able to find this outpouring of love and caring to be healing and regenerative. Indeed, the hospital will become an embodiment of loving energy, and love will occupy a central place in the healing of the individual.

"Wait," you might object, "I don't want love, I want a skilled surgeon, and I don't care about his or her mental state." I understand the feeling, and I felt that way myself until I recently underwent surgery and found that these other factors mattered a great deal, not only in unnecessary delays that made the surgery more dangerous, but also in the whole recovery process. Just talk to anyone who has been through the hospital experience today and you begin to learn that having a skilled surgeon is a necessary but not a sufficient condition for effective healing.

But where are you going to find medical professionals who could be healers in a holy hospital? Today, it would be quite a stretch. But we need to redesign medical training so it includes this way of thinking about health and a whole new way of treating medical students. Today, medical students and interns are treated as though their lives and feelings are irrelevant; they are asked to sacrifice themselves for the sake of the hospital. In a spiritually shaped medical school, the well-being of the healers becomes an important focus, and training, rotations, internships, and residencies are designed not to exploit the novice, but to help her or him enter a holy sphere of work. From the beginning, this means developing in the medical student, intern, resident, nurse, social worker, chiropractor, doctor of homeopathy, and all other healing professionals an ability to pursue his or her own spiritual development and time to do so as well as an ability to hone his or her capacity to be loving and caring.

Many of the people who enter the healing professions today wish they could develop their capacities for caring and loving, but they find that these are undervalued and even cynically dismissed at various internships and residencies. Far more will be attracted to health-related careers, even though the pay will shrink, once we have a new spiritual orientation to the practice of medicine.

Meaning as Medicine

Practicing physician Raphi Kelman, M.D., has made some important observations about the centrality of spiritual meaning as a source of healing. The need for meaning in our lives has significant physiological consequences. Kelman says that his research as a medical practitioner confirms my argument that the need for meaning is as significant as the need for food or economic well-being.

Spirit Matters—because the deprivation of a spiritual dimension to our lives and the absence of a sense of meaning has drastic physiological consequences.

So, Kelman argues, if one lives in a society in which health care is available to some but not to others, one is living in a society in which the sphere of caring has been severely restricted—and that will have immediate health consequences. When people are just out for themselves, there is an inevitable loss of meaning. Conversely, if we live in a society in which people take care of each other, which would certainly manifest in adequate health care being available, then we will have direct health benefits that flow not from the availability of the care but from the framework of meaning that promotes our well-being.

Similarly, Kelman continues, caring about the environment is good for our health, even when we have not yet succeeded in stopping the polluters or restraining those who are misusing the earth's resources. A doctor's very concern, and involvement with others in this issue produces health-inducing meaning with its positive consequences.

Many people think there is a clear separation between what we do as individuals and what the country or the larger economic and political sphere is like. They imagine there is no point in bothering to try to change the larger picture. But, Kelman maintains, "What I've learned in my medical practice is that when someone activates the concern in themselves for ecological improvement, they are simultaneously activating a transpersonal aspect of one's being that aspires to meaning, which has significant physiological effects. So even when we can't win on ecological change or health care change, being so engaged can have positive health effects."

Kelman emphasizes that the issue is not just social change activity, but the inner reality that produces this activity. As American politics has become narrower and technocratic in focus, many people begin to address health care, ecological change, or other social justice issues with a kind of mentality that is more like an intellectual game than an act of love. If your involvement in these issues reflects an ability to transcend ego and connect to a life of meaning aimed at the well-being of all, you activate the heart in ways that have significant impact on our physiology. The success of any social action depends on the consciousness that one brings to social transformative activity.

The reason some people might be shocked to hear this is that we have come to think of ourselves only as machines. Our materialist philosophical framework is so entrenched that it seems almost incomprehensible to us to recognize what people throughout most of human history recognized, namely the deep connection between spiritual and physical well-being.

Ironically, most of the people who tend to dismiss spiritual insights on scientific grounds actually have little familiarity with the latest developments in science, developments that make us question the wisdom of seeing the world from the standpoint of matter. The mechanistic worldview has little plausibility to those on the cutting edge of physics today, yet it continues to dominate the kind of science that is taught to doctors and that is popular in the larger society. Popular attitudes on science today fit with the science of fifty years ago.

Medicine, Kelman points out, got into this error a long time ago. It developed its "medical science" through the study of the anatomy of a corpse. Much important information was gathered, but deep philosophical mistakes accompanied the new knowledge. A human being is not a corpse—we are something that needs to be understood in a different way. Mind and body are not separate entities—and we need to rethink our philosophical frame.

Similarly, it's sometimes helpful in medicine to compare a human heart to a mechanical pump. But it's fundamentally different from a pump—and indeed unlike anything we know of in the rest of the universe. We know that experiences of compassion and tolerance affect cardiac function, but a computer or a mechanical pump won't change its function even if it looks like it's experiencing compassion, but a human heart will change! Numerous studies show that compassion and tolerance improves cardiac functioning, whereas anger, intolerance, and hostility worsens heart functioning.

It would be better to think of health as a flowing of energy that may occasionally get blocked.

At the annual meeting of the American Psychosomatic Society, medical researcher Margaret E. Kemeny, PhD, recently reported that a group of 330 people infected by HIV were followed for seven years. Six were found to have remained healthy, while the rest proceeded to AIDS. Psychological questioning revealed striking differences between those people who had remained healthy and those who had progressed to AIDS. Those who had remained healthy were found to score much higher in the areas of Meaning, Creativity, and Giving and Receiving Love!

In the Study for the Advancement of Medicine in 1995, researchers showed that when patients experience caring and compassion, salivary SIGA, the body's first line of defense against viruses and other pathogens, increased significantly. A study[1] by D.C. McLelland at Harvard University showed that an experience of compassion raises SIGA—even in people who claimed that they had no subjective feeling of compassion. On the other hand, experiences of anger suppress immunological responses and reduce cardiac functioning. One qualification: anger for the sake of humankind or to express that you are being hurt or oppressed can be healthful anger.

When people see their interconnectedness and overcome their alienation, their stress is reduced in a good way—other forms of stress reduction that really don't have this impact. The stress reduction groups that have a positive impact are those in which the experiences of compassion, caring for each other, and interconnectedness are generated, and it is these aspects of the group that make their stress reduction work.

Kelman's work has important consequences for medical practice: "If we can't get patients to activate their interest in meaning (however they define it), we will not be as successful in healing. So this should be a high priority for medical practice (of course, not in circumstances of acute crisis, but in most other circumstances).

"Of course," Kelman writes, "I don't deny the physical dimension either. Spiritual healing doesn't have to be counterpoised to chemotherapy. We need to approach people on all levels because interventions on many different levels all have a synergistic effect.

1.   McClelland, D.C., and Chariff, A.D. 1997, "Immunoehencie Effects of Humor on Secretory IgA and Resistance to Respiratory Infections," *Psychology and Health*, 12: 329-344

But neither is approaching someone purely on a physical level adequate. And I say this not only about the traditional forms of medicine, but also about the 'alternative medicine' techniques. If you give people a regimen of vitamins or other physical interventions like nutrition that are separate from any meaning-level of intervention, it will be less effective" (TIKKUN, March/April 2000).

Kelman's point is a caution for those who think a spiritual approach to healing is simply to give out vitamins or to eat organic. That may be an important part, but what is also needed is a certain kind of consciousness. There are some health-care practitioners who present themselves as "alternative" because they don't use traditional medicine, but who nevertheless approach health in a mechanistic way. The alternative I am recommending may include non-traditional methods as well, but must include the issues of meaning and spiritual practice.

Consider, for example, the question of what we take into our bodies and how to do that in a spiritual way.

When people see that food is an act of giving on the part of the earth and that we have a corresponding need to give back, they begin to approach a spiritual level of understanding. So, eating foods that are products of exploitation of the earth or that were produced through alienated labor that was wildly underpaid and demeaned has negative health consequences. As Kelman puts it, "The earth gives to us so that we can give in turn to others—because we are all fundamentally interconnected and interdependent. Our atoms are constantly being shuffled from the earth and the air through us and back to a tree, or to other human beings, or to the earth. There is a constant dance of sharing that is occurring, but when we block this whole cascade through fear or greed, we interfere with the life-giving and nurturing qualities that are available and were meant to sustain us."

We return, here, to one of the core points in this book: we have lost our sense of wonder and appreciation. Awe and wonder must be part of our process of eating, and if they are not, their absence will have adverse health consequences.

So part of a spiritually oriented medicine is that a doctor must try to instill an understanding of the integrated nature of our health—that on the one hand the health of one part of our body is linked to the health of other parts, and, on the other hand, that the health of the body is linked to health of the economic, political, and ecological systems outside the body. Then the doctor must support the patient in developing a meaning-orientation toward life and encourage the patient to activate the capacity for compassion and connectedness between people (because it is in those moments that the deep healing begins). The initial taking of a history would include these dimensions, and yearly checkups would also address the entire life situation of the patient. When they begin to think in these terms, many doctors will find they have much to learn from their patients about the various levels of interaction between health and other aspects of life.

The underlying point here is that the reality of each part of our bodies and of the total body is rooted in a much larger totality, a spiritual/emotional/intellectual/physical unity, and that all work together. Spirit Matters—and one dimension of our health problems lies with our inability to understand the full implications of this body-mind-spirit embodied unity that is who we are.

A Spiritual Exercise

Try the following exercise in your own life, and you'll reap many benefits: as you sit down to eat, stop and give yourself three minutes to contemplate the goodness of the universe that has supplied you this food. Bless the food and all who have contributed to the causal chain that brought the food to your table. Then, take ten minutes in the middle of the meal to eat in silence. Focus on the tastes. Chew slowly, and be aware of each movement of your tongue and teeth as you chew the food. After the meal, spend three minutes of silence with a focus on thanking the universe for the food and on renewing your commitment to spend time and energy to ensure that all those who do not have enough to eat will be given food.

If we can get ourselves to slow down in this way and respond to the world with awe, wonder, and radical amazement, we will certainly develop a healthier attitude. This kind of attention and consciousness will eventually become more prevalent and will contribute to a healthier world.

None of this is to suggest that we abandon drugs or other forms of high-tech medicine. It is a plea, however, to open up our understanding of what can be healing in meaning.

A First Step

Make it a legal requirement that doctors take a "meaning/spiritual" history when they do their intake and examinations. This information will soon be shown to predict health or disease, and that could lead to a deeper attention to meaning and the spiritual development of patients.

Require that part of the continuing education of the profession be a course that encourages doctors and nurses to allow themselves to be utopian, to fantasize, to imagine, to be creative in envisioning the kinds of changes they would like to see in their own professions. Let doctors and other health professionals learn that Spirit Matters. Health care and medicine could look very different if we had a new bottom line of love and caring, a new sensitivity to the world of spirit. As the new spiritual awakening deepens in the coming centuries, we will see fundamental transformations in the way we practice healing and health care. Engaging in this kind of envisioning, seemingly utopian at first, will free doctors to do the kind of thinking they were never taught to do in medical school—and could be the beginning of a very significant transformation in medicine.

eight

The Spiritual Transformation of Law

As it's currently constituted, the legal system plays an important role in shaping the dominant individualism and selfishness of society. The very word lawyer conjures up the image of a lone shark seeking money and power without regard to the consequences for others, ready to hurt or betray everyone in his path toward success, and lacking any moral compass. Though this kind of stereotype is unfair to many who practice law, it is rooted not only in bitter experience with many contemporary lawyers but also in an intuitive grasp of the way the entire legal system has lost its mooring in transcendent notions of justice and righteousness.

Most young people enter law school because of their concern for justice and fairness and their desire to help create a decent society. Yet the framework of law is quickly imposed upon them, encouraging them to think about their own interests and the interests of their clients without regard to the consequences for others.

The responsibility to represent their own clients without regard to the well-being of society is built into the "code of ethics" to which lawyers can be held legally accountable. The original idea was to protect the individual against an oppressive government—the kind of liberal approach that emerged as a defense against communities that, throughout centuries of feudalism, had become unconscionably domineering and intrusive. The lawyer emerged as the hero who would push for laws and legal practices that provided all of us with a shield from the arbitrary decisions of the powerful.

But today we live in a different world from that dominated by a feudal aristocracy. Our society is one in which the most important problem is the preponderance of isolated individuals who barely know how to connect to each other or how to see their personal lives in some higher moral frame.

Peter Gabel, my partner in building a spiritually oriented practice of social healing, has taught me many of the insights I want to share with you here. Gabel is a professor of law at New College of California and was one of the founders of Critical Legal Studies (CLS), an organization of progressive legal scholars. But Gabel broke with CLS when he realized they would not take into account the hunger for meaning and love that are so central to our contemporary needs.

Neither of us wants to see the important civil liberties gains of the past dismantled, and so we support efforts to bring a deeper understanding of the importance of protecting the individual from a coercive state into public understanding. But we also believe the legal arena has a tremendous impact on public consciousness, and that it tends to reinforce a paranoid vision of what human relationships are about. The central goal of legal practice becomes that of defending the individual against unfair or irrational demands of others or of the community as a whole. The task of the lawyer becomes that of vigorous representation of the stance of one's client (employer)—regardless of the consequences to others. Moral judgment is put on permanent hold. The need to get everyone a counsel becomes the highest value, and this translates into the responsibility of "zealous representation" without regard to the consequences of what one is representing and what one's client has done or may yet do to the rest of us or to the planet. The goal is to win—at any cost.

A morally neutered legal ethos frees lawyers of any responsibility for the social consequences of their legal activities.

Technique separated from moral accountability leads to the moral depredations of the contemporary world. The corporate business person follows the same line of argument: "I am only hired to maximize the profits of this company, so don't bother me with ethical considerations, because they have no place in my public role as a corporate manager. But after work, I'm moral in the way I treat my children and I'm even involved in my church or give money to charities." This is

the line that was used by some of the lawyers for the cigarette industry, and I see nothing in its logic that would prevent others from being
active advocates for Adolph Hitler, even were he poised to continue
genocide after being acquitted in a court of law.

Presumably, this irresponsibility is justified by our belief that the
presumption of innocence combined with the right to counsel justi-
fies the criminal defense lawyer to do whatever is legally allowable to
secure his or her client's acquittal. But when taken as a social practice, this way of thinking reinforces the extreme individualism and
irresponsibility of the contemporary world. So, even if you know that
your client is guilty and might reasonably be expected to return to a
life of violence and hurting others after acquittal, you don't have any
responsibility to the larger society. Similarly, this way of thinking
encourages lawyers who represent large corporations to use every
possible legal trick to destroy the rain forest or protect the polluter—
because it's "not their job" to pass judgment on their clients' ends.

Law as a Moral Calling

Imagine how different the norms of the legal profession would be
if we began with the notion that law was a moral calling, a calling to
serve the public good. As Peter Gabel puts it, law should become a
social practice "aimed at healing the ingrained distortions in human
interaction that disable us from repairing our communal fabric."

Gabel was challenged in the pages of TIKKUN magazine by Alan
Dershowitz, one of the lawyers who defended O.J. Simpson and
helped obtain his acquittal(TIKKUN, July/August and September/
October, 1997). Dershowitz demanded to know how Gabel would
handle a case where he'd been asked to represent a woman facing the
death penalty for killing her abusive husband. What, for example, if
police broke into the defendant's home without a warrant and discovered evidence suggesting the murder was planned. Would Gabel
preclude the women's appointed lawyer from invoking Fourth or Fifth
Amendment protections so as to exclude this evidence? Dershowitz's
point, of course, was that it was the obligation of the lawyer to do

whatever he could to manipulate the existing system to find defenses for his client.

Gabel's response took up the challenge directly: "If I believed she did kill her husband, I would only be reinforcing the amoral individualism of the existing legal culture if my first act were to seek to exclude the evidence that formed the basis of my belief. Instead, I would seek to have a profound encounter with my client that revealed to both of us the tragedy and violence of their relationship and, if she did kill her husband, the awesome nature of that act even if it were a response to her own suffering at his hands. True justice in these circumstances calls for a public telling of this story and public acknowledgment and a public taking of responsibility for what she did. Then I would seek to defend her on the grounds that her act was justified, or understandable if not entirely justified, depending on a moral consensus that she and I sought to arrive at together. In Mr. Dershowitz's hypothetical case, the use of the Exclusionary Rule (suppressing evidence unlawfully obtained) would serve to deny the client the opportunity to be vindicated for what she actually did by pretending that she did not do it."

Of course, Gabel recognizes that we don't yet live in a society in which we are free from the distortions that have led to developing protections like the Exclusionary Rule (for example, the tendency of police to raid the homes of innocent people without a warrant, the way class and race factor into crime and punishment, the inhumanity of the present prison system, the irrational criminalization and sentencing practices associated with drugs, and many other things that need to be changed). But the point is how to develop different society, and Gabel's point is that we can't get there if we allow ourselves to become morally blinded to the kind of "do anything for your client" thinking that might have been a factor in Alan Dershowitz's helping to acquit O.J. Simpson. The lawyer, says Gabel, if he could reasonably conclude that a batterer (perhaps like O.J. Simpson, if we are to believe the findings of the subsequent civil trial against him) had probably killed his wife, might be morally required to demand that his client acknowledge his act and the suffering it has caused, while seeking some mitigation of the sentence based on compassion for the cultural brutality the defendant himself had suffered. (In the case of O.J. Simpson, Gabel speculated that there might have been some discussion of the story of a black man raised in the projects of San Francisco who made it in white society by adopting what the writer Franz Fanon called a white mask, and the effect of this history, if any, on his experience of rejection by his wife.)

But if the lawyer uses the Exclusionary Rule to secure the acquittal of a known batterer of women who may have brutally murdered his wife without doing anything to ameliorate the client's past victims or to protect the potential future victims, that lawyer is behaving unethically.

Equally important, argues Gabel, this kind of social practice contributes to the larger and pervasive notion that we are all disconnected individuals without responsibility for each other's fate—the very means by which the existing legal system contributes to the spiritual decay of the larger society.

The legal profession needs to reorient itself toward justice, rather than toward the self-interest of the client. "Justice," says Gabel, "is a spiritual and moral healing of a distortion in human relationships." Attorneys, then, must present themselves to their own clients as moral beings rather than as technical experts in the law, and they need to learn how to see each case as a potential link in their primary responsibility as lawyers—which is to create a less alienated and more spiritually connected world.

This is a new conception of lawyers, to be sure. Lawyers would no longer be perceived as technocrats who manipulate rules for the benefit of the highest bidder, or as experts in serving their own and their clients' selfish or even vengefully motivated interests, regardless of the impact on others and on society as a whole.

This vision is articulated in "The Declaration of Legal Renewal," which is the law plank of the Law and Meaning Task Force of the Foundation for Ethics and Meaning, an organization that Peter Gabel and I helped form in 1996 to work on issues of building for a spiritual transformation of society.

End the Adversary System

Gabel and the Task Force have called for an end to the adversarial system.

At the simplest level, possible before we've made a total transformation in the way we do law, lawyers could take two very important steps:

They should stop characterizing the motives and actions of opposing counsel and their clients in distorted and demeaning ways.

They should stop making legal claims known to be unjustified or misleading simply because there may a semblance of plausible evidence or legal theory that can be deployed and manipulated to support them.

But ending the adversarial system would be a much deeper and more profound transformation. Today, courts are set up as a kind of arena for a fight to the death between two parties whose interests are counterpoised.

Imagine, if you would, a legal system in which the goal of lawyers was to find the best way to serve the interests of everyone involved—and that would include the best interests of the society as a whole.

In such a circumstance, the jury of peers would have the task of making a decision after listening to all the relevant information. But relevance would have to change, because the jury would be concerned with figuring out how to contribute to the rectification of all the distortions in the social fabric that had been uncovered in the process of hearing a specific case.

So, if you can remember the O.J. Simpson trial, one of the things that a jury in the new system I'm envisioning might have done would have been to order changes in the Los Angeles police department so that racist policemen were removed from the force. They might also have sought changes in the way domestic violence calls are treated, so that Nicole Simpson's earlier battering would have resulted in O.J.'s being exposed and prevented from having any further contact with her, or at least, after the fact, that future calls for help to the police would have been given more serious attention. And, of course, attorneys on both sides might have taken steps to find out what really happened, rather than being prevented from doing so by legal "protections" that did not serve the interests of justice. But my point here is that in a new system lawyers would be looking not only at the main crime but at all the peripheral material about the distortions that led to the crime.

Certainly the Bill of Rights was an enormous achievement in protecting the presumed innocence of those accused of crime and protecting our culture against a police state. For all these reasons, I deeply appreciate the work of civil libertarians.

But in criminal cases where you know your client is guilty, these rights should not be invoked in the same way.

Murder may still be a hard case for my suggested changes. So, even if you don't quite agree with me about eliminating the adversarial system in those kinds of cases, perhaps you might see that it would be a good idea in many lesser crimes and certainly in most civil suits. There may be lots of money at stake, but there is no reason why our legal system should not try to promote the best interests of all parties, including the interests of the larger community. With such an orientation, lawyers would be working cooperatively rather than antagonistically.

Reconciliation and Atonement: Restorative Justice

If the goal is to promote the best interests of all parties and to promote social harmony, then criminal law would no longer have identifying who committed a particular act and punishing that person as its sole aim, but rather would expand its focus to help rectify the disruption to the fabric of love and trust that was generated by a given criminal act. Similarly, civil law would aim not at determining "who was right" so much as at reestablishing goodwill and harmony among participants in any given dispute.

With this new focus, part of the responsibility of all officers of the court (including lawyers) becomes encouraging repentance. Repentance, however, becomes a multidimensional reality. Sure, we want "the criminal" to repent his or her misdeeds. But we may also have to inquire deeply to see if other parties involved have some responsibility that may require their own repentance.

For example, in a world in which there is vast inequality of wealth, we will *not* excuse those who think that the way to rectify this situation is to steal for their own benefit. This kind of selfish and individualistic solution tears at the social fabric, making people less trustful of each other, and hence less open to hearing political ideas about sharing one's own good fortune or caring for others. If the individuals engaged in poverty-generated crime put the same effort into building a political movement for social change, their situation would be far more likely to improve.

Yet every time people act in this irrational manner and then repent, their repentance needs to be matched by a genuine repentance on the part of the rest of us who managed to turn away and ignore the fact that within a few miles of where most of us live there are people whose desperation to feed their own families has led them to engage in criminal activity. Our ability to shut our eyes to the ongoing pain created by the obscene inequalities of wealth and power in most advanced industrial societies should be cause for shame and repentance—and the criminal justice system should encourage that repentance and demand that society change the way it organizes itself.

As a society becomes more infused with Emancipatory Spirituality, it will become more focused on rectifying the conditions that so obviously manifest an insensitivity to the spirit of God in every human being. No society that recognizes the sanctity of each human being would put a significant section of human beings into circumstances in which they could not earn a living wage doing work that was respectful of their intelligence and creativity. Nor would a society governed by principles of Emancipatory Spirituality allow conditions in which people felt so underrecognized and underconfirmed that they began to lash out in irrational ways.

Yet we cannot promise that there would be a full resolution of every form of human pathology even as Emancipatory Spirituality increasingly sets the political and economic agenda in the centuries ahead. There may still be irrational acting out and hurting of each other, and to that extent there will be a need for reconciliation and repentance. Yet those who are concerned with creating social peace and harmony should try to understand the complexity of the forces that generated the problem, and hence they should seek repentance not only from the individual who seemed to be the problem but also from the social system in which that individual festered and was in pain without being adequately loved and cared for.

One important step in this direction has already emerged in the past few years: a movement of lawyers who seek what they call Restorative Justice.

The Restorative Justice movement recognizes that crime is not only an offense against the specific person being ripped off, but against the whole community. Crime makes us all fearful that we are going to be ripped off or hurt, and it makes us feel that we need to be protected against each other. The deeper we go into that fear, the more we each see ourselves as an isolated "I," and the less we are able to feel part of any "we." Ironically, the more we feel unable to trust others, the more we create the psychodynamics that lead to crime, because people are far more likely to turn to crime than to political action or to seeking help from others when they live in a society dominated by fear and mutual distrust.

The Restorative Justice movement points out that incarceration rarely solves these problems. So Restorative Justice focuses on the needs of the victims of crime and on repairing communities rather than simply jailing individuals. David Lerman, a Milwaukee county assistant district attorney, and an activist in the movement, argues that by focusing in this way, rather than solely on how to punish the person who broke a law, the victim, offender, and community can use the event "as a sort of 'fuel' from which to reengage and empower victims and community members toward building stronger communities" (TIKKUN, September/October, 1999).

An important step in this process is for the offender and victim to meet at a Victim-Offender Conference in a safe setting in which the basic premise is that one party has been wronged and the other is there to accept responsibility. The offender is able to learn how much he or she has hurt the victim. And, according to Lerman, it is common for the offender to apologize directly to the victim in Victim-Offender Conferences. Storytelling is an important part of this process. Victims and offenders are encouraged to tell the stories of what really happened and the impact of the criminal wrongdoing. "By focusing on harm, harm reduction, and accountability, as opposed to simply finding guilt followed by punishment, Restorative Justice opens the door for understanding the human consequences of crimes. The victim feels much more empowered this way than when the entire focus is on punishing the offender and, as a result, the offender never really feels safe to tell what actually happened or to acknowledge guilt or responsibility."

Acts of restoration for the community and the specific victim must be tailored to the specific realities of each criminal act. Instead of working from a menu of crime and punishment, the victims and prosecutors work out an acceptable scheme for restoration of repair of the damage done.

While Restorative Justice is in its infancy at present, it represents a consciousness that will expand as Emancipatory Spirituality plays a larger role in our society. Eventually, we will find society placing repentance, restoration, and reconciliation at the heart of the legal system.

The Truth and Reconciliation Commission in South Africa shows a new way to deal with justice without retribution. In *No Justice without Forgiveness*, Archbishop Desmond Tutu argues that this new way of dealing with law has actually worked in South Africa.

Mediation Outreach and Community Problem Solvers Replacing Police

An important precedent for moving away from adversarial ways of thinking has already become established in some Western societies through the movement toward mediation and arbitration of disputes. Divorce is one example; minor traffic accidents are another. And the more cooperation, the less pain for everyone involved.

Mediators do not seek to determine who is right and who is wrong, but rather reach some common solution to a shared problem. While this is not always appropriate in our current society where some people and some economic institutions are willing victimizers, it becomes increasingly appropriate as more and more people turn from the ethos of selfishness to the ethos of caring for others. Without endorsing moral relativism that sometimes inappropriately accompanies mediation in this society, we can nevertheless see that there are many situations in which mediation would be a better way of resolving conflict than the adversarial approach of our current legal system, and that in a future legal system, it will play an increasingly prominent role.

In our own society, it is all too often the police who are called in to resolve disputes and who are forced to deal with individuals who are disruptive to others around them. The police are given all the wrong tools for this, trained more for their use of violence than for their ability to understand the complexities of human needs and find ways to address them.

As Emancipatory Spirituality becomes more prevalent and the resulting goodwill makes people more trustful of each other, there will be much more room for a different kind of professional increasingly supplementing and eventually replacing the local police officer on the beat: the local community healer and problem solver. Community healers, problem solvers, and police officers would be chosen for their outstanding capacities for empathy and compassion as well as for their exceptional smarts at problem solving and mediation. And because of these traits, they would earn the respect and trust of people in the few blocks of a neighborhood in which they were employed to help counsel individuals and families about their own personal and familial problems as well as serve the community in facing neighborhood problems.

Instead of waiting for a problem to get to the stage at which it might turn into abuse or criminal activity, the community healers and problem solvers would be involved in early intervention, seeking to provide the love, support, and practical assistance that would undermine the tendency to "act out" in pathological ways.

Because we want to preserve a realm of privacy, the healers and problem solvers would not have coercive authority to intervene in situations where they were not explicitly asked to become involved. Yet in a society in which the norms of cooperation and mutual caring had replaced the paranoid fear of others that dominates our own society, people would be much more willing to seek this kind of neighborhood assistance long before problems had erupted in hurtful ways. In the period of transition, which might be many decades, there would still be a need for police. Increasing energy would be given to training police in the skills that might enable them to become the first generation of healers and problem solvers. As part of that process, police would be required to live in the neighborhoods they patrolled.

The deepest form of mediation: when the mediator allows the

underlying hurt that each person is experiencing to emerge and be recognized by the other person. The best mediator doesn't focus only on the specifics of the case, but also on the underlying desire for recognition, compassion, and empathy.

The Obligation to Care for Others

In Jewish law, each individual has a legal responsibility to care for others in need. The Torah explicitly commands us to not turn our backs when we hear the cry of the oppressed, and even not to hide ourselves when we see our neighbors' property being placed in danger.

We have a positive obligation to take care of our neighbors and to worry about their well-being. Legal courts can enforce this obligation.

The opposite has been true in Western law. If you see someone drowning and you could save her, but you don't want to be bothered, you have no legal obligation to do so. The drowning person's family would have no recourse were you to stand idly by as your neighbor sank into the water, even if only the slightest action with little or no personal risk might have saved the person from drowning.

An important step toward reframing our understanding of law would be to reintroduce the sense of caring for each other as a legal obligation. In the transition to a society based on Emancipatory Spirituality, it would become possible for an individual to sue those who had not exercised sufficient responsibility in caring for those in need of immediate help. It would no longer be sufficient to claim, "It was none of my business."

Of course, as in all arrangements aimed at fostering mutual caring, the possibility of overzealousness might risk another goal of a spiritually oriented society, namely, the goal of creating safety for people to be alone and focus on their inner lives. A run-away "political correctness" could take the principles of caring articulated in this book and turn them into a crusade of all against all—because the amount of pain in this world exceeds the capacity of any given individual to pay attention, and the nut case politically correct crusader could sue all of us for not paying attention to everyone else's pain. I know that any call for love and caring can be misused, and any legal arrangement can be perverted. But we've gone so far in the direction of excessive individualism that we need to take significant steps in a different direction toward mutual caring, and the legal obligation to take care of others could be a valuable step in that direction.

Here, as in all the other changes suggested in this book, we need what Aristotle called "practical wisdom," the ability to find the mean between extremes. It is important to remember that a spiritually aligned society is one that seeks balance and wholeness, not extremism. Intolerance and excessive moral haughtiness in the name of love and caring is just as much a distortion as are the extremes of individualism and selfishness that predominate in our current reality.

Justice and Righteousness

The real aim of a legal system should be to promote justice and righteousness.

Righteousness, however, is not fostered through coercion, but only through love.

And that is why the ultimate goal of the lawyer must be the same goal as all the other professionals of the society: to encourage more loving toward every human being and toward the totality of all being.

The particular challenge of the lawyer is that she or he must face human beings at times when they have somewhat lost contact with their highest selves and have diminished capacities to see the spirit of God in others. The task of the lawyer, then, is to repair this damage and help the client, others who have been interacting with the client, and the larger society to return to their most loving and nurturing and spiritually alive selves.

I'm not surprised if your first reaction to this notion is to think "I don't want the lawyers I know to be involved in trying to teach me love or caring." I share this sentiment in the case of many (not all) lawyers. My point is not about retraining our current lawyers but about restructuring the legal system entirely in ways that would make it consonant with a world that manifests Emancipatory Spirituality.

Yet there are many lawyers, more than most of us suspect, who want to live lives more consonant with the original moral values that led them into the legal profession, lawyers who would not laugh at the notion of seeking justice and righteousness but who instead feel deep pain at how far away from those ideals the actual practice of law has taken them.

These kinds of lawyers have formed organizations like the Law and Meaning Task Force of the Foundation for Ethics and Meaning and the Restorative Justice movement precisely because they aspire to a different set of values than those that are currently practiced in their profession.

If lawyers can get together to envision these kinds of changes, so too can professionals and working people in every type of work. If lawyers can allow themselves this kind of freedom and exercise the creativity to think so far outside the box, so can anyone.

And this is the way change will actually happen. In every profession and every work situation, people will begin to allow themselves to participate in these kinds of discussions about what their workplace or their profession might look like in a society governed by a different ethos. In such discussions, they will give themselves permission to challenge the fundamental assumptions (such as: law is an adversarial system designed to protect the individual from the possibilities of coercion by others or by government) and to rethink their entire work enterprise based on the notion that the highest goal is to create a society that nurtures the soul and allows us greater opportunities to live lives of the Spirit, lives filled with awe, wonder, and love.

A First Step

Campaign for a law that says that no one should be sent to prison for crimes that do not involve physical violence until he or she is first given an opportunity to participate in a program of restorative justice as democratically defined by the people who live in the community in which the offense took place. Creating an ethos of repentance and forgiveness is a first step in the process of creating a new vision of how to do law, and it opens the possibility of having this much larger conversation.

nine

THE SPIRITUAL TRANSFORMATION
OF EDUCATION

Nowhere have liberals more consistently missed the mark than in the way they approach education. Over and over again, their focus is narrowly extrinsic and superficial.

Liberals correctly point out that teachers need better pay, that the teacher student ratio needs to decrease so that one teacher has enough time to work with individual students, and that school buildings themselves need to be upgraded.

All this is true, and the liberals' program should be quickly adopted.

But then, in order to show that they are "tough-minded," liberals have joined with conservatives to demand "performance" skills as demonstrated by early and frequent tests to ensure that students acquire the necessary skills to succeed in the economic marketplace. "We are showing that we really care for students and really care about the possibility of equal opportunity," they argue, "when we insist on quality schools teaching the skills that will be needed for economic success." They often strike a chord with parents who have been convinced that the system is unchangeable, and that the smart thing to do is to position your own child in such a way that she will be most successful in the competitive marketplace. If the market demands skill X, and the parents believe that the market will always remain the arbiter of their children's success, they will demand that schools teach X.

If the goal of education is to ensure your competitive advantage in the marketplace, you will educate in the way that we currently educate. The consequences: huge amounts of unhappiness, a population that has few of the skills that would make it possible for them to access the richness of a spiritual life, and a society that thinks being rational means being selfish, materialistic, and cynical.

As Emancipatory Spirituality becomes more prevalent, more and more people will begin to demand a fundamentally different kind of educational system.

If your goal is to create a human being who is loving, capable of showing deep caring for others, alive to the spiritual and ethical dimensions of being, ecologically sensitive, intellectually alive, self-determining, and creative, there are ways of restructuring education to foster this kind of person.

In describing an educational system with a true "new bottom line," I am seeking to provide a vision of what the goal of educational reform could be if it were inspired by Emancipatory Spirituality. None of this will seem particularly plausible given the current bottom line of "making it" and using education for that purpose. So the picture being presented here may seem disconnected from the immediate struggles likely to be waged in the coming years. Yet from my standpoint, it is the absence of a compelling vision that inexorably leads so much "educational reform" into narrowly technocratic tinkerings with a fundamentally misguided system.

The task of Emancipatory Spirituality is not to present minor educational reforms within the context of contemporary "realistic politics." So I present a more sweeping alternative, as I have in the case of medicine and law, in the hopes that a vision of what the world could be might help generate a new commitment to transformation. I realize that what I'm presenting here is no more likely to become reality in the next thirty years than is a legal system that eliminates the adversarial pose or a medical system that gives prominence to the spiritual dimension of healing. So if the picture I draw seems utopian, it is meant to be utopian in exactly the sense that it seems utopian today to envision a society with a new bottom line of love or caring. Yet before you dismiss the picture I'm painting, remember how utopian it seemed a mere fifty years ago to talk about full equality for women, African Americans, or other minority groups. Yesterday's utopian visions can become the realities of today or tomorrow.

Of course, there may be other objections to building an

educational system that seeks to foster loving human beings. Consider, for example, this objection: "You are talking about indoctrination of your values, and thereby undermining the two-hundred-year struggle of liberals and progressives to get religious indoctrination out of schools. What you are advocating is dangerous."

This line of argument seems persuasive only to the extent that we are unwilling to acknowledge to ourselves and understand our own experience of schooling. One reason the whole enterprise of this book may feel counterintuitive to many people is that we have been so deeply educated into a set of values that tells us that the social system we have is the inevitable outgrowth of human nature and that its values are really not values at all but the manifestations of the further development of rationality. What I've shown in this book is that the alleged ideological neutrality of contemporary social and economic institutions is actually a thin veneer covering a powerful commitment to competitive individualism, scientism, materialism, and selfishness—and that a spiritual world would seek to replace the dominant values with other values (described in chapter five).

The alleged neutrality of contemporary education is a sham that covers up the systematic indoctrination of students into the dominant religion of the contemporary world: the slavish subordination of everyone to the idols of the marketplace and its "common sense" that all people should seek to maximize their own advantage without regard to the consequences for others, that all that is real is what can be validated through sense observation, that it's only human nature for people to compete with each other and seek "individual excellence," and that schooling should aim to promote economic success, which is available to anyone who has accumulated the requisite skills and who has the requisite intelligence.

Once one recognizes that public schools today are set up to teach the dominant values in this society, it seems a bit less outrageous to suggest that there are other values around which schooling should be structured. And that is precisely what I'm about to do.

Eliminate the SAT
and other Odious Forms of Testing

Nothing eliminates a sense of connection to others more effectively than the way contemporary schooling teaches students that
their own success depends on their ability to do better than others.
And nothing reinforces this more than the current approach to testing. Limited testing for diagnostic purposes may be of some use in
some subject matters, but objective testing in schools has become
something very different—a method to provide a supposedly objective warrant for recreating a hierarchical system of rewards.

Perhaps the most destructive of all the tests is the IQ test, with its
claim to measure a socially constructed but supposedly inherent quality called intelligence. The assumption that intelligence can be measured is the result of massive societal indoctrination: people did not
think of themselves or each other as differentially intelligent in societies without tests. Many people believe the validity of IQ tests is a
reflection of the degree to which they have internalized the dominant
message that testing is meant to reinforce: you deserve to be where
you are. As Peter Gabel wrote in an editorial in TIKKUN
(October/November 1995), "We have created a society where we are
addicted to feeling dumb, inadequate, and like failures, no matter
how inaccurate and even childish the 'measures' which create and
reinforce this impression."

The whole warrant for testing lies on the empirical foundation
that all forms of emerging spirituality seek to challenge: that what is
real is what is publicly observable and repeatable under controlled
conditions. From this limited perspective, that which cannot be tested is not real, and hence is not worthy of our attention. Over and over
again, the use of testing has had a mind-corroding effect, because as
a social practice, it begins to legitimate this pernicious doctrine about
reality in mass consciousness. Anything that cannot be "measured" in
these kinds of ways is dismissed as purely subjective and as not worthy of our attention or respect.

This same kind of fallacious reasoning leads people to say that
love and caring should not be at the core of our educational system,

or that awe and wonder cannot really be taught, because there is no objective way to measure them. That this is seen as obvious is a testimony to how destructive the pervasiveness of testing has become in our society.

Consider the SATs, the primary test determining entrance to colleges. They do not measure your capacity to be creative or caring or to connect to the deepest truths in literature, philosophy, or art. What they do measure, Peter Gabel points out, is "your capacity to think like a machine—by which I mean to think without employing the faculty of human understanding (or more accurately, while suppressing the faculty of human understanding)—under highly abusive competitive and authoritarian social conditions."

Gabel goes on to capture this brilliantly:

"The abusive conditions consist of herding together in one room young people who since early childhood have been conditioned like rats to believe that love and approval depend on the quick and correct public answering of magical questions, and then subjecting them under extreme time pressure to what they are told is the one Big Test that will determine the degree of cultural validation they will get for the rest of their lives."

What Gabel means by "thinking like a machine" is this: the SAT measures meaningless thought, thought that has been purposely separated from the actual emotional situations and ethical and spiritual concerns that fill our real lives. The multiple-choice format is meant to test the ability of the student to "disconnect him or herself from any such understanding and adopt a hypothetical rather than an engaged relationship to reality."

Of course, those who do best on these kinds of tests are those who are best able to make this kind of disconnection. The tests will accurately predict who will succeed in the universities and the alienated institutions of a society that separates skills from moral or emotional wisdom.

The kinds of people who are selected to be trained to be our scientists and engineers, our doctors and our university professors, are people who have learned how to close their eyes to the ethical, spiritual, and emotional damage they are doing to the planet, to each other, and to themselves as they work within the framework of the society as currently constituted. If, by chance, some of them manage to maintain an ounce of ethical and spiritual sense, it is only by accident or by their consciously working to resist some of the most degrading aspects of the education they receive. But the empathic understanding of human longings; the connection with a sense of stewardship or responsibility for the planet, the ability to experience empathy, caring, or love for others—these are precisely what gets stamped out as attention is focused more and more on objective testing. Though this kind of detachment is an ingredient in every aspect of the educational system and the institutions into which we graduate, "the trial by fire that we all must go through in late adolescence," says Gabel, cements this pervasive cultural distortion into consciousness. It is, concludes Gabel, "brutalizing to the soul of everyone who is subjected to it because it requires that we alienate ourselves from everything that matters to us in order to be recognized by the prevailing criteria of merit as deserving, worthy, intelligent members of our community."

It becomes clear how people who have been selected by such criteria of merit could be able to both "know" that the current arrangements of the world are leading to ecological destruction and nevertheless explain to themselves that they have to be realistic and focus on the requirements of their job and self-advancement.

Challenging the world seems as pointless as challenging the SATs—"it's just how it is, so we might as well do well at it." In other circumstances people join fascist parties; in the current world they do nothing more than attend to their business and ignore the larger social context and the larger spiritual, ethical, and ecological crises facing our world.

Moreover, those who have succeeded by the criteria of the SAT and other objective tests feel that they have an "objective validation" that may offset the other messages they've internalized that tell them they do not deserve love and caring. So they frantically cling to the validity of the tests and are furious at anyone who dares challenge them. With fervor equal to that of any religious fundamentalist, many of these people dismiss those who would dare question the validity of this system as not only irrational, but evil. I remember having that feeling myself when my own high 700s came back in both math and English. So now I could show everyone that I was in the top 1 percent of students nationwide! Within months, I was attending an Ivy

League school filled with others who had similarly proven their capacities, and we all thought we were so very special. Many of us went on to take positions of power in the society, feeling perfectly justified in having much more money and power than others—after all, our scores had proven our worthiness. It was only years later that I thought more clearly about the tremendous cost to me and to others of competing so desperately for this kind of validation and of the ways it had guaranteed mutual estrangement and loneliness for us all.

I don't mean to suggest that testing can never be useful. I'd like the people who perform surgery to be tested on their capacities to do that, though I don't care much about whether they get tested on their math skills in high school or their ability to memorize formulas for bio-chem prerequisites. I'd like the person who flies my airplane to be tested on his or her capacity to do that, and that will probably involve some skills in reading and deciphering complicated computer information. I'm happy if the very few professions where measurable skills are required teach those measurable skills and test on them, but I don't want to see five year olds or twenty year olds who have no interest or intention of ever using those skills to find that their chances of getting into college or grad school are decreased because they show no interest in or capacity to perform well on "objective" standardized tests.

In a spiritually balanced society, measurable skills will play the same role that, say, the tests measuring a carpenter or an architect might play today. We certainly need good carpenters and good architects, and part of what that means involves the ability to demonstrate intersubjectively verifiable skills. I don't want everyone to have to learn how to be a good carpenter or architect, I don't want the skills that are common to the architect and the airplane pilot and the machinist to be imposed on the rest of us, who probably would get through life very well with not much more than the capacity to do algebra plus instruct a computer to consult its memory bank to answer most (not all) of the other questions that are intersubjectively verifiable.

For a further discussion of the distortions brought to us by objective testing, please consult *The Big Test*, by Nicholas Lemann and *Standardized Minds*, by Peter Sacks.

Multiple Forms of Intelligence

Another way to understand what's so wrong with the SATs, the IQ tests, and many other objective tests is to recognize that there is no one right way to understand the world. There are multiple forms of intelligence, and that insight underlies the work of people like Daniel Goleman (in his book, *Emotional Intelligence*), Michael Murphy (in his emphasis on cultivating somatic understanding), Jurgen Habermas, and many who have talked about left and right brain functions. The same insight is captured by those who talk about the aesthetic imagination and how different it is from linear forms of knowledge.

Important work by Carol Gilligan has helped us understand that gender differences may foster different visions of knowledge and intelligence. Masculine approaches emphasize "objective," distanced, and abstract ways of knowing, whereas feminine approaches may be more "subjective," relational, concrete, and focused on specific contexts. I tend to doubt whether these differences are ultimately rooted in sex differences, because much of the spiritual wisdom I've been seeking to reclaim in this book fits the feminine side of this dichotomy. But it has been developed by both men and women throughout spiritual history.

Part of our Western conception of knowledge was shaped by a Hellenistic culture that saw perfection in the form of a God who was the unmoved mover, totally self-contained, needing nothing else in the world. Knowledge was a way to see the world the way God saw the world—a way that involved universal, abstract, and disconnected knowledge.

Judaism was in open conflict with that Hellenistic worldview. Jewish theology (now articulated in strains of Christianity and Islam as well) saw God as a Being who had a fundamental need for relationship with human beings, who cared about our lives, who had emotions and did not feel totally complete as long as the world was filled with cruelty and injustice. From that very different and non-Western approach, relationship to others is central, and knowledge is shaped by how it affects our human relationships. Non-Western forms of knowledge also put a greater emphasis on the link between study and action in the world. Again, the Biblical view of knowing is directly linked to intimacy and action.

In part, what is at stake here is an expanded sense of the goals of knowledge. If real knowledge involves cultivating the ability to love and receive the love of the universe, to be attuned to the spiritual and ethical realities of life, to be deeply connected to the presence of Spirit, and to understand how the world needs to be healed and how best to do so, then this will require a greatly expanded notion of intelligence.

I don't intend to try to develop a spiritual theory of knowledge here, but only to remind you that the attack on SATs and IQ tests is the tip of a deeper iceberg that questions the significance of the kinds of knowledge that could possibly be measured in a nonrelational context. As with all things spiritual, the point is not to delegitimize the type of knowledge that could conceivably be tested (mathematical skills or the ability to remember the definitions of words), but to insist that our education system needs a profound transformation so it can ultimately reflect a better balance among the different forms of knowledge. Western rational models of knowledge can take their place alongside somatic, emotional, aesthetic, and spiritual ways of knowing (compare with Don Rothenberg's instructive essay, "Transpersonal Studies at the Millennium").

But Don't You Need Objective Criteria for Excellence?

Sometimes yes, sometimes no.

Excellence must be related to what our human goals are. If our goal is to find the person best able to construct a nuclear weapon, yes we might be able to do that without trying to ascertain his or her moral or loving capacities. But that produces a certain kind of expert: the kind that has never been asked to develop his or her moral and loving capacities. Such people are all too good at "just following orders," while the science and technology they produce is used to undermine our chance of survival on this planet. It is a human disaster to separate the moral and spiritual from the technical when we assess excellence.

When it comes to moral and spiritual excellence, there is no "objective test." We have no choice but to use our own spiritual and moral intuitions when assessing how well others are doing.

Of course, this has the potential to be abused. Who does the choosing when it comes to moral or spiritual excellence—and how can we trust that the choosers will not be bribed or corrupted or become enamored of their own power, no matter how high the moral and spiritual principles they articulate? This was precisely the kind of thing that happened in the former Soviet Union when people who articulated wonderful principles actually used those principles as fig leaves to cover their own elitism, hunger for power, and inevitable human fallibility. Won't the same thing happen if people are empowered to make subjective judgments of others?

This is an important objection, though not decisive because "objective" criteria themselves are biased toward those who are best at being out of touch with their feelings, least connected to the spiritual dimension of reality, and most agile at separating their "personal" moral judgments from their sense of what they should be doing in the public arena to achieve success and recognition. It's not that "objective" criteria are morally neutral—they just reflect a different set of moral priorities. And the people they select for positions of power can be every bit as morally obtuse as any other system of selection.

Still, it behooves us to take important steps to block against the possibilities of corruption, favoritism, and abuse. There are two ways this can be built into the system of rewards and advancement. First, if decisions are going to be made evaluating people's spiritual and ethical capacities, these judgments should be made not by a longstanding committee of professional evaluators, but rather by the relevant communities out of which people emerge. So, for example, a neighborhood high school might seek to create its own criteria for moral and spiritual excellence and then provide some rankings based on its assessments of how well different students are doing.

This, too, may have its problems—the imposition of local prejudices under the guise of moral or spiritual evaluation. To protect people against that, there need to be alternative tracks in which people could seek to have their ethical and spiritual talents evaluated. For example, students should turn to their religious, ethnic, social action, or other voluntary communities and ask that they make such evaluations. The idea here is to create a series of options so that no one community would get too much power and begin to operate with its own form of "political correctness" that can stifle rather than enhance individual creativity and eccentricity.

The principle is clear: We want to preserve the subjectivity of evaluation that comes from our teachers and peers. We want to value the kinds of moral, spiritual, and loving capacities that will never be measurable but that are just as real and sometimes even more relevant to our central goal: to create loving, caring, spiritually alive, and morally and ecologically attuned human beings. And we want to achieve this in ways that do not allow political correctness or community totalitarianism to undermine the process or make it feel as unsafe as the current "objective tests" do to most who confront them.

Education for Awe and Wonder at the Sacred

Let awe and wonder be the first goals of education. Let our teachers be judged on how successful they are at generating students who can respond to the universe, each other, and their own bodies with awe, wonder, and radical amazement at the miracles that are daily with us. I don't mean teaching students *about* awe and wonder—as a new subject matter, memorizing facts and passing objective tests. (Ludicrous as it sounds, I once had a course on Eastern religions in my undergraduate days at Columbia University in which the entire focus was precisely this kind of ridiculous memorizing of facts, none of which I could remember the week after the course concluded.) Rather, I mean we should teach students to actually embody awe and wonder in the ways that approach their own experience of the universe.

Educating for awe and wonder would require a whole new pedagogy.

It would begin with a focus on integrating "knowledge about" (in the external left-brain sense) with a deeper right-brain emotional and experiential focus.

Students in kindergarten through sixth grade should spend a significant part of their school time in natural settings. (Urban students could be bussed from their metropolitan centers to parks or country settings.) In those settings, teachers should combine free play with instruction aimed at eliciting a way to see the grandeur of the universe. Yes, that way of seeing can be taught, and if you start young enough, you can succeed. It's difficult in this society, where media cynicism conveyed to children in the cartoons they see at ages three to five may already preclude it—but remember, I'm trying to describe what could happen in a society where a powerful pro-spirituality movement supports rather than undermines our spiritual consciousness.

On the days students spent inside classroom buildings, the focus would be on art, music, storytelling, history, science, and theater. Science would be taught through experimentation with nature, and reading would be taught in noncoercive ways, free from the anxiety that so many parents and teachers transmit as they approach this arena today.

The more education is seen as "useless" (that is, not aimed at achieving some future economic success), the more successful it would actually be, because students would be able to learn for the joy of learning, not to fulfill internalized parental expectations or to ensure future marketability. But when I say it would be successful, I mean successful in creating of human beings capable of participating in a society based on love, caring, solidarity, and awe.

Grade schools should be places where students can experiment with a wide variety of different activities to see what grabs them and speaks to their souls. So, we'd have lots and lots of free time in which students might wander in and out of rooms dedicated to providing opportunities for them to delve into a wide variety of activities: art, drama, music, archaeology, history, literature, poetry, biology, chemistry, physics, astronomy, ecology, cooking, computers, mathematics, dance, movie-making, mechanical and woodworking shop, health, and much more. Let students explore without feeling that they need to master some specific skill or talent by the time they are eleven!

In the upper grades, students would be rewarded for the extent to which they could pioneer new avenues for manifesting and deepening awe and wonder. Their goal would be to learn to see the sacred in the ordinary.

The person who was most grateful and most awe-filled would be the person most likely to succeed in building a fulfilling life and most likely to have the qualities of soul desired by the institutions that eventually do the hiring and promotion at every level of the society.

I do *not* favor teaching a specific religion or a specific concept of God in our public schools—nor is that implied in teaching awe, wonder, or awareness of the sacred. There are good reasons to prevent schools from being committed to any particular religious tradition, and they do not have to do so in order to teach awe and wonder.

But it does make good sense to teach students about all the different religious and spiritual traditions—all the manifold ways people have responded to awe and wonder and the sacred throughout human history.

There is much to gain from having students who have been exposed to the wide variety of religious and spiritual traditions, both those rooted in native peoples and those that developed in class societies. First Amendment purists rightly worry about the slippery slope to indoctrination, but today we've seen the opposite extreme and the destructive consequences of students graduating from high school without ever having been exposed to the rich spiritual heritage of the human race. But teaching about religion without religious indoctrination can be tricky; it requires the kind of sensitivity and respect for spiritual differences that would be a central value of societies seeking to embody Emancipatory Spirituality.

Well, you might think, then let's teach spirituality in a kind of anthropological mode: "strange lands and peoples." But this distancing actually teaches nothing more than the capacity to distance. If you want to expose children to the range of spiritual wisdom of the human race, you have to allow for some level of experience and advocacy of different traditions. And the legitimate fear, of course, is that students will be co-opted into some spiritual trip other than the ones being introduced by parents at a stage in their lives when they are ill prepared for it.

However, nothing is as destructive to spiritual wisdom as the attempt to present spirituality in "neutral" or "objective" and distanced ways. It's like teaching music by teaching music theory to students who are never given a chance to listen to actual music. Whatever they are learning, it's not music. Similarly, you can't teach about spiritual or religious traditions without any experiential exposure.

To ensure that religious traditions are presented in the fullness of their spiritual richness, they need to be presented by people who are excited about their perspective and are good at communicating what it is that excites people who are part of that tradition. I don't expect that classroom teachers in any given school could do that with equal commitment and without communicating their own biases. So, one way the "exposure to world religions and spiritual traditions" course might work is this: students would view a set of video tapes prepared by different religious and spiritual communities on a set of specific questions, adjusted for grade level and growing sophistication, beginning in eighth grade and continuing through high school.

These tapes would present advocates of different religious and spiritual traditions and would show forms of worship, the history of the traditions, their philosophical underpinnings, and their music, dance, and silence. Starting in eleventh grade, students would be given Internet capacities (and whatever else technological breakthroughs make possible) to connect to practitioners of different traditions so they could pose their various questions, explore their own thinking, and, if they so chose, find out how they could pursue a particular spiritual practice outside of school. One option presented in this panoply of possibilities would be the voice of those who argue for a nontheistic approach to awe and wonder.

Using videotapes and the Web are very imperfect ways of introducing spiritual and religious voices, but they may be temporarily necessary as a transition to a more trusting and loving society. In the meantime, as a Jew, I don't wish to have Jewish children taught these subjects by a classroom teacher who may give a covert messages that "the real" approach to Spirit is only through Jesus, Mohammed, or Buddha. The technology approach can be monitored for fairness and balance (though it should not be neutered or made "safe" in the sense of eliminating the potential for students to find themselves attracted to other spiritual traditions than the ones in which they have been raised).

The main focus of spiritual education in schools will not be this introduction to other spiritual traditions, but the focus on generating an aliveness to the sacred in students themselves. And the key to that is to have teachers who are alive to the sacred themselves and who are allowed to use their own creativity and spontaneity to open this awareness to their students.

One element of this training: teach students how to be alone with their own thoughts and feelings. In part, this can be learned through instruction in meditation and other techniques of inner awareness. The goal is to learn how to be fully aware of one's own experience in a gentle and nonjudgmental way, and to lovingly and nonjudgmentally observe all that is happening both outside and particularly inside oneself.

Schools can begin to teach this consciousness from the earliest grades, and by the time students are in high school, they can learn fairly sophisticated techniques of meditation, compassionate awareness, and spiritual aliveness. This capacity for mindfulness is a fundamental prerequisite for increasing one's capacity to notice the wonder of the universe that appropriately elicits radical amazement and joy.

There's an important societal benefit to teaching mindfulness and the development of an inner life: the development of inner resources to resist totalitarianism in all its overt and subtle forms.

We used to be afraid of external power-driven maniacal dictators, but today we are growing equally fearful of a gentle totalitarianism that gets indoctrinated through the media, the World Wide Web, and the globalized marketplace. For this reason, it is a high priority for people to develop the capacity to maintain their own perspectives and not allow the community to undermine their own views. Helping your children develop the capacity for meditation and for attention to their own inner lives will allow them to resist the various forms of totalitarian mind control that can sometimes present themselves as democratic or even spiritual. Here we encourage a regulative principle that should follow every lesson: to thine own self be true!

Thus educated, students will have the ability to develop their own private space, fully resistant to the demands of public space. This capacity will also provide a foundation for resisting the potential abuses in implementing Emancipatory Spirituality. The spiritual approach must always insist on the limits of our own knowledge, a deep humility about the appropriateness of the means to our ends, and a willingness to recognize that even the highest spiritual goals can and often have been misused for destructive purposes. For these reasons, we must resist every attempt to allow any spiritual system to colonize every aspect of personal life and to insist that the personal and political should never be fully coextensive.

Education for Love, Caring, and Cooperation

One of the tired old saws of the educational reductionists is that schools can't substitute for a good and loving home environment. The underlying assumption is an old version of the public-private split: school is the public realm where spirit, emotion, and ethics have no place; whereas home is the private arena, where all this "nonobjective, nonverifiable" material can be addressed. To protect the sanctity of the home, schools should stay away from "private matters."

I respect the importance of a realm separate from the public sphere. As I've argued in the previous section, the cultivation of an inner life is meant to foster our capacity to have that separate realm, not to undermine it. But love, caring, and cooperation are not only matters for inner life, but also for our lives together in society, so we all have a stake in ensuring that each person in this society is encouraged to develop loving capacities. In chapters two and three, I showed how much contemporary family life, schooling, and the world of work are structured to undermine or limit our loving.

There is no reason to believe that schools that support love, caring, and cooperation will undermine the love and caring available in families and communities. On the contrary, as I've shown here and in *The Politics of Meaning*, a society that puts selfishness and materialism at the center of its values and at the center of its schooling constantly undermines the capacity of families and communities to teach love; and a society that values and teaches the importance of love will serve as an important accessory to parental attempts to foster loving children.

In a loving society, schools themselves will be embodiments of loving energy, just as in the medical and legal arenas. There is no reason to want schools to be impersonal and bureaucratic factories pouring out little beings with narrowly defined and testable skills. Far better that they should turn out beings who are bursting with love and caring for others.

A loving education requires teachers who are capable of demonstrating love and caring in their own being and in the way they interact with each other and with students.

Moreover, teachers will have transcended the mistaken notion that love is a zero sum game and that the more you give the less you have. Teachers will know and embody the opposite truth—that love is a capacity that develops and deepens the more it is used and manifested.

I've already seen a few experiments with fostering a more caring environment in some schools, and they have been powerful. At one school, students were rewarded for the degree to which they showed cooperation and caring for each other. Each day began with students being asked to give examples of behavior they had seen the previous day in which some fellow student had been generous or caring toward someone else. Each week the school had a schoolwide assembly (approximately eight hundred students), and the actions of generosity or caring of at least five students were publicly described in a sensitive (not overly bombastic) and supportive way, and those students were rewarded with a book or video. At the end of each semester, two students at each grade level were selected for their acts of kindness and generosity, and their families were given a free weekend vacation at a vacation resort.

Though the model of rewards and material incentives may ultimately be transcended as Emancipatory Spirituality becomes more widespread throughout the society, rewarding cooperation and caring behavior in the classroom had a remarkable impact. I spoke to students aged twelve to sixteen who were deeply motivated in their school work, successful at their studies, and highly motivated to care for other students. They saw their success in "we" terms: "we are learning" and "we can figure out how to make sense of our world together."

One of the features of this kind of learning is that students are encouraged to work in small groups at every level, including work together on papers, tests, and end-of-term projects. I witnessed this at some schools in Israel and saw how well it fostered a sense of community. I had originally worried that this kind of community learning might eliminate students' ability to think as individuals, but, to the contrary, I found that it made it easier for them to express their individuality because they felt more supported and less scared of embarrassment at revealing themselves to be inadequate. These students went on to become capable scientists, electronic specialists, doctors, college professors, teachers, social workers, etc. The group experience they had in school did not make them incapable of functioning on their own. It did not reduce their individual creativity but actually fostered creativity, and did not produce a passivity that is often feared if people are not taught to compete.

One feature of a cooperative learning environment is that students are encouraged to be mentors to younger students. At the beginning of the school year, students aged twelve to fifteen are paired with students aged eight to eleven and assigned to work with them and assist them in learning. The mentors feel enormous pride in helping the younger students succeed in "getting" the skills they are taught. One of their central tasks is to help those students feel good about themselves and their capacities. To do that, the older students have a supervision seminar with a teacher who helps them think about what younger students need to feel good about themselves and how to foster that.

Growing up in this system, students end up feeling enormous excitement about the possibility of becoming a mentor and deep gratitude at the opportunity to help someone else.

The joy of giving to others can become a central aspect of the experience of school, something quite absent from schools that focus on developing lone individuals who see everyone else as potential competitors for scarce rewards.

Schools that educate for caring and cooperation will teach a very different perspective on what it is to be a human being.

In many schools today the history of the human race is framed as a struggle for survival, and the main events taught are wars and the successions to power of kings, queens, presidents, and political parties. History and literature classes focus too often on self-aggrandizing individuals, ruling elites, and the cultures they have formed. But what distinguishes human beings from other animals is not our cruelty but our capacity to be creative, caring, innovative, and conscious of our ability to heal and transform.

In a world increasingly alive to Spirit, students will learn about the great movements of cooperation throughout our evolution as humans. The powerful accomplishment of developing language, the incredible achievement of mastering fire, the wonder of developing agriculture and cooking, and the emergence of science and technology—all of these will be taught with a sense of wonder at the amazing things people can do when they cooperate and when they share information, learning, and experimentation. The levels of cooperation necessary to protect human infants, and the wide variety of ways people have found to raise children, will be part of the exciting story of the history of cooperation that has been central to the survival of our species.

Of course, history cannot be told in a Pollyannaish way—it must also describe the distortions, the cruelty, and the ways that humanity has sometimes gone astray. Truth is, the course of human history has been rocky and filled with unnecessary pain and cruelty. Suffering is real and should not be hidden. The shadow side of human history must be fully acknowledged. In a society that tilts toward spirituality, it's very important to teach the history of the ways that religious and spiritual traditions have functioned as bulwarks of oppression and cruelty.

It is one thing to acknowledge the shadow; quite another thing to be taught that the shadow is ontological, built into the structure of necessity, an unchanging and necessary feature of what it is to be human, and hence a good reason to develop personalities and styles of behavior aimed at protecting oneself from everyone around. That kind of negative expectation is usually self-fulfilling and should not be part of the educational systems of the future.

It will take several generations to get to the place where schools are fully successful at educating for caring, cooperation, and love. One major obstacle is that many students come from homes in which they are not given enough love and recognition. Students who have been deprived of adequate recognition and support come to school in various stages of woundedness, and in the contemporary world teachers are given neither the tools nor the time to address the wounds.

As Emancipatory Spirituality becomes an increasingly powerful force in our society, more and more schools will begin to take a central transitional task seriously: helping to heal the psychic wounds of children and teens. Until these wounds are healed, educators face an almost impossible burden.

Yet today we are far from even acknowledging that this healing is a societal necessity. So, the first thing that needs to happen is the acknowledgment that differences in capacities to learn are usually differences in levels of fear and emotional pain. This kind of pain creates huge "attention deficits" whose cure is less likely to be found in drugs than in changes in the way we parent and the way we educate. Today students are burdened by fears of physical deprivation (not enough food, clothing, and shelter), fears of emotional deprivation (not enough recognition for being someone who deserves love and attention), and fears of spiritual repression (not enough support to see the world as magical and alive, filled with miraculous beauty). However, if educational systems can work in tandem with parents to overcome these fears and create space for students to pursue their interests in wonder and joy, those students are likely to be far more successful at learning.

Differences in innate capacities may exist. I'd be willing to accept that hypothesis if, after a thousand years of living in a loving, caring, and spiritually alive society, there continued to be marked differences in people's capacity to learn subjects they really wished to learn. But in our own society, there's ample evidence that much of what we see as an innate range of intelligences and capacities may actually reflect a range of levels of pain and coping strategies for that pain. Many students who have trouble learning are not "less intelligent" but are less capable of handling the pain they've experienced as a result of the twin traumas of having their spiritual awareness denied or debunked and having their need for recognition systematically thwarted. On the other hand, while some students who do well in school today are healthier psychologically, most are not, but only are better at coping and denying or repressing their most fundamental needs—a capacity for which we are well rewarded in schools and professional training but which will eventually explode in the form of spiritual pain, social alienation, or psychological depression.

So, in the transition to a society congruent with Emancipatory

Spirituality, we must seek to create caring schools that see their first priority as developing an environment in which students are supported to recover from psychic and spiritual wounds. This can be done in a vulgar way (some of the educational reform attempts of the 1960s and 1970s had a kind of "laissez faire," or "students always know what's in their best interest," ideology that undermined their otherwise strong commitment to creating social healing, and schools have consistently responded to struggling students by "dumbing down" material, making it even less interesting, never questioning the way the material is taught) or in a sophisticated way (for example, rewarding a commitment to learning, because in a society that values caring and cooperation, one person's knowledge benefits everybody). That's why, even though I favor students having a wide variety of options to experiment with all kinds of interests, I also favor providing them with competent teachers who can, in fact, show them the difference between a well-made poem and a sloppy one, or between historical or literary thinking that is rigorous and thinking that is shallow. To be loving is not to be sloppy, and avoiding objective tests doesn't mean that there are no standards.

In the transition period to a more spiritually oriented world, schools will provide a variety of ways for students to learn about how they may have been taught misinformation (for example, that they are not smart, that they do not deserve to be loved, that if they see things in different ways than others do they are not being mature, and that if they don't like the way things are in the adult world they are not being adult).

At every grade level there will be time, energy, and classes devoted to teaching students how to understand the tensions their own parents may be facing in the larger world, the stresses that sometimes evince irrational or even hurtful behavior, the ways students learn to internalize negative feelings and act them out on each other, and the ways they can recognize when they feel bad about themselves and about others and how to overcome some of the hurt involved.

As a peripheral addition to a curriculum, this kind of focus would almost certainly have little impact. That's why it must be introduced in contexts where school systems recognize it as an urgent need, and as a basic prerequisite for making schools successful. In the current world, where people have good reason to be suspicious of schools and schooling, they would likely resist such efforts and feel that the school was meddling in their private lives. But as a movement for social healing begins to win more public support, more and more parents will be open to the idea that a public school system could be their ally, not a hurdle on the path to getting their children a good start in the competitive market.

In the current climate in which the materialism and selfishness of the marketplace has infiltrated and shaped the agenda of schools, attempts to introduce this focus will face ridicule and derision at first. But as the struggle for an Emancipatory Spirituality heats up, more and more parents will feel empowered to demand changes in the way we educate our children. More and more parents will begin to feel critical of the school system not because of its failure to help their children get high scores on objective tests, but rather because the schools have failed to support their own efforts to raise children who are loving, caring, and morally, spiritually, and ecologically sensitive and alive. As parents begin to demand a new bottom line from their local school systems, the impact of these struggles will strengthen the resolve of people in law, medicine, and other spheres to struggle for a new bottom line.

Won't parents object to a decrease in their authority if schools start to break down the barrier between public and private in this way?

Some will.

Some will feel immensely threatened and fearful that their personal distortions might be revealed by their children, and they will fight tooth and nail to keep these kinds of discussions from taking place in schools. They will be panicked at the thought that their own failures will be exposed and that they will be publicly shamed. In response, they will scream about the dangers of schools becoming instruments of totalitarian control, they will imagine that the last vestiges of freedom are about to be eliminated, and they will argue that teachers should stay out of anything connected to love, caring, and cooperation and should focus exclusively on "the basics" of reading, writing, and computer skills.

Incidentally, the same kinds of arguments were used just a few decades ago to argue that teachers should not bring feminist consciousness into public schools. The notion that the teaching of history or literature should be changed to include the experience of women was seen as subversive and revolutionary, and it was argued that those who sought to "impose" their feminist agenda on schools would actually subvert the entire educational system. These changes certainly were a bit of a shock to many teachers, and many schools have not yet integrated this new understanding into their curricula or the way subject matter is taught. But today thousands of schools have succeeded in reshaping the way people teach so as to include more understanding of the experience of women and more validation of the potential for equality in social and economic institutions. The same kind of change will take place as spiritual values enter the public arena—and there will be similar struggles, similar fears, and eventually a similar triumph of the spiritual orientation.

One reason the spiritual orientation will eventually triumph is that parents will eventually feel grateful that their children feel better about themselves as they learn categories to explain their world, categories that empower them to succeed as learners. In the transition period, where parents are still tied to oppressive forms of work, the potential support they can get from schools, particularly in fostering the psychic health of children, will ultimately be acknowledged and welcomed (after a few decades in which it is likely to be resisted and denounced.)

As the movement for Emancipatory Spirituality becomes more present in public discourse, more and more parents will realize that their children need the kind of caring that can only be gotten in an atmosphere in which competition and the values of the cutthroat marketplace are not at the center of the educational venture. Witnessing the societal dysfunction and the tremendous unhappiness that pervades our schools today, more and more parents will begin to opt for a spiritually oriented school system.

I imagine that this will be hotly contested for the next fifty years at least, but as Spirit becomes a more central force in other arenas, parents who support spiritually oriented education will become more and more successful.

As Emancipatory Spirituality becomes a shared goal of tens of millions of people, the separation between teachers and parents will decrease, and they can build real alliance based on shared values and can work together in the best interest of the children. Instead of fearing that teachers will steal parental prerogatives, parents and teachers will share information, strategize together, and do their best to show children that they are cared for, respected, recognized, and valued as embodiments of Spirit.

Education for Tolerance and Diversity

There is no one right way.

No one has the only way to God, to love, or to spiritual truth.

But one thing is certainly wrong: to demean others and to not recognize them as intrinsically valuable and worthy of respect and caring. It is wrong to prevent others from realizing their fullest potential, as long as they realize that potential in ways that are not hurtful to others.

This is the opposite of moral relativism. Moral relativism teaches that every path is equally good. We need to teach that the path of demeaning others, not recognizing their value, not treating them with respect and caring—all of these are wrong. We have a positive moral obligation to help others.

But there is no necessary right way to implement this objective value. There are many ways, many paths.

Riane Eisler talks about one path—what she calls Partnership Education to distinguish it from the "dominator model," which has been so deeply embedded in previous forms of education. Boys and girls will be taught to see each other as equally valuable and to overcome the long history of education that devalued the contributions and wisdom of women and that dismissed caring and caretaking work as "merely women's work." Students will learn that caretaking work "is the highest calling for both women and men, that nonviolence and caretaking do not make boys 'sissies,' and that when girls are assertive leaders, they are not being 'unfeminine' but are expressing part of their human potential."

One element in partnership education is respect for difference, starting with respect for the differences between the female and male halves of humanity. "They will have mental maps that do not lead to the scapegoating and persecution of those who are not quite like them. They will learn to regulate their own impulses, not out of fear of punishment and pain, but in anticipation of the pleasure of responsible and truly satisfying lives and relationships" (Eisler, TIKKUN, January/February 2000).

That's why it's important to teach the experimental method in school—the possibility of trying different approaches, learning how to assess outcomes, and then deciding, based on the evidence, how to proceed. At each stage in this process, one's own intuitive capacities are brought to bear, not only in framing the experiment but also in assessing the outcomes.

To figure out what kind of supports you need to build a bridge, you look for one kind of evidence. To figure out how to be most caring toward people who have suffered childhood emotional wounds, you look for a very different kind of evidence. Assessing evidence in the second case may often depend on empathic intuition. The Greek philosopher Aristotle pointed out that the kind of evidence you seek is always shaped by the kind of issues you confront.

The importance of an experimental method is that it suggests that our conclusions about the best way to maximize love, caring, and ethical, spiritual, and ecological sensitivities are almost always tentative, subject to refinement and reformulation.

In such a world, there will be a wide variety of options for how to live and how to teach. We will recognize alternative ethical and spiritual traditions and alternative visions of how best to achieve shared goals and we will make space for diversity of goals as well.

Not everyone sees the good life in the same way, nor should they. So, we want to build an ethos of mutual respect and tolerance.

Sharon Welch teaches about this two-sided spiritual approach: an absolute commitment to our highest ideals and infinite suspicion of our own motives—because we don't have all the answers, and we need to be circumspect. Henry Giroux calls this task developing a provisional ethic. In the language of the spiritual tradition, we must have a deep sense of humility rather than the kind of self-righteousness that has all too frequently dominated the practice of religious and political movements.

In this context, we seek not a single path but a multicultural plurality of paths and a societal respect for difference. As I argue for my particular perspective, I'm committed to building a society and a school system in which a wide diversity of traditions are taught. But diversity doesn't mean tolerance for everything, and so I'll side with an active intolerance for intolerance.

It is central to my spiritual vision that every human being is a reflection of the God energy of the universe (in Biblical terms: created in the image of God). If so, then every person's story is worth hearing. So history, literature, and many other fields of intellectual inquiry must be reshaped to reinclude the experience of those who have been previously marginalized or ignored: women, ethnic and religious minorities, gays and lesbians, and others whose perspective has not been fully heard in public discourse.

Ecologists are teaching us to expand that consciousness to include the story and needs of other species and of the entire planet. Our schools must become places in which the voices of all are heard and treated with respect. But to treat with respect does not mean to listen uncritically or without one's own perspective. Genuine respect involves an encounter between an I and a Thou. To have such an encounter, one's own "I" must be developed and fostered. Turning ourselves into mush out of fear that we might be imposing our own views should we hold them too strongly actually undermines the possibility of genuine dialogue and real respect.

If we take this qualification into account, classrooms can become meeting points, bringing people with different histories and cultural backgrounds together. In fact, we should seek to use new technologies to allow people from all different cultures to interact. Imagine, for example, if for a few hours each week students participated in a global classroom in which they met twenty students from every part of the world, and through simultaneous translations, were able to learn from each other.

The key, of course, is that the communication be real—not passive acceptance of some "lesson" to be taught by a teacher, but rather active engagement in which the goal was to allow people to speak and tell their real stories to each other. Accompanying this kind of direct encounter could be a more structured lesson in which students learned about others' culture, history, and literature.

Multiculturalism must not be taught as a branch of postmodernist relativism. Emancipatory Spirituality insists on multicultural education precisely because we hold the objective, universally applicable "master narrative" that all human beings are precious and sacred, deserving of respect and love, entitled to the fullest opportunities to develop their intellectual and creative capacities, and entitled to be supported in freely choosing and shaping their own life paths.

There's nothing relative, however, about our underlying ethical stance—that every human being deserves love and compassion, and that a good society is one that promotes not just the "opportunity" for people to be loving, joyous, intellectually alive and creative beings, but also the actuality of that (in short, we are not talking about the opportunity to compete for self-actualization, but rather about creating a world in which everyone does, in fact, get to self-actualize—provided that this self-actualization does not come at the expense of others).

Learning about the diversity of experience and insight from all the world's peoples may provide a foundation for another central value of Emancipatory Spirituality: a humility about the limits of our knowledge and understanding, and an openness to learn from others. The more we learn from others, the greater chance we have of strengthening our sense of mutual connection and interdependency, shared interests, and shared moral vision.

One danger is that the forces behind the globalization of capital will advocate for a form of multicultural education whose hidden goal is to subvert differences and to convince people across cultural boundaries that they can overcome the negativity, rivalries, and hatreds of the past through the universal religion of consumption, materialism, and cynicism. Emancipatory Spirituality, on the other hand, will oppose the homogenizing aspects of the new global melting pot and will instead champion the importance of preserving difference and multiplicity of cultural heritages—within the context of a shared respect for every person on the planet and a commitment to the notion that everyone has a part of the truth and is partly a manifestation of God's presence.

Education for Citizenship

Building a democratic society is one of the elements in the central spiritual belief that every human being is a partial embodiment of Spirit. One of the keys to building democratic participation is to learn to see other human beings as fundamentally deserving of love, caring, and respect.

An equally important tool is to provide students with the capacity to think for themselves, to evaluate the ideas of others, and to view the world with a critical perspective that enables them to recognize that the world can be transformed and that they can be agents of that transformation.

Through the works of Paulo Friere, Maxine Green, Herb Kohl, Ira Shor, Henry Giroux, and Svi Shapiro, a powerful movement for critical pedagogy has taught us that students today are trained to learn specific ideas, but they are not taught how to participate in a democratic society. A democratic society requires the ability to look at any given reality critically, and to imagine alternatives to that reality.

Developing this kind of critical consciousness becomes increasingly difficult as young minds are shaped by television and the Internet, where the dominant message is: you can make changes in your life, but beyond that, "reality" must stay the same; don't expect to change it.

Contemporary education all too often puts the mind to sleep. Spiritual education wakes it up and teaches us to recognize that every aspect of reality can be fundamentally healed and transformed, and that each of us is the agent of that transformation. Spiritual education is about learning how to look at all that exists, including all that we are being taught, with a lovingly critical attitude. Or, to put it in the words of Maxine Green, it is about making the familiar strange and the strange familiar—a kind of shaking up of our ordinary attitudes and assumptions so the things we take most for granted can be questioned.

The danger in the rest of my prescriptions for education is that they may be taken as a new "content" that can be used to deaden the mind just as well as the old content—because every content and every set of values can be transformed from something spiritually alive into a new ideology, a new dogma, a new religion.

So much of contemporary education is based on a kind of banking method: you get a certain course material and you put it in the mind bank; when you have enough of these courses in the bank, you are supposedly educated and ready to graduate and teach others. This produces people who know a lot but who can't think critically. They can operate complex technology, do careful scientific research, or analyze a novel, a poem, or a painting. They can teach someone how to read; they can even be psychotherapists, lawyers, or doctors, but they are unable to ask themselves what kind of a world they want to live in or how their activity contributes to building that kind of world. They are unable to understand how their own activity contributes to the creation of the status quo, much less how that status quo might be shifted.

So pedagogy itself must change. It must be directed at engaging the student in asking critical questions and learning to see the possibilities in every given actuality. Even the deepest spiritual truths are of little value if taught as a new catechism. Unless students are awakened to do their own thinking and exploring, much of the rest of what we teach is going to be useless, no matter how wonderful its content.

It's not enough to see through the phoniness or moral vacuity of what is—we must also learn how to act in the world to change it. For that reason, students must be given opportunities to become involved in social change activities as part of their education. Reflecting on that activity, learning to think about the strengths and weaknesses of their own actions, can be an important element in preparing students for participation in democratic transformation.

Emancipatory Spirituality adds another element into the mix: we want students to be lovingly critical—to bring a spirit of compassion and love to the act of criticism and the practice of social transformation. We need not approach contemporary reality drenched in anger and upset, but rather with a deep knowledge that what has happened so far in history and in the organization of our society can provide us with a springboard for a deep healing and transformation of all that is.

When students learn to look at reality as filled with opportunities for change, they avoid the frustration that often accompanies pedagogy that is laden with critique and not balanced with celebration. Sure, there is much to generate anger—the injustice and suffering of millions, the irresponsible destruction of the life support system of the planet, the willful obliviousness of advanced industrial societies about the hurtful consequences of our narcissism and self-indulgence. But we also have much to celebrate in being alive, being conscious, and watching the world develop the tools that will make a much higher level of spiritual evolution and social solidarity possible. Teaching students to see both the importance and necessity of social transformation, giving them the tools to think critically and act powerfully, while nurturing their ability to celebrate the universe and acknowledge all that is good in what we have already accomplished as a human race, provides the kind of balancing a spiritually sensitive education must achieve.

But Isn't There Some Knowledge We Should Be Transmitting?

One of the great joys of life is to learn some of the accumulated knowledge of the human race. It's one of the most fun things that can happen in life, so it would be wrong to withhold that knowledge or not put serious attention and creativity into finding ways to share it with the next generation.

If schooling has tipped too far away from wisdom and knowledge of the heart toward knowledge of facts we don't want to rectify that by tipping so far toward knowledge of the heart that no one ever learns how the body works, how our ecological systems operate, or how to operate a computer.

Spirituality is about balance. We want to avoid the tendency to rectify a previous historical wrong with an innovative new lack of balance in an opposite direction.

So, while we make it possible for our children to be as loving and spiritually alive as they possibly can, we want to teach them all that we've discovered about history, literature, philosophy, anthropology, science, ethics, religion, and technology. But we want to teach these things in a very different way than they're being taught today, where these subjects are presented as divorced from the awe and wonder at the heart of their enterprises, and from spiritual and ethical wisdom. Instead, we want to encourage a new integration of knowledge and wisdom, matter and spirit, detached thinking and intuition, and emotional understanding of reality.

There are no limits to the creative possibilities for how to reorganize learning once the goals are clear. For example, I envision a curriculum for junior high and high school that might be organized around a few core streams in which different courses were offered each year building on the knowledge that had been accumulated the year before. I share my thinking only to stimulate your own, and with the humility of knowing that others will come up with better formulations in the future. In fact, I'd be delighted to hear your own perspective; I hope you'll get together with others to read this one and brainstorm your own vision of what the junior high and high school curriculum should be in a society committed to a new bottom line. With those caveats, here are my core streams around which courses could be built.

1. The World of Work

In this stream, students would learn about the different ways people work. At each grade level, they would spend some months actually engaged in doing a different kind of work as an apprentice or assistant (perhaps as much as half of each day) and then spend the remaining months preparing the skills for their next apprenticeship. In some cases, children would already know about the world of work from exposure in their families, but all too many children, regardless of class background, have little direct experience with what it is their parents and neighbors do with their lives all day in the world of work. I could imagine students spending several months at the end of fifth grade working in an agricultural labor situation, the end of sixth grade working in a service job (for example, with restaurant or hotel workers, janitors, hospital orderlies, sanitation workers); the end of seventh grade working in an office doing secretarial and computer work; the end of eighth grade helping to build a road, a clinic, or a school or in some other hands-on, nits-and-grits kind of physical labor; the end of ninth grade working in a factory, the end of tenth grade working in a court or law firm; the end of eleventh grade working in a hospital, and at the end of twelfth grade spending a year in public service in some community on the planet that needed assistance in developing its own strengths and capacities. Each of these students would meet weekly for a few hours with other students who had similar placements and with a field placement supervisor whose task would be to assist students to develop critical capacities to observe and assess the strengths and weaknesses of each workplace in terms of its ability to produce or help sustain loving and caring behavior and its degree of ethical, spiritual, and ecological productivity and its degree of encouraging and fostering awe and wonder at the universe.

2. The Miracle of Body

In this stream, students would focus on the miracles that go on inside their own bodies, how to care for their bodies and the bodies of others, and how to understand the operations of the human body and the bodies of animals and plants. Students would learn nutrition and diet, sports and exercise, meditation, dance, music, community singing, and techniques of deep relaxation and focusing. Then they would learn biology, chemistry, physiology, and physics and the development of consciousness—all focused on understanding the ongoing miracles of body. They would learn about sexuality, about birth and sickness, about medicine and healing, and about death and dying.

3. The Meaning of Life

In this stream, students would learn about the various ways people have sought to discover a framework of meaning for life. Students would study art and poetry, music and dance, world literature and philosophy, religions and forms of spirituality. They would be encouraged to consider their own paths for finding meaning, and to develop rituals, poetry, music, and dance that fit the lives they were shaping for themselves or as part of ongoing communities of meaning.

Students would also be exposed to the range of human suffering, projects, and strategies for ameliorating or reducing suffering, and the range of responses and attempts to give meaning to the suffering and the attempts to be with the suffering without giving it any larger meaning. They would also be exposed to the ways people have sought to find meaning through community action, mutual support, and love. Many students will have already had their own exposure to suffering in their families and communities, but the school situation will give them a different take: an opportunity to reflect on suffering and its meaning. So, too, students will explore the experiences of unity and mystical luminosity and joy that are as much dimensions of life as suffering and cruelty.

Within this stream, students would be encouraged to prepare for a rite of passage that they, together with parents and teachers as advisors, devised for themselves: a kind of "hero's quest" in which they were initiated into the realities of some aspect of adult life. Adapting from suggestions made by Joan Halifax, I suggest that such a rite of passage would involve going through a process of (a) plunging into some arena of activity, (b) allowing oneself to separate from the familiar paths and ways of coping so that one can "not know," (c) allowing oneself to experience confusion and fear and disorientation, without jumping into denial or easy resolution of conflict, and (d) healing oneself and incorporating into one's being the knowledge learned as part of this process with (e) a firm determination to liberate oneself and the world from suffering. It could be argued that many students surviving the modern urban high school already go through stages "a" through "c," but rarely get to "d" or "e."

4. Cooperation and Community

In this stream, students would learn about the history of the human race and all the ways that we have learned to cooperate with each other. Students would learn about the development of languages and cooking and agriculture, about technology and scientific discovery, about the creation of mythology and shared stories, and eventually about the emergence of history and self-reflection.

Students would study the emergence of class societies and the various forms of oppression and pain as well as the systems of legitimization for those oppressions. At the same time, they would learn to appreciate the remarkable creativity and innovation that came from those who faced oppression as well as from those whose time had been freed from work so they could use their talents to develop culture and science. Students would learn about the subordination of women and the history of patriarchy, the history of children and childhood, the history of art and culture, and the history of liberating movements as well as the myriad ways in which those who were oppressed managed to keep their dignity and expand their possibilities.

An important theme would be to teach cooperation and to help students learn how important it is to avoid violence in all of its nefarious forms and to actively embrace an attitude of nonviolence and active involvement in reducing the pain and the legacy of past cruelty and oppression.

One major focus in this stream would be the evolution of our relationship to nature. Students would work together in a project designed to rectify and repair the damage to the earth done by previous generations that had been environmentally challenged.

5. Birth and Death

In this stream, students would study the various stages in the development of life, from conception to death. Students would be exposed to the various ways that people throughout history have developed systems of meaning to explain and ritualize the stages of life and to sanctify death or to deny it. They would learn to assist in the process of pregnancy and childbirth, as well as in the process of death and dying. Instead of denying death, students would learn how to assist people in developing spiritual readiness as they learned the wide variety of spiritual practices concerning death and dying.

Traditional Fields of Study

I hope you will note that the streams above would be taught in a way that would include much of what is traditionally taught in classes on science, literature, history, and social science. However, these streams are not intended to supplant subjects like algebra and world history, but rather to offer the holistic curriculum these "basics" were originally intended to provide. So, for example, in the stream on "cooperation," students would study physics, chemistry, and other sciences as part of learning how the human race had learned to cooperate and develop knowledge that could be shared. Yet in that same stream they would study much of the literature of the world. Or they would learn biology and organic chemistry in the framework of studying the body. Still, there will be some "basics" that may not fit these streams. Those would be taught in separate courses.

Finally, in the schools of the future, many electives would be available through Internet, video, and television that were not available when the teacher had to be physically present. It's perfectly possible for a student today to learn Greek, a Chinese dialect, Portuguese, or Tamil without having anyone in the high school competent to teach them. The high school of the future would have a wide capacity to teach electives. Though it would be possible for some students to finish high school without ever having taken a course in geometry or physics, students would learn much about science, literature, philosophy, and history through the streams described above—and most would emerge with far greater competency in these areas than they do in schooling that teaches them as separate subjects rather than trying to integrate them within a framework of meaning that might excite the interests of students. Still, we would make sure through electives that students who are interested in a particular subject area would be able to use the Internet resources to pursue that area to as high a level of sophistication as he or she chose.

Are you wondering if all this would really be too advanced for junior high and high school students? My answer is: not at all, unless they were turned off to school by the repressive experiences of earlier grades, or unless they had otherwise been taught to believe that they couldn't figure out how things were in the world. Don't judge what students can learn by the students of today, who have been subjected to immensely negative conditioning throughout their entire schooling.

But don't students need some basic skills in order to learn any of the subjects discussed above? Yes, it's important that they learn how to read by the time they reach sixth grade. But those who don't will learn quickly if they have the motivation and if the school allows for the possibility that they can pick up that skill at a later grade level without being humiliated in the process. The reality is that most students can learn skills if they want to learn the subject to which the skills give them access and if they find themselves in a context where the skills are available to be learned.

Let me remind you again that the curriculum I've outlined is one particular way a school system might look, not the only way. I've presented one way to facilitate the development of human beings who are loving and caring and filled with awe and wonder, and one vision of a society that might be willing to go a bit slower in technological innovation so that it ensured a population that developed its ethical, spiritual, and ecological sensibilities. Every school district would be free to innovate and develop its own curriculum, and I imagine that many possibilities and formats would be tried. All power to the imagination.

Life-Long Learning
and the Sabbatical Year

In our current system, we give children an intensive overdose of formal education grades from kindergarten through college, and then that's it—"now you face 'the real world.'" If you don't teach a particular topic in high school, children may never learn it. In a spiritually integrated society, education could be very different. Not only would everyone be guaranteed access to a college education, but education would be life-long.

First, the division between education and "the real world" would be overcome. Students would have significant periods during each school year in which they were given the opportunity to be at work with their parents or with other adults, to experience the operations of nonschool reality, and to integrate that experience into what they are learning and teaching each other in school.

Second, schooling would become an ingredient in every level of life. As the human race dedicated less of its time to production of new goods, in part to protect the planet, in part to protect our inner selves, there would be far greater possibilities for leisure and education. One way this would work would be to give our whole society a sabbatical year once every seven years—a time in which everyone would be able to return to the drawing boards, enriched by the experience of working the previous six years, and now ready to rethink directions both on an individual and communal level.

Because we would have at least six or seven such sabbatical years in the course of the fifty or more postcollege years an ordinary citizen can expect to live, we would not need to seek to cram all knowledge into the kindergarten-to-college experience. Thus, for example, you might have responded to my suggestions for a curriculum for junior high and high school with a panic-laden, "But when will they learn X or Y or Z?" Well, the answer is, there's plenty of time.

We wouldn't rely exclusively on the sabbatical years. Once we gave up the idea that school only goes to a certain age, we could begin to fund public education on a modified "adult education" model. If some of the most gifted teachers were available in evening schools, weekend educational programs, or on-line, and if these programs were publicly funded and the teachers given significant salaries, we'd soon have a model of education that emphasized life-long learning. One might choose to learn a foreign language or advanced calculus or painting or dance or forestry or poetry writing or chemistry at any point along the way, without regard to whether or not it was going to be relevant to getting a job or "advancing one's career."

If we succeeded in engendering a love for learning in our earlier grades, people would gravitate to these adult learning opportunities.

"Learning for its own sake" would become the norm rather than a utopian fantasy. And all those who worry that we'd learn fewer facts or have fewer "basics" would be reassured as these adult opportunities began to generate massive enthusiasm in a population whose previous educational experiences had made them excited about learning.

The Wisdom to Be a Spiritual Teacher

In a spiritually oriented society, the people most highly regarded will be those whose skills are concerned with nurturing others, helping them to develop their own capacities to be loving, conscious, self-determining, wise, playful, joyous, and filled with awe and wonder. Parenting will be one such occupation, and teaching will be another. To be acknowledged as a teacher will be one of the highest honors, and people will hope that their children might be worthy of growing up to be a teacher in this society.

Whatever their specialty, teachers will first and foremost be selected and promoted to the extent that they can show themselves to be good role models for their students, people who embody a capacity to be loving and caring, people who are themselves joyous and playful, people who are filled with awe and wonder and evince an excitement and genuine desire to share this with young people and a joy and creativity in doing so. And a teacher will be someone who genuinely cares about promoting the uniqueness of each child, who notices each child's needs and interests, and who works to develop the child's strengths and to help the child overcome fears and feelings of worthlessness or helplessness, rejoicing in the child's strengths and choices.

Teaching cannot be reduced to a technique, and much of what gets taught in contemporary schools of education is more than a waste—it is counterproductive and often stifles the creativity and intuitive wisdom of the teacher in training. As Parker J. Palmer explains in his extremely important *The Courage to Teach*, what good teachers need is the capacity to fully and proudly claim their own identity and the integrity to be real about who one is and to struggle with one's weak points while lovingly affirming one's own value and beauty and the miracle that we each are.

Good teachers also need the capacity to see God in others and a true sense of the miraculous and the preciousness of the universe, life, and consciousness. A true teacher is one who can stay in touch with his or her own heart, nourish it, and get nourishment from others.

But how can a teacher become this kind of person and develop these capacities? The first place to start is with a recognition that this is a lifelong process, and that the key is not to demand that every teacher be the fullest embodiment of these ideals, but rather that teachers be on a spiritual path aimed in this direction. As a result, one of the important goals of any school system must be to support the spiritual growth of teachers and to give them a real feeling of being supported and cared for by each other.

Some examples of the form that support might take:

• It may prove useful for teachers to meet with each other each day to share their inner process and to nurture each other and provide peer counseling for problems that arise in the classroom. If teachers can't be models of cooperation and mutual caring among themselves, they are unlikely to be able to teach cooperation to their students.

• The school itself must be a learning environment for teachers. Part of each school day should be devoted to teachers learning with each other—studying a text or analyzing a movie or a piece of art, reading and discussing poetry or fiction or in some other way learning from each other.

• Teachers need to have time during each school day for meditation and for reconnecting with their own spiritual center.

A First Step

Try this: Encourage your local school district to place the teaching of empathy at the center of its educational program. Devise criteria to assess how empathic students are becoming to the needs of others. In earlier grades, the goal could be to develop empathy for fellow students. Through junior high, the focus of empathy could be directed toward the outsiders of our society, for example, the homeless, minority groups, gays, and lesbians. In ninth grade, it could switch to people in other countries around the world; in the tenth through the twelfth grades, it could focus on developing empathy for one's own parents and family.

Then, propose that state universities set aside 10 percent of their admissions for people who have excelled in empathy, just as they might for students who have excelled in math or in football.

The focus on teaching and rewarding empathy would be a powerful place to begin the discussion of a new bottom line for education, particularly if you were armed with the picture of where we could go eventually in transforming education. Get a group of parents together to discuss this picture, and consider acting together to educate other parents about the value of teaching empathy. Once you've got a group of parents who feel committed to placing empathy at the center of the education they want for their children, encourage them to develop their own picture of how that might play out in specific curricula and to publicize their vision so they can find other like-minded parents who will work together and begin the process of transforming education.

ten

SPIRITUAL PRACTICE
AND THE SOCIALLY ENGAGED SOUL

The globalization of Spirit requires that we overcome the false dichotomy between changing ourselves and changing societal structures. At times we may be inclined to say, "I need to work on my own head first, then later I'll try to change society." But this strategy can be the beginning of a slippery slope toward narcissistic self-absorption, just as the "I'll change society first and then worry about inner life" strategy can be a slippery slope to the insensitivity and spiritual obtuseness of most contemporary political movements.

Emancipatory Spirituality encourages a living synthesis of individual and social transformation.

No amount of social change can replace attention to one's inner life. The fruits of social change won't last if they're implemented by people who are out of touch with their own spiritual dimension—and the change won't ever be achieved, because most people eventually drop out of social change movements that lack nourishment for the soul. However, no amount of inner enlightenment can adequately nourish a spiritual life if one's day is drenched in soul-destroying social realities.

From the Inside Out

More and more people are coming to realize that we will not be whole until our inner and outer realities are congruent. That's why an integral spirituality and integral politics go hand in hand. Inner healing and social transformation are like horse and carriage: you can't have one without the other. So where do we start? Both places—with spiritual practice in our own lives and with attempts to transform the world of work and other aspects of our political, economic, and social institutions.

In this chapter, I'll start with some of the changes we need that begin internally and then move to larger societal change.

Meditation and Prayer

The inner change we need to make most is to recognize ourselves as part of the Unity of All Being, manifesting the goodness and love of the universe.

It sounds so simple: recognize and rejoice in the Unity of All Being, stand in awe and wonder at the glory of all that is, bring about as much consciousness, love, solidarity, creativity, sensitivity, and goodness as we possibly can.

But living this way involves much more than holding a correct opinion or subscribing to a good idea. To actually dwell in this experience, to sustain this kind of consciousness is extremely difficult. A momentary elevating thought—sure. But as an ongoing frame of our awareness—not so easy. For thousands of years, spiritually oriented people have struggled with a major stumbling block: *the ego is typically out of control*; its fear of its own obliteration is so overwhelming that it cannot calm down enough to allow this new awareness to take root.

Spiritual teachers talk about "monkey mind," the chatterbox tendency of the mind to jump constantly from one thought or feeling to another, unable to slow down and take in the essential unity of all.

Much of what we call spiritual practice is actually exercise in slowing and quieting the mind. It is only in this relaxed state of being that the mind is able to recognize itself as part of something larger.

This is where meditation enters the picture. Meditation trains the mind to be still and attend only to the present moment, rather than jumping forward into fears, or backwards into angers and regrets.

Meditation trains us to notice and accept the various states of the mind as it rushes around on its various trips. We sit quietly, gently noticing how our mind wanders, and gently returning it to focus on something specific (often on our breathing, but sometimes on a particularly evocative phrase or mantra).

The more we succeed in quieting the mind, the more receptive it becomes to the Unity of All Being. And the more deeply it can acknowledge the truth of this experience and hold onto it, the less frenetic it becomes. Eventually, we become far more capable of integrating this awareness into our daily lives.

Don't underestimate the degree to which the organization of daily life in a competitive, obsessive society like our own tends to undermine many of the benefits of meditation. Even spiritual masters often retreat to monasteries to seek a supportive environment. But for most people on the planet, life in a monastery is not really an option. The solution is to work on one's meditative practice, and to work on changing social institutions as well!

Prayer too, can help quiet and focus the mind on a deeper awareness of ultimate Unity. But too often prayer is rushed through, as though the main goal were to get certain words said and have it over with. In those cases, prayer becomes just one more instance of monkey mind, not a counter to it. Yet prayer *can* be a rich opportunity to connect with Unity. I generally do daily prayer after morning meditation, and I find that the two reinforce each other in a very powerful way.

Along with prayer and meditation, try singing and dancing. Try them by yourself, but even better, try them in groups. I often sing a blessing before and after each meal, and when possible, I invite people to join in other mealtime singing. If you have teenagers in your family, they may think it's weird, but they think everything their parents do is weird. And even they have a great time when they do it with enough of their peers. Similarly, dancing can be approached in a meditative mode or as a form of prayer. Moving one's body often helps connect with aspects of reality that words cannot access by themselves.

Prayer, meditation, singing, and dancing are extremely nourishing and health producing. But they are only rarely sufficient in themselves to sustain a spiritual consciousness through a normal day in the contemporary world. Think back to the world of work I described in chapters two and three—with Samuel, Joan, and the others—and recognize that spiritual consciousness faces a massive wall of resistance in the world around us.

Every interaction, every bit of language, every work situation, every communication we receive from television, radio, e-mail, or the Web tends to restimulate the fragmented, anxious, lonely, and frightened consciousness that finds its expression in monkey mind.

My conclusion: a healthy person will combine inner work like meditation and prayer with outer work aimed at transforming the institutions of our society.

So, if you've gotten this far in reading this book, and you are convinced now that Spirit Matters, then this might well be the right time to begin the process of deepening your inner life. For those who wish to develop some of the appropriate skills, I suggest the following resources:

Lorin Roche's book, *Meditation Made Easy*, is a user-friendly place to start meditation practice. Then turn to Sylvia Boorstein, teacher at Spirit Rock Meditation Center in Woodacre, California. See particularly *Don't Just Do Something: Sit There: A Mindfulness Retreat* and *It's Easier Than You Think*. Another brilliant teacher is Sharon Salzberg (cofounder of the Insight Meditation Center at Barre, Massachusetts, at www.dharma.org), particularly in her 1997 book, *Lovingkindness: The Revolutionary Art of Happiness*.

Finding a way into prayer is more difficult. I suggest you start with a book by Tamar Frankiel and Judy Greenfeld, *Minding the Temple of the Soul: Balancing Body, Mind and Spirit*.

Mindfulness

The more we can clear the mind of its tendency to be everywhere but here and now, the more we are able to develop *mindfulness*, the active attention to what is.

To be mindful is to know ourselves, to feel our bodies, to be in touch with our emotions, to honor our intuitions. To be mindful is also to be present to others, to experience them in their fullness, to allow ourselves to know what we intuit from them. To be present is, most of all, to not impose our preconceptions, judgments, and cunning commentary on what is happening, but to allow ourselves to be receptive to it and to take it in.

There is no way to fully overcome seeing reality from the standpoint of who we are, individually. Even the greatest spiritual teachers were limited beings, and they understood truth through the framework of their own reality. Gandhi could see the suffering of the Indian people, and he taught people how to effectively resist British rule, but he was remarkably silent when spiritual leaders should have been teaching the world how to resist Hitler and the Holocaust.

We can reduce the distorting lens of ego so we stop seeing other sentient beings through the lens of our own needs. But we don't want to reduce that awareness *too* much, because our ego orientation provides useful information, and because our own needs are also valuable and worthy of attention.

The goal is not to annihilate the ego, but to make it an object of awareness. Part of our task is to heal it through gentle acceptance rather than to repress it through harsh self-criticism.

Part of being present to "what is" involves opening ourselves to the omnipresent possibility of possibility, to the presence of the Force of Healing and Transformation (YHVH) or, to put it in other terms, the Voice from the future drawing us toward what could be. To hear that Voice in the present, to know that the potential for transformation is in everything, is to touch a central truth of Biblical religion.

Yet that is not all there is to being mindful of what is before us. We will also be overwhelmed by the beauty and luminosity of all existence. We will be filled with radical amazement at its grandeur. We will feel unable to articulate the wonder that we see. And at the same time, we will be filled with sadness and compassion for all the pain and suffering that fills our world. We will feel joy at the life force that flows through us all.

Here are some resources for enhancing mindfulness:

Joel Levey and Michelle Levey, in *Living in Balance*, provide a very useful account of how to achieve a spiritual balance in one's mind, in one's relations, in the rest of one's life. Its subtitle, *A Dynamic Approach for Creating Harmony and Wholeness in a Chaotic World* may overpromise, since it lacks a serious sense of social transformation, but the book contains a lot of good tips for a mindfulness approach.

So, too, does Larry Rosenberg, in *Breath by Breath*, and Lama Surya Das, in *Awakening the Buddha Within*—both rooted in a non-sectarian approach to Buddhism. Also very accessible is Thich Nhat Hanh's wonderful *The Miracle of Mindfulness*.

For a powerful integration of mindfulness with the need for tikkun (healing and transformation), see Ram Dass and Mirabai Bush's *Compassion in Action: Setting Out on the Path of Service*.

Getting in Balance: Steps on the Spiritual Path

When we begin to experience the joy of being liberated from "getting and spending" and the extraordinary personal gifts that come from a regular spiritual practice, we sometimes begin to lose perspective and think that we have found the *one true answer* that will work for everybody or the one truth that obliterates all others.

Spirit Matters—but, as I've learned in my life, it is not the only thing that matters. It changes many things, but not everything.

The Buddhist teacher Chugyam Rinpoche wrote of the dangers of "spiritual materialism" when people reduce the spiritual life to yet another product to be consumed.

Balance requires a certain maturity that cannot be fixed by formula. Aristotle talked about it in terms of the need to find the mean between two extremes, but when asked how one could know the mean, he talked about finding and learning from a person who already exhibited "practical wisdom." But how to identify that person? Any formula can be misused. "It takes one to know one"—you have to develop your own life experience and wisdom to know from whom you can learn.

The reason we need accomplished spiritual therapists is that all the spiritual truths must be applied in complex situations. In my own work as a spiritual counselor, I've found that people sometimes may need to develop a particular understanding at one point in their development, and they may need a move in just the opposite direction at another point. No formula can replace practical wisdom and openness to one's own experience.

One excellent place to read about achieving this kind of balance is Elizabeth Lesser's *The New American Spirituality: A Seeker's Guide*. Lesser's book combines practical lessons with a stunningly comprehensive review of new spiritual thinking.

Letting Go of Control

One of the great illusions of the ego is that it can control everything. Fearful of its own dissolution, the ego seeks to convince itself of its own solidity and power.

We've all suffered the consequences. In our own lives, we've tried to control others, only to find that doing so has ruined our relationships. Or we've succeeded, and then found that the person became less filled with life, less like a real partner, because in succumbing to control they lost what we valued in them, the ability to be themselves. Or we've belonged to groups only to see a member or leader intent on controlling everything and everybody make the rest of us feel so uncomfortable that we eventually dropped out. Or we've allowed others to control *us*, only to find ourselves filled with anger and resentment—and we've eventually abandoned the situation.

Ironically, the best way to build a different kind of world is for each of us to learn the practice of giving up control. This is not easy. But it's a powerfully important experience: to allow things in our life and in relationships to develop without us always needing to be in the driver's seat. Even allowing ourselves to think about the world without putting ourselves and our desire to control things at the center is an important first step. The world is continually being recreated by each one of us, and we must never minimize the amount of power we have. But neither should we forget that we are just one part of a vast picture.

And we must recognize that we are on this planet with six billion other human beings. The world was not created just for you or just for me but for all of us.

Giving up control is actually giving up the arrogance of imagining that we *are* in control when, in fact, we rarely are, and giving up the futile ego drive for control over all things. Ironically, once we give up this fantasy, we are better able to take control of things that ought to be under our control (for example, the ways we pollute the environment or the ways corporations shape the economic and political life of our planet). Giving up our grandiosity is a first step toward increasing our actual power.

In the current historical moment, the spiritual task is to reverse our energies so we are willing to share control in our loving relationships and communities and take *more* control over our economy, political life, media, and the other major institutions that shape our lives.

There Is Enough—You Are Enough

The world is not running out of food, shelter, or clothing.

If we share the world's riches, and plan sensibly, there is enough for everyone.

When we see that there is enough, we can get off the endless cycle of producing and consuming more and more, while always feeling empty and unsatisfied. So what if we didn't produce a new model of car or supercomputer each year? What if we just slowed down? We'd still have enough.

We need to focus on seeing the world from the standpoint of gratitude for what is already there, and we need to learn how to share it in a loving and caring way.

One reason we have trouble slowing down is that we feel internally that we ourselves are not enough, that if only we accomplished some great feat, won some trophy, got our picture in the newspaper, had an attractive lover or partner, had a bigger house, a more powerful position at work or a more successful stock portfolio, *then* others would recognize that we are okay and then we'd start to feel okay.

The deep truth the spiritual tradition has to teach is this: *you are ALREADY enough.* You don't have to *do* anything You are created in the image of God, an embodiment of sacred energy, a miracle that is already happening, an heir of the greatest possible wealth, namely the goodness and love of the universe. There is nothing more you have to do but rejoice in who you are and all you have.

Once you realize that you are *already* enough, you can begin to feel good about being promiscuous with kindness and concern for others. Just as there is no shortage of goods, so there is no shortage of love. Love is like a muscle: the more you exercise it, the stronger it becomes. Or, as a pop song puts it, the more you give away, the more you have. This simple wisdom is so counterintuitive to marketplace consciousness that we need to remind ourselves of it every day.

Give to Give, Not to Get

Generosity to others means giving for the sake of giving without expectation of a "return on the investment," without feeling hurt or angry if we do not get back from them in equal measure.

Giving to give quickly becomes its own reward. The inner pleasure of giving can be one of life's great joys.

Model the kind of love you want to receive and you will receive that kind of love in return. Be the goodness you wish for in the world.

If you give to get, you will likely distort the quality of your giving, and the gift will feel more like a demand to those who receive it.

Even prayer can be like that: not a statement of awe and wonder and celebration, but a demand on God to deliver something.

If you are calculating and controlling, if you make a move for some personal advancement, people know it, the universe can feel it, and you end up being disappointed by their response and by yourself.

So giving to give is the key: give without hope of reward and without anticipation of gratitude. Imagine that people around you are in so much pain that they are not going to be able to really appreciate your goodness, and so distorted that no good deed will go unpunished. Nevertheless, in the midst of that world, see your task as lighting a beacon of hope by being the one person who gives goodness without expectation of real appreciation and knows that others who feel unable to be equally giving may even be somewhat resentful.

Start with this simple exercise: Every day, find some way to be giving or loving or to do some act of kindness and generosity for someone you barely know, someone who has not done something to "earn" this favor. Spontaneous acts of giving for the sake of giving are good places to start your spiritual practice.

Money and Meaning

If you are someone who has been blessed with financial well-being or wealth, you have a special opportunity to advance the process of spiritual development. You can become a living proof to others that it is possible to live a life in which the pursuit of money is not the bottom line.

But money can also be a burden and a curse.

I've worked with families that have been broken apart by the anticipation of inheritance or by the resentments that developed when one family member became wealthy and others remained under financial pressures. I've watched as parents lavished wealth on children and found their children becoming distant and rejecting the parents' best values. I've seen people born to wealth unable to trust others, fearful that everyone they met was more interested in their money than in their souls. I've seen people who earned lots of money spend much of their psychic energy worried that their success would never last and hence felt unable to act with generosity toward others. Many people who have money are so sure others will resent them for it or put demands on them that they feel they have to hide what they have.

So let's start with this: if you have money, rejoice in the opportunity it gives you. There was a time when liberal and progressive circles thought money was a contamination and that the highest goal was to live a life of poverty. Poor people never shared this philosophy.

Emancipatory Spirituality does not call upon you to be poor. It rejoices in well-being and seeks to build a world in which everyone can enjoy a life of plenty. And that does not depend on you giving up all that you have.

The first challenge in dealing with money is to give up your attachment to it, and instead see it as a momentary gift that you have received and for which you are the steward. Your task is to learn how you can use your resources to best serve God or Spirit.

There was a time when this meant: give it away to some charitable institution and let them worry about it. I know many decent people who do this still. But increasing numbers of those who have suddenly come into wealth, either because of good fortune in the marketplace or through inheritance, are becoming involved with their charitable giving, taking a more hands-on approach. As this involvement grows, these people are beginning to ask themselves a central question: do I want to do more with my money than put Band-Aids on societal problems?

For some, the answer is "no!" They are afraid that asking those kinds of questions may force them to challenge the very institutions and economic practices that gave them the money in the first place. Others are excited about the possibility that they might use their money to make a real difference, to provide ways to fundamentally change our world.

From my standpoint, the key in evaluating any potential recipient of support is this: Are they explicitly helping people with whom they have contact to recognize themselves as part of a growing spiritual movement that seeks a new bottom line for our society based on love and caring, ethical, spiritual, and ecological sensitivity, and awe and wonder? If they are explicitly developing that consciousness, please help them. I've seen so many good people and foundations squander huge amounts of well-intentioned charitable giving on projects that provided Band-Aids, because they never really were clear enough to ask: how exactly do we ever expect to create a society that might reflect the values in which we believe? Charitable giving should focus on supporting those projects that, in your opinion, seem to be providing the best answer to that question.

Of course, there are many other wonderful and important ways to be of service. Every time you enable others to act from the standpoint of their own inner goodness, or empower them to recognize that they too are manifestations of Spirit, you make an important contribution.

One important practice: talk to your children about money and about the responsibility to use it to serve the advance of Spirit in the world. Share your most idealistic feelings about how to use money, with them and involve them as early as possible in the discussion of how they might use any money you are able to give them. Talk to them about the fears and the hopes you have for using money in a spiritually healthy way.

If you're unsure how to begin the conversation, spend some time writing an ethical will. Talk about the values you hold and how you wish they could manifest in the world. Then talk about what you wish your children could do with whatever money they might inherit or earn in the marketplace—and how they might embody your values. Then, invite family members to read that will out loud and discuss it together.

You don't have to be "rich" to engage in these kinds of conversations. Many of us are struggling financially and don't share the problems of the wealthy. Yet talking about money can be an important spiritual practice for us as well. Helping family members talk out their fears and their hopes around money will make everyone feel less alone. Dr. Stephen Goldbart's Money, Meaning, and Choices Institute described in TIKKUN, March/April 1999 provides assistance in this task.

The universe has been amazingly generous to each of us. One of the traditions in Jewish life is that even a poor person who receives charity should give to others in need some of what she has been given. The opportunity to give to others is one of the great blessings of life.

Hospitality

The Biblical Abraham kept his tent open in all four directions to make sure he could greet passersby and invite them in to share his hospitality. Today, we treat our homes as fortresses against the world. The Biblical command, "Thou shalt love the stranger," seems the most foreign element of ancient spirituality. Many a spiritual practitioner will soar high in feeling connected to all but will not invite a homeless person in or take active steps to reach out to the shy and the lonely.

Jewish Biblical commentators have argued that the sin that drew down the destruction of Sodom and Gomorrah was the result of the way those cities closed their doors to the homeless. If so, contemporary America needs to reform itself quickly. We have passed legislation denying social services and other important benefits to immigrants, both legal and illegal. We have created an Immigration and Naturalization Service that harasses rather than greets the stranger.

As long as the advanced industrial societies have so much more than the rest of the world, others will want to immigrate.

But the solution to that is obvious: if we do not wish to be overrun, we have to share. If we were to devote fifty years to building up the productive capacities of third world countries and sharing and transforming the way we produce, we could have a world in which the incentive to immigrate would dramatically decline.

Similarly, local governments in the United States argue that "We can't be too generous lest we start attracting homeless people to our city from all over the country, thereby overwhelming our capacity to be generous." The answer, of course, is to have these cities coordinate with each other and for each to make a solid commitment to building adequate housing for tens of thousands of the homeless.

But, in the meantime, we face the situation by ourselves.

The place to start is right here and right now. We could work to create an international peace corps made up of people who voluntarily go to Third World countries and to our inner cities, and whose first task is to rebuild the economic infrastructure. I'd like to see every young person take two years of national service to do this kind of work before going on to college. But in the meantime, the first step is for you and me to practice hospitality in our own lives.

Hospitality means inviting the homeless to your home. But it should also include people who aren't homeless but who would benefit from more connection with others—which is almost everyone around you. Invite more people to come over for a dinner, a picnic, a pot-luck gathering.

You don't have to have a big or fancy apartment or house to invite others, it does not have to be all neat and orderly, and you don't have to "make a good impression" by having the right clothes or the right decorations or furnishings. If you don't have time to cook, ask people to bring something to share. In the Jewish religious world, where the custom of inviting people to come home for Shabbat (Sabbath) lunch is widely practiced, I've frequently found myself with a group of ten to twenty people stuffed into a tiny, tiny apartment space in which we shared very unfancy food but had a wonderful time singing together, talking about the weekly Torah reading or politics. or shared stories about our lives—and almost everyone feels nourished by such occasions.

Open your home like Abraham opened his tent. Reach out and invite people in your workplace, your church, synagogue, mosque, or ashram, your community organization, or your political movement to share a weekday evening, a weekend afternoon, a walk in the park, a swim at the beach, or some other opportunity to open your life and your abundance with others. If this sounds overwhelming, start by taking one day a month to work on this practice.

Graceful Simplicity

Ecological sustainability and spiritual wholeness both suggest that we learn to detach ourselves from our frenetic accumulation of things. While it's an illusion to believe that we can change the world without collective social action, in transforming our individual patterns of consumption we can make an important impact on our own psyches. For example, we don't really need a new car every five years, and we don't need to upgrade our computers every two years. We won't need many new clothes if we refuse to pay attention to those whose job it is to make us feel awkward if we aren't keeping up with what they define as "fashion." Many of us buy far more than we need. Next time you are invited by some advertisement to surf Web pages devoted to selling you things, "just say 'no.'"

Generosity can be shown in other ways besides buying material things. One step on the path may be to give away some of the "stuff" that fills our homes, the stuff we don't really need. Others might actually need some of what fills our closets—and if we each understood this kind of sharing as a spiritual practice, it would be less awkward to ask others to take what we don't need.

An equally important spiritual practice is to learn to give to others what they need, and often that is not just stuff.

Imagine if people in our society could stop buying so much for Christmas, Chanukah, birthdays, anniversaries, and weddings and instead asked themselves, "What does person X really need in her life and how could I help her get it?" For example, imagine if you gave someone a gift certificate that said "I will give you five hours of child care or care for your elderly parent," or "I will supply you with five hours of grocery shopping," or "I will give you X hours of assistance in painting your house, working on developing a garden for you, or doing some form of housework."

Imaginative giving is only one of the steps toward simplifying our lives together.

Jerome M. Segal's insightful book, *Graceful Simplicity: Toward a Philosophy and Politics of Simple Living*, provides a fascinating introduction to how to build such a life for ourselves.

Treasuring the Body

Our bodies are a gift and we need to learn to treasure them. This may sound strange to those of us who grew up in religious or spiritual communities that identified the body with a lower, material existence that was suspect at best and prone to sin and evil at worst. The truth is that many forms of spirituality have denigrated rather than treasured the body.

Yet there has always been a countertradition that understood bodily existence as inherently good and potentially sacred. Rather than repress our enjoyment of the body, contemporary versions of Emancipatory Spirituality unequivocally affirm bodily pleasure and consider honoring the body a high spiritual task.

As with all spiritual practice, balance is the key. Bodily pleasure cannot be pursued without regard to the consequences for others. Profligate sexuality divorced from loving relationships has been a quintessential aspect of contemporary narcissism. The contemporary obsession with looks and with a single societally sanctioned ideal of the attractive body is just as limiting.

Similarly, the focus on providing food in a way that is healthy, sustaining, aesthetically pleasing, and joyous can be turned into an obsession with the perfect gourmet experience that becomes a new enslavement.

Emancipatory Spirituality, on the other hand, seeks to affirm pleasure, sexual joy, and ecstasy, yet places them in the context of a balanced life, integrated with attention to the needs of others and our sense of Unity with All.

One place to practice this joy is in eating. You can start and finish each meal with a blessing.

Bless the universe or Spirit or God for making the planet Earth, which has so many wonderful things that can sustain us. Then, shift your focus to the hundreds of generations that developed techniques of agriculture and cooking to make this available, and bless them. Bless the people in our own generation who grew the food, harvested it, and brought it to market. Bless the person who bought it, who brought it home, who prepared it, and set it before you.

Eat slowly. Enjoy looking at the food. Taste every bite—and be aware of the tastes buds that are being stimulated. Pay attention to the decision to stop tasting and to start swallowing. Allow this to be the moment you reconnect to the Unity of All Being, as you consume that which the goodness of the universe has made available.

Let me suggest one guided visualization to try each morning. Close your eyes and form a mental picture of your body. Put your hand on each part of your body as you think about it. Start with your eyes, and say something like "Thank you, God (or thank you, universe), for having given me eyes that are still functioning, and thank you, eyes, for bringing to me the visual stimuli that make it possible for me to see." Then thank God or the universe for your smell, hearing, taste, and touch and thank each part of your body involved. Then go to your heart. Form a mental picture of your entire blood system and thank God or the universe for creating this incredibly complex system. Then thank your heart for working so hard to propel the blood, and thank your blood for carrying the oxygen and food to each cell of your body. Promise your heart you will eat more sensibly and do exercises to lighten its load. Thank your lungs for bringing in oxygen and excreting carbon dioxide. Promise your lungs you will do all you can to challenge corporate practices that are pouring waste into the environment and slowly poisoning them. Do the same for your stomach, thanking it and promising you will do more to challenge corporations that have been poisoning our foods, changing their genetic makeup in irresponsible ways, or whatever other technological nuttiness interferes with our ability to get the natural foods our earth provides. Envision your genitals and thank God or the universe for sexual pleasure and our ability to create the next generation of the human race. Envision your brain and nervous system and thank it, and God or the universe, for this most complex and marvelous part of your body. Go through each part of your body, including parts I haven't mentioned, visualize them and offer similar thanks.

Try this each day as one way to offer spiritual support for nurturing and honoring your body.

Read *Sins of the Spirit, Blessings of the Flesh*, by Matthew Fox, to get a fuller sense of the ways you may be unconsciously carrying some of the anti-body messages that Hellenistic and Christian traditions managed to introduce into the mainstream of Western culture. A more healthy affirmation of body and pleasure accompanies some variants of contemporary renewal in the Christian world.

Build Compassionate Community

It's easier to love humanity in the abstract than real live human beings in all their complexities. But only the latter brings about real spiritual connection to the Unity of All Being. I know some intellectuals who write about community but who will never be part of one— so all their fine words don't give them the real experience, joy, and inevitable frustrations of building community.

Each week put some energy into helping build and sustain a community of people that shares some of your goals.

Imagine that you have joined a community of people committed to building Emancipatory Spirituality. You'll hope to find people who are spiritually evolved. Imagine your surprise when you discover, as you almost certainly will, that many of these people have dramatic flaws and inadequacies. Some of them say things that are hurtful to you or others. Some act in obnoxious ways at meetings, obstructing the purpose of the group. Some seem less committed and serious than you believe they need to be to keep the group working.

Don't be surprised. People who have been shaped by a world that systematically denies their need for meaning and frustrates their capacities to love will necessarily be somewhat "screwed up." Chances are that applies to the rest of us as well.

The appropriate attitude is not to say, "I tried that, but the people were so disappointing" but rather to develop a sense of compassion for each other and for ourselves.

"But how can screwed-up people be vehicles for spiritual and social transformation?" Well, that's what we have, so that's what we have to work with. And that includes ourselves. We need to recognize our own limitations and to develop a sense of compassion for ourselves as well.

Building a spiritually centered community means incorporating spiritual practices at each stage and staying focused on the highest goals for which the community is being built.

Democracy and good process are not enough.

Many communes, collectives, and social change projects have failed in part because they thought that it was enough just to share a commitment to democracy. Some communities thought they were "alternative" simply because they shared the notion of collective decision making without hierarchy or patriarchy, shared a commitment to eating organic food, or even were willing to share resources and income. But that was not enough. Communities need to be about something more than themselves and their own flourishing.

I remember hearing exciting stories about the democratization of factories in Yugoslavia under communism. Certainly with workers' control, we were told, a new society would be built! Imagine our surprise when that same society became a racist bloodbath as the former Yugoslavia broke down into ethnic violence. People had not been transformed by having power in their workplaces, because the workplaces still reinforced the old ethos of looking out for number one, even though the number one was now a larger community instead of just an individual. That's why communities need to be connected to a transcendent spiritual vision and purpose of the sort that emerges from Emancipatory Spirituality.

The same is true for retirement communities. Today, retirement communities are built around the theme of serving the needs of the elderly, and the frequent outcome is isolated groups of people who find their lives boring and focused on shared medical problems. Spiritually oriented retirement homes or communities of the future can be built around a different vision of aging: one in which the emphasis is on all that our elders have to teach and to share with the rest of the society. Elders frequently have many life lessons they could teach to the young, and they often have time that could be mobilized to offer important services to those in need. Imagine retirement communities organized around the themes of service to others and celebration of all the good the universe has already brought to us in our lives. We need not romanticize aging (it's often very painful and disabling) or assume that everyone who has lived a long time understands his or her experience, but neither should we underestimate (as our society systematically does) all that could be learned and all that elders could contribute to the rest of us. Retirement communities built around these themes and aimed at empowering elders so that they can, in fact, share and contribute would provide an invaluable service to society and would be internally sustainable and spiritually nourishing. Building such communities is a sacred task that should be given high priority and could be a powerful stimulus to the emergence of Emancipatory Spirituality. In fact, the retiring generation of baby boomers has an incredible opportunity to return to its most visionary and hopeful moments and lead a societal transformation, if it is willing to build retirement communities based on hope rather than communities based on the assumption that everything else has been McDonaldized and that there is no choice but to sink into an aging dominated by white bread, one-dimensional television, isolation, and resentment that nothing ever happened. If this generation is to assume its rightful role as elders, and embrace an Emancipatory Spirituality, it can still play a transformative role.

Embodied Compassion

Put conscious energy into developing a compassionate attitude toward all of being, all animals, and all human beings, including yourself.

I know the sappy version of this that predominates in contemporary psychobabble that seems to suggest a nonjudgmental attitude so complete that you are no longer allowed to think about who is hurting you and who are your real allies. That's disempowering and not part of an Emancipatory Spirituality.

A fuller-bodied compassion is one that actually sees other human beings from the standpoint of who they are and how they came to be that way. For example, it is valuable to understand the full story of how your parents may have made their love conditional on your acting a certain way, of how these messages were reinforced by schools and the media, and of how, in that context, you maneuvered as best you could. When you fully understand that you've been doing the best you could within the circumstances you've faced, work to develop a similar understanding for everyone else around you, with as much detail as possible so your compassion is concrete and embodied.

If we really develop this kind of compassion, we can get past unconscious but pervasive beliefs that we don't deserve happiness, pleasure, joy, or connection to Spirit. Moving past these pathogenic beliefs is not easy. Spiritually sensitive psychotherapy may often play an important role in developing this kind of compassion.

So how do you know you've reached the level of embodied compassion sought by Emancipatory Spirituality, rather than the sappy compassion of New Age flakedom? Here are the markers:

1. You will feel an overwhelming desire to attend to the legacy of pain and oppression around you, not only by caring for others, but also by putting your energy into changing societal arrangements that have hurtful consequences.

2. When people around you do not live up to their own professed ideals and do not manifest the loving energy that would be better for them and better for the world, instead of being angry or depressed you'll feel compassion and a desire to help them feel safe and loved.

3. Instead of being angry at those who are weakening the spiritual, religious, or political communities in which you participate, you'll see the disappointing behavior of people in these communities as an opportunity to serve, to heal, and to repair. When you meet people in spiritual communities who

manifest racist, sexist, or homophobic ego distortions, instead of wanting to quit the community, you'll rejoice at how successful they have been to reach out beyond their previous circle to attract people who could benefit from your capacity as a loving and healing being. Instead of being impatient with them (or with yourself), you'll recognize that it may take many years of spiritual and psychological work before they (or you yourself) actually embody the ideals you hold.

4. Armed with that compassion, you will play a role in soothing the anxieties and disappointments of others in your community. When some people fight for leadership positions, play a disruptive role in meetings, demand more attention than the group can reasonably give them, or make things difficult in other ways, you will model compassionate leadership by (a) showing them compassion, while at the same time (b) not letting them dominate the dynamics or scare others away. It is this balance of firm resolve to not let the hurts of others undermine the group activity while at the same time giving real compassionate attention and caring to those hurts that the key to compassionate leadership.

For a fuller account of how this can work, see my book, *Surplus Powerlessness*. Developing compassion for parents may be the hardest step—but it is crucial. For assistance in this part of the process, try Barry Grosskopf's *Forgive Your Parents, Heal Yourself: How Understanding Your Painful Family Legacy Can Transform Your Life*, a book that tries to put psychological issues in a spiritual context. For a deeper level of compassion, I recommend you try the Hoffman process, a powerful transformative childhood-oriented nine days of healing (www.hoffmaninstitute.org).

Purity of Language

One of the most powerful ways to undermine our faith in the possibility of healing and transformation is to be part of a community that claims to be spiritually centered but is filled with people who frequently criticize each other in hurtful ways or who share negative stories about each other. Over a period of time, the most sensitive people feel uncomfortable and unsafe in such an environment, and they often quit, leaving the community to the people who are most adept at saying hurtful things.

So here is an important spiritual practice: avoid saying negative things about other people. I don't mean that you should avoid criticizing the actions of people who have disproportionate power (political leaders or the managers and owners of corporations), but even there, it's important to criticize their public actions, not their personal identities, their private lives, or their inner motives.

Don't repeat stories that have a negative or even potentially negative twist about others, unless you are 100 percent sure your reason for doing so is to help people stop a particular form of oppressive behavior. Talk about what your boss (or anyone else in your world who has disproportionate power) is doing if your goal is to bring people together to stop her or him from doing something hurtful and oppressive. But be cautious: focus on someone's power to do harm, don't go looking for personal weaknesses (for example, attacking a politician's personal or family life or critiquing the minister of your church for faults that everyone else on the planet also shares).

Don't be a passive recipient of negative stories about others. When someone feels the need to tell you such a story, interrupt and say you don't want to hear that kind of talk, or simply walk away, change the topic, or end the phone or e-mail conversation.

Of course, even the concern about purity of language can become misused by rigid people and made into a form of "political correctness" (as in, "I speak less negatively than you do").

Avoid assessments of who embodies spiritual values and who doesn't. I can easily imagine a community devolving into personal brutality as members challenge who is or isn't spiritually evolved enough, or who does or doesn't do spiritual practice in the correct way, or even who is best at avoiding brutal or negative language about others. Avoid all of these kinds of judgments, except if someone comes to you and asks for personal advice, and then focus on supporting the positive rather than denigrating the negative.

Argument as Spiritual Practice:
Generosity in the Clash of Ideas

In attempting to validate the importance of right brain capacities, including feelings and intuitions, some spiritual activists have made common cause with the popular anti-intellectualism of American society and decided that serious thinking and argument must be the polar opposite of spirituality.

There *is* a form of argument that runs counter to spiritual life: the kind of male-chauvinist posturing and clashing that's more about the enhancement of ego than about clarifying ideas. As a faculty member at various prominent universities, I watched my colleagues enter the intellectual arena with the intensity and self-involvement of great matadors. Usually their goal was more to symbolically kill or at least disgrace the opponent than to secure a deeper understanding of the world. Read the posturings in a magazine like the *New York Review of Books* or the *New Republic* and you get this same combination of inflated self-importance, breathless self-promotion, and endless infatuation with the trivial as the self-anointed great thinkers of our day engage in a never-ending celebration of their own narrow circle, and in vitriolic and angry put-downs of anyone outside it. If this is intellectual life, no wonder so many people rebel against it.

Yet argument and rational discourse need not be filled with anger nor guided by ego. Jewish and Christian theological traditions, for example, often encourage a vigorous counterposition of different positions and intense argument over these differences, while simultaneously promoting a sense of camaraderie and loving commitment between alternative positions. In the case of the contending schools of Rabbi Hillel and Rabbi Shammai, the Talmud recounts that, after years of struggle, a voice came out from heaven announcing, "Both of these are the voice of the Living God." In short, you don't have to win or lose, because the process of argument itself can be done in a way that is a testimony to God's presence.

What is the path of sacred argument? First and foremost, it is a path that recognizes and continually remembers that the other person is created in the image of God and deserves to feel respected and cared for no matter how deeply you are convinced she or he is deeply mistaken. Be generous in acknowledging what is true and compelling in the position against which you are arguing.

Some people fear that argument will lead to anger. Well, sometimes it may—but sometimes anger can also be part of a spiritual life. Insofar as it is motivated by a righteous caring for the downtrodden, anger can serve an important healing role. Anger directed against a set of oppressive social conditions can be healthy, and when balanced by feelings of compassion, can be a useful part of a spiritual life.

Balance is necessary here. Some psychological processes give so much focus to anger that they have trouble moving beyond it to compassion and love. Yet there are some who are so fearful of anger that they define it as an enemy, rather than recognize that it, too, can be integrated into a balanced spiritual life—and can, manifesting as righteous indignation, play an important role in energizing people to struggle for a more just society and for ecological sanity.

Forgiveness, Repentance, and Atonement

Try taking a bit of time each day to forgive people who have offended or hurt you. Forgiving may involve developing a sense of compassion for the other person and trying to understand him or her. But it also involves a willingness to let go of past hurts.

Forgiveness does not mean giving anyone a carte blanche to hurt you or others. In fact, it is very important to do what you can to stop the offending behavior. And in the course of doing that, it is often important to liberate righteous indignation toward those who continue to act in hurtful ways.

Still, it's important to curb our tendency to direct anger and hostility at people in our immediate lives when it would be more appropriate to direct that anger at people who have far greater power but are less accessible to our rage. I've seen community or spiritual organizations torn apart by this kind of inappropriate dumping in which people seem filled with fury over issues like what's on the agenda, who did or didn't do some particular task, who is invalidating whom, or who did or didn't correctly understand what some other person in the room said or did. Almost always this comes from people who have not gotten adequate recognition in their lives. They take it out on those closest to them rather than on those who have actually been responsible for the hurts they feel.

Getting beyond the tendency to misdirect rage requires an ability to forgive others and forgive ourselves for not being all that we wish to be. But forgiving ourselves can only be done fully once we recognize the ways we have failed to be, as Neale Donald Walsch writes, Who We Really Are. The ancient Hebrew concept of "cheyt" has been translated as sin and was used by some strands of Christianity as a guilt-laden focus on essential human defects. But it actually means something closer to "missing the mark." We are beings created in the image of God, but we have gone astray, departed from where we really want to be, and become different people.

The task of repentance is to get us back on track.

As David Wolfe-Blank's interpretive translation of the Hebrew penitential prayers puts it, "Who are we? We're light and truth, infinite wisdom, eternal goodness. Yet we've abused, we've betrayed, we've been cruel, yes, we've destroyed."

To have this spiritual sense is very different from approaching human beings from a pathology model. At our core, we are pure; the holiness of our true selves can never be completely fouled. The task is to evolve our lives toward greater connection with God or to become more fully embodiments of Spirit.

Yet in our collective and individual lives, we have gotten very far away from our pure core beings. Individually and as a society, we need a period each year for repentance and for atonement. Imagine if each September, as we reentered our lives again after the summer, our whole society dedicated itself to exploring every social institution and every part of our own personal behavior and we could all focus on the changes we wish to make.

One important note: don't forget to include your parents in the list of those to whom you need to direct forgiveness, repentance and atonement. This may be the most difficult task of all, because parents have often earned our anger for the ways that they were not there for us, betrayed us, or emotionally (and sometimes physically) abandoned us. Learning to see them as people whose own psychological and social inheritance may have crippled them, or at least made them less than who they really are, is an important component in the development of real compassion. As long as our anger overshadows our compassion for our parents, we are unlikely to be able to really recognize and forgive all the others in our lives who have disappointed, wounded or betrayed us.

Impermanence and Death

A central spiritual practice is to learn to disidentify from our own egos and accept our own mortality.

We need to look at the universe with full candor and recognize that the particular configuration of feelings, ideas, and transcendent connection to the universe that we experience as ourselves will not persist for very long in its present form.

Impermanence is a reality in all things. When King Solomon developed a ring he could wear with a message that would always be true, he inscribed on it: "This too shall pass."

Ego attachment leads us to imagine that we can do something that will make us live forever. Ernest Becker's powerful book *The Denial of Death* chronicles some of the many ways that human beings have distorted their lives on this planet to ensure a permanence that can never be achieved.

This is equally true of planet Earth and even of the universe. This too shall pass. The world came into existence and it will pass out of existence. Only Spirit or God will remain forever.

But in the meantime, we can rejoice in being alive and in participating in the development of the consciousness of the universe.

If we could each see ourselves as momentary expressions of the consciousness of the universe—very important moments on which future moments will build—we might have a better understanding of our place. We could see ourselves as part of Spirit and hence as participants in the eternity of the All. That only seems unsatisfying if we remain committed to keeping our own particular consciousness alive forever. Overcoming that particular fantasy is a core spiritual practice.

The Jewish holiday of Succot aims to develop this awareness of impermanence. Every fall, religious Jews move out of their homes and spend seven days living in flimsy booths with roofs made of tree branches separated far enough to let the elements enter. Reexperiencing the insecurity of the wilderness and letting go of the material possessions we use to give ourselves the illusion of solidity and permanence can help us understand that we are just passing through. Holy saints from many different traditions have developed methods to remember impermanence. Bernie Glasman, a Buddhist teacher, has developed a similar practice in which he encourages practitioners to live on the streets with the homeless for a week without any money or support system to protect them from the difficulties homeless people face all the time. People who do this may be motivated to help eliminate homelessness and in the meantime can experience the reality of our own vulnerability.

In developing this consciousness, reading the Biblical book of *Ecclesiastes* can be helpful.

Try Shabbat

You don't have to think of yourself as religious or a believer in God to get the benefits of the Bible's most brilliant spiritual practice. It's called Shabbos, Shabbat, or the Sabbath.

The way the Sabbath is observed in many official religious communities has often felt spiritually empty—a set of restrictions and rituals, usually focused on attending a religious service. It was only when I encountered people who were deeply engaged in spiritual Judaism that I found Shabbat to be a powerful meditative practice that took a full twenty-five hours and that grew more and more powerful the more it was practiced.

The idea is this: an entire community takes one full day (in Jewish practice, from before dark Friday night to after dark Saturday night—but Muslims celebrate on Friday and Christians on Sunday) and dedicates it to celebration. Celebrate what? The Bible says that Shabbat is "in remembrance of the liberation from Egypt" (in other words, a celebration of the possibility of moving from oppression to the fullest realization of our human capacities) and "in remembrance of

Creation" (in other words, a celebration of the grandeur of the universe).

The basic principles of this practice are the following:

• Rejoice! Dedicate this day to joy, celebration, humor and pleasure.

• Let Go of Worry! It is forbidden to worry about work, money, power, control, or anything else. Of course, we all have real and important things to worry about—but the idea is that for twenty-five hours you agree to let go of any focus on those worries.

• Gratitude! All week long we focus on what is not yet happening and what needs to be changed in the world and in our lives. Our energy goes to "getting things together" and "making things happen." On Shabbat the energy goes in a different direction: it is focused on what is *already there* in your life, and on what you *already are*. The goal is to celebrate all that—to be grateful.

Like every meditative practice, it's hard to enter into the consciousness of Shabbat. You may have spent all week concerned about your work, finances, how to get people to think and feel about you the way you wish they would, about how to get your house to be neater or in better repair, how to get your garden to grow, how to get your shopping done, how to get your bills paid and bank account balanced. It's hard to stop thinking about these things on Shabbat. But that's what's necessary in order for this spiritual practice to work.

Jewish tradition designed a set of *"restrictions"* for Shabbat, but if you start to do this practice once a week you'll quickly come to experience them as a *liberation*. Based on the accumulated wisdom of people who have been trying this practice for the past thirty-two hundred years, this is the list of things to avoid:

• Don't use or even touch money.

• Don't work or even think about work.

• Don't cook or clean or sew or iron or do housework.

• Don't write or use the computer, e-mail, the telephone, or other electronic devices.

• Don't build a fire. Don't even turn on the light.

• Don't fix things up or tear things down. Leave the world the way it is.

• Don't organize things, straighten things up, or take care of errands. Put your "to do" list away for a day.

• Focus on pleasure. Good food, good sex, singing, dancing, walking, playing, joking or laughing, looking at the magnificence of creation, studying spiritual texts, communing with one's inner voice, or whatever else really generates pleasure—all this is on the Shabbat agenda.

For one day out of the week, don't try to change, shape, or transform the world. Respond to it with joy, celebration, awe, and wonder.

Open yourself to the miracle and mystery of the universe.

And play! Whatever feels playful and light to you—make that part of your Shabbat. One of my favorite play activities is humor. I love to share jokes and hear them from others, or read a novel written with humor and playfulness. In an earlier draft of this book I tried to share some of my favorite jokes, but I succumbed to editorial advice to cut the length and so . . . you only get the heavy side here. Part of my own work in trying to bring more of Shabbat energy into the rest of the week involves sharing that humor with others all week long. A central message of the Hasidic tradition: serve God with joy. My own neo-Hasidic amendment: serve God with humor!

In actual practice, not all of these rules work for everyone. You and your community need to find a way to observe Shabbat together. Some people find that using the telephone, listening to music, or taking photographs works to enhance their experience of spiritual joy and relaxation. Others report that the continued disconnection from all mechanical devices for twenty-five hours is a real liberation that creates a unique experience they can't get any other way. Some people find that a ride in the country on Shabbat afternoon can bring them to the spiritual space they seek. Others report that the freedom from riding in a car on Shabbat is liberating.

In our individualistic culture, many people respond to this whole idea by saying, "It's a great idea, but I think I'll fit it in when it feels right," or "I'll do the parts that feel good at the time." There's a big danger in that approach: it underestimates the way the dominant culture and its market consciousness have shaped "what feels good" at any particular moment. Working through our unconscious, the voice of the dominant order is constantly goading us for not "doing something productive." It's hard enough to take half an hour each morning for prayer and meditation. If you wait for the moment when it feels right to take a full day off, you will wait a long time. If you let "what feels right" guide your sabbath practice, you'll soon find yourself making bargains with yourself to do just "this one little errand" and make just "this one little business call." You'll tell yourself that it makes you feel more relaxed to get these tasks out of the way. But once that takes over, you will never experience the joy of a full Shabbat experience. In fact, that's one reason why it's best to make Shabbat not only a personal but a communal experience.

Ideally, there should be moments when you join others for communal celebration, moments when your focus is on family or friends, and moments when you focus on being alone and communing with nature, caring for your soul, and connecting to God or Spirit.

I recently counseled a couple in my community who had resisted the idea of Shabbat on the grounds that they wanted to take the restful energy of Shabbat and have it every day. "Why not build more balance into every day and bring a sense of the spiritual into everything we do?" they asked. I certainly agree with bringing Spirit into every aspect of life—that's what the spiritual practices recommended in this book are all about. So, I invited them to do that—and to report back to me in a year on how well they had managed to create that balance every day. Not surprisingly, half a year later they reported what many others have reported: the pressures of the world of work are so powerful that they had not been able to create that kind of balance.

I agree with the goal of bringing spirituality into every day—and that's the goal of Emancipatory Spirituality. But recognizing all the obstacles, Shabbat offers a historical compromise: a single day focused on spiritual life, the conquest of one day from the logic of the marketplace. Take that one day and you'll want more—and this will make it easier for you to bring spirituality into the rest of the week. But take that one day. Make it real.

When I told them that, they began to observe Shabbat, and half a year later they came back to tell me that, in fact, Shabbat had become the high point of every week and that they felt far more spiritually nourished than they had ever felt while they were trying to work the energy of Spirit into the rhythm of every day. They had discovered that one fully immersed-in-Spirit day was a powerful experience that gave them confidence about the possibility of extending some of the energy of Shabbat to the rest of the week. It was a "base camp," or "liberated territory," from which they could launch their struggle for greater spirituality in the rest of their lives. Far from becoming a substitute for spirituality in the rest of the week, it strengthened their ability to lead a full spiritual life in the other six days.

Try it—you might like it!

Observing the Shabbat is a classic case of getting free from the tyranny of the marketplace by taking on a spiritual practice with a set of restrictions of its own. Every spiritual practice has rules and restrictions. If you retire to an ashram for a week of meditation, don't be surprised if the rules prohibit you from answering your cell phone during meditation. Focused attention on a particular practice allows you to experience it in a way that simply can't happen when you are bouncing about, responding to the demands of the marketplace and its "do something" mentality.

To build the foundation for this practice, read *The Sabbath*, by Abraham Joshua Heschel; *Renewing Your Soul: A Guided Retreat for the Sabbath and Other Days of Rest*, by David Cooper; and *Sabbath: Restoring the Sacred Rhythm of Rest*, by Wayne Muller. For people practicing within the context of a Jewish religious practice, I've developed a short manual to make it easy to learn the steps of the practice. My wife Debora and I have created an audio tape to help you sing traditional Jewish chants and Shabbat songs (send $30 to Beyt Tikkun, 2107 Van Ness Avenue, Suite 302, San Francisco, CA 94109). But you don't have to be Jewish or sing Hebrew melodies to make the Sabbath a central spiritual practice in your life!

From Outside In

What about the rest of the week? This brings us back to the nits and grits of economic reality and our to need to create a new bottom line of love and caring lest the logic of the marketplace continue to infect our thinking and shape the way we relate to each other and to our environment.

How do we develop the external dimension of Emancipatory Spirituality?

Well, I can make some specific suggestions, but I want to share my hesitations in doing so. I've been part of many social change movements, and most have collapsed because the inner dynamics were so unsatisfying. Any of these ideas can be turned into their opposites or amount to nothing of value unless they are part of a larger spiritual movement that actually radiates love and caring, compassion and thanksgiving, generosity, awe, and wonder—and unless its practitioners are conscientiously involved in the spiritual practices I've listed in this chapter. Without that, the rest will accomplish little of permanent value.

A Movement and a Spiritual Party

We need a political movement that can bring together people who wish to build a society based on Emancipatory Spirituality. Such a movement should see itself as a place that encourages and facilitates the spiritual growth of those who participate in its activities, as well as provides support and coordination among those who are seeking to bring a new bottom line into every workplace and profession. People who are struggling for Emancipatory Spirituality need a way to share their wisdom with each other, learn about strategies that have worked or failed, and coordinate activities and resources.

What would such a movement be about? I've already presented some of its goals in chapters seven, eight, and nine. If we can create groups of people throughout society who envision changing societal practices and institutions in accord with a new bottom line, they can provide the details for a programmatic focus for many areas not addressed in this book.

The first step after creating a movement is creating a political party that would enter into the public debates by participating in elections. Watching how the electoral process continually marginalizes those without huge amounts of money, I am aware of the dangers presented by too much focus on an electoral strategy. Though we claim to live in a democracy, the "winner take all" system means that minority voices get no representation in our Congress or state legislatures unless they have a majority in one particular location. The supposedly "crusading" campaign finance reformers in Congress have only timid ideas abut restricting the power of money in elections. A spiritual movement should seek elections that are fully financed by public funding, and that are accorded free television and radio time, as well as Internet space to present the whole range of candidates and positions including minority positions. In putting this forward, a spiritual movement should remind people that the airwaves belong to all of us, and that private companies that use them should be required to make adequate time available for a full discussion of the political issues facing the community free of charge, with adequate representation of minority views.

A spiritual party should be unequivocal in its commitment to democracy and human rights. It should seek to dramtically increase the number of decisions that are put directly to the people through referenda (but only if there are powerful measures to ensure that those with money do not have a better chance of getting their views presented than the rest of us). It should be committed to economic democracy both for our own regions and for the global economy.

Here are some of the key guidelines:

—Its specific political projects must never be given greater weight than the focus on spiritual growth and healing of the people involved. The goal is not to "win" but to be an embodiment of its vision of the good.

—It must put its fullest utopian vision of a world based on love and caring at the center of its public activities, and it must never seek to win immediate victories by compromising its willingness to articulate its highest goals.

—It must be decidedly nonutopian in the way it seeks to achieve the goal of embodying of its vision of the good. It must place compassion for its own members, and then compassion for everyone else, including people who disagree with its ideas, at the center of its spiritual practice.

—It must encourage awe and wonder at the glory of the universe as part of its activities. Its meetings should include music, poetry, prayer or meditation, and thanksgiving.

—It must demonstrate loving and caring not only with high-minded ideals, but through an internal practice of care that includes: visiting the sick, feeding the hungry and sheltering the homeless, providing child care and assisting in elder care, and providing spiritual counseling and psychotherapy. But it should not allow its meetings to turn into therapy groups, and it should be firm in assuring that meetings feel good and productive and accomplish the goals set for them.

—Most of all, it would seek spiritual balance as described above. The truth is, any one of the guidelines can always be taken in an extremist direction and turn into its opposite. That's what so often happens with political movements—and that's one reason people have good reason to distance themselves from politics. There can never be a formula for exactly how to achieve the balance, only an injunction to seek spiritual balance and to make that balance a conscious element of building the movement.

Economic democracy is a second part of extending democratic decision making. As the central decisions facing us are increasingly being made on a global basis, we would want to take steps to ensure global economic democracy.

Here are some specific steps that a spiritual party could take in extending democracy:

•Global standards for all countries, including basic human rights (as embodied in the Universal Declaration of Human Rights), rights for working people to be protected from sweatshop conditions and from child labor, rights to be free from ecological pollution and degradation of the country's environment, rights for working people to organize and bargain collectively, and rights for all people to enjoy democratic participation in the political life of their country.

•Eco kashrut, a notion from the Jewish Renewal movement, says that goods that have been created in ways that are environmentally sound and ethically sensitive (for example, by workers who are treated with respect) should be labeled as such so that consumers can choose to support these practices through their patterns of consumption. We need to develop a universally recognized symbol of goods that are prepared according to these standards.

•Universal corporate codes of conduct and reporting.

•An alternative global media that would provide full information and help peoples of the world learn about each other and develop strategies for cooperation.

•An international network of support that mobilizes people all over the globe in projects to improve education, health care, nutrition, housing, child care, and elder care for everyone on the planet. In such an international effort, we might not only share technology with materially underdeveloped countries, but we might become the beneficiaries of citizens of those countries coming to the technically advanced countries to teach us new ways to embody spiritual values in our daily life activities—and helping us overcome our spiritual underdevelopment.

•Shift taxes away from taxing income and tax pollution, resource depletion, and energy use. As Lester Brown suggests in *The State of the World, 2000*, we should tax fossil fuels at a level that reflects the full costs associated with air pollution, acid rain, and climate disruption.

• Shift the focus on gross national product to a focus on the quality of life.

• Take first steps toward the creation of a legal, medical, and educational system as outlined in previous chapters.

• Encourage socially responsible investing.

• Create a fund to support alternative advertising that would expose not only untruths but forms of manipulation in corporate advertising—to educate the public about how to recognize ways advertisers seek to manipulate them.

• Create councils of elders and an ethos of learning from the wisdom of the aging.

• Provide support for ecologically sustainable forms of transportation.

• Rebuild cities with public spaces that encourage our ability to respond to the natural world with awe and wonder, that give people the ability to meet together in large and small groups, and that enable people to expand public participation in the arts, humanities, and political life of the community.

• Create a variety of models for housing that include single-family as well as cohousing, urban communes in which people share kitchens and public living space while retaining private space as well, and encourage community brainstorming about forms of housing that will make care for children and elders easier to share among many families.

Many of the above suggestions were developed by Hazel Henderson; others came from discussions in TIKKUN magazine.

Endless specific policy ideas are possible in creating a world with more ethical, spiritual, and ecological concerns.

For that reason, both the party and the movement must place the struggle for a new bottom line at the center of their activities.

The biggest problem creating a political party is that there is almost always a distorting pressure to change what you stand for in order to be practical and win. This would be less of a problem for a spiritual party that took the message of Emancipatory Spirituality seriously. Such a party will put its fullest utopian vision of a world based on love and caring at the center of its public activities. Yet at the same time, it will treat its members, and the people outside who do not share its vision or ideas, with compassion and caring. It will resist the kind of destructive dynamics that sometimes occur in progressive movements in which a ferocious "political correctness" can lead people to turn on each other and focus on the ways that they are not adequate embodiments of their movements' highest ideals. It's this balance between insisting on utopian ideals, and nevertheless treating each other with compassion, that will make this party a manifestation of Emancipatory Spirituality.

Imagine a political party that:

• encourages awe and wonder at the glory of the universe as part of its activities.

• includes music, poetry, thanksgiving, and prayer or meditation as part of its meetings.

• demonstrates love and caring through an internal practice that includes visiting the sick, feeding the hungry, providing child care and assisting in elder care, and providing spiritual counseling and psychotherapy (without turning its meetings into therapy groups, but insisting that meetings feel good and productive and accomplish the goals set for them).

• seeks spiritual balance.

I believe such a party would become powerful enough to play a major role in transforming our society within one or two generations.

The major obstacle to its creation: The pathogenic belief that no one else will be part of it, leading everyone to think it rational to vote for "lesser evil" candidates of the major parties rather than to vote for their own highest ideals. So a spiritual party will only emerge when the actual practice of Emancipatory Spirituality has become so widespread that this pathogenic belief's hold on our minds has dramatically decreased.

But such a party must always be subordinate to the larger movement of which it is an expression. And that movement can make important advances right now in the first quarter of the twenty-first century by popularizing the notion of a new bottom line, embodying an ethos of love and caring, awe and wonder, and by bringing the nation of corporate chartering into popular discourse Perhaps the most impressive thing such a movement could do would be to actually embody in its daily activity the spiritual practices I've outlined in this chapter. If it did, it would spread like wildfire, because people hunger for a context in which they can actually feel and experience the caring and spiritual-aliveness that is denied them in so many other corners of reality.

The Social Responsibility Amendment to the U.S. Constitution

A surge of interest in preventing child labor and exploitation in Third World sweatshops that serve multinational corporations has heightened awareness of yet another destructive potential in the globalization of capital. As the World Trade Organization finds ways to undermine national efforts to restrict environmental degradation and the exploitation of workers, growing numbers of people wonder if there can ever be a way to change the global system.

Tens of thousands of demonstrators amassed in Seattle in November 1999 to protest the World Trade Organization's practices and to force the world's political agenda to confront how much power we give to multinational corporations to proceed unimpeded with their form of globalization.

Globalization itself is not the enemy. Rather it is the fact that the particular form of globalization brought to us by corporations gives them so much power to move resources and production from one country to another that they are no longer accountable to any particular governing force for the consequences of their actions.

In my experience with the corporate world, I've found most people there are decent and ethically sensitive. From top corporate executives to the lowest paid employees, I encounter people who care about the environment, worry about the moral deterioration of the society, and seek spiritual nourishment in their personal lives. Many of these people would love to see Emancipatory Spirituality succeed and provide a new bottom line.

But there's one caveat: they know that the way the society is currently structured, they must focus on maximizing money for their corporations, lest they lose their own income. Even the corporate executives with the highest-level of spiritual sensitivity will tell you that they have no choice but to accept corporate profits as the absolute bottom line. Some will tell you that occasionally (particularly if they can advertise this fact and increase their public "goodwill") they will make environmentally sensitive or ethically aware decisions, but only if they can be reasonably sure those decisions will not significantly lower their capacity to generate revenue. It's important that we not demonize these people. Most would act differently if they thought they could do so without risking their livelihood for the sake of ideals that at the moment seem unrealizable.

There are some businesses (particularly those that sell products aimed at environmental cleaning) that clearly see their profits and their morality working hand in hand, but while the number of these will grow in the coming years, they still represent a small percentage of the total investment dollars at this time.

The Social Responsibility Amendment (SRA) to the U.S. Constitution is one powerful way to help the many very decent people in the corporate structure who are stuck in this dilemma.

Here is what the SRA says: Every corporation doing business in the United States (whether incorporated here or elsewhere) with an annual budget exceeding twenty-five million dollars (in year 2000 dollars) must receive a new corporate charter every twenty years. It will only qualify for a new corporate charter if it can prove a history of social responsibility as measured by an Ethical Impact Report. No branch of government shall make any treaties or enter into international agreements that limit the right of the United States to insist on corporate social responsibility and ecologically sustainable behavior. Any such treaties or agreements already concluded are hereby declared null and void.

The Ethical Impact Reports will be compiled by three different sources: (a) the corporation itself, (b) the employees of the corporation (under conditions of strict confidentiality), and (c) community organizations that can make a reasonable case that they represent people whose lives have been affected by the corporation (for example, people whose health has been affected by a corporation's products or people whose lives have been affected by the messages conveyed through the corporation's media advertising presence).

The Ethical Impact Report would ask the respondents to rate how much the corporation:

- encourages and rewards workers for using their intelligence and creativity in their work,

- rewards cooperative behavior,

- rewards workers who trust each other,

- encourages supervisors to demonstrate respect for employees,

- protects and/or enhances the natural environment, both in the United States and around the world,

- gives global environmental concerns a high priority in making corporate investment and production decisions,

- produces in ways that are environmentally sustainable,

- contributes to the environmental health of our planet,

- produces socially valuable products,

- promotes the value of truth-telling and personal integrity in its day-to-day operations and in its presentation of itself and its products to the public,

- encourages employees to take the societal, ecological, and moral consequences of corporate decisions into account,

- rewards employees whose decisions reflect significant concern for the common good even when that may conflict with corporate profits,

- provides mechanisms of accountability for corporate executives and members of the board of directors,

- reduces unnecessary stress on the job,

- provides workers a decent living and adequate opportunities to organize themselves,

• provides stable employment,

• shows loyalty to its employees,

• avoids discrimination in hiring and promotions,

• aggressively combats discrimination in the workplace,

• provides adequate attention to the family needs of its workers,

• makes information about its operations freely available to the public and to relevant community organizations,

• creates time for workers to have a short period each day (minimum twenty minutes) for emotional and spiritual renewal,

• rewards an openhearted attitude toward the world and toward others,

• encourages humility, gratitude, and a sense of awe and wonder at the glory of the universe, and

• advertises its products or services in ways that are sensitive to the emotional and spiritual well-being of the society.

This is only a tentative list. One thing I want to ask you, the reader, is this: What else ought to be part of an Ethical Impact Report for corporations?

Please bring this discussion to your fellow workers, friends, and others you know. Discuss the SRA and the Ethical Impact Report with them. Discussions about what should be part of the Ethical Impact Report may become an important part of the process by which people in our society begin to grapple with the idea of "a new bottom line" and to see that it could actually be adopted.

To implement this process, and to avoid the creation of a new governmental regulatory bureaucracy whose employees might soon be influenced by corporate seductions, I propose that each evaluation be carried out not by some government agency but by a Social Responsibility Grand Jury (the SRGJ), composed of twenty-five citizens whose task would be to read the Ethical Impact Reports and receive oral testimony from the corporation, employees, and relevant community organizations—and then assess what they had learned.

There would be thousands of such SRGJs convening hearings every year all around the country (and eventually around the world), charged with deciding whether to renew a corporation's charter or not.

Inevitably, there would be differences of perspective. Just as we put the fate for life and death in the hand of juries who are drawn from sectors of the population that have different values and different perspectives, so the fate of each corporation would be decided in a similar process.

If an SRGJ decided, after assessing the history of a corporation's social responsibility as measured by its ethical impact report, that the corporation should not be granted a charter renewal, it would then move to stage two: what to do with corporate resources. The SRGJ would listen both to corporate management, which could present a plan for how it was going to significantly alter its behavior in order to become more socially responsible, and hear testimony from other for-profit or nonprofit groups that could propose how they might run the same corporation with more socially responsible policies.

The SRGJ would then decide to either award the corporate char-ter to another group, and with it the assets of the corporation in ques-tion, or to put the corporation on probation for three years.

If it gave the corporation a three-year probation, the SRGJ would reconvene three years later to determine if the changes had, in fact, taken place, in which case it could restore the charter for the next seven-teen years (thus making up the full twenty) or it could determine that the corporation had failed to adequately implement significant changes and award the corporate charter to some other management group.

Grand jurors would be selected at random from the population, but the jury would be balanced in order to guarantee racial, religious, spiritual, gender, and economic diversity. Jurors would be paid (by a corporation's charter renewal fee, not by taxes on the citizenry, a salary equal to that which the corporation paid its middle-level man-agement). Juries would have subpoena power and could impose con-tempt citations and prison sentences on corporate leaders for up to two years if they found that the corporate leaders were withholding vital information or otherwise attempting to disrupt or distort the evaluation process (for example, by trying to restrain the testimony of workers or community groups that had negative things to say). The

SRGJ would be assisted in obtaining information on corporate behavior by a corps of Social Responsibility Agents, which would operate much like today's public defenders' office, except with funding written into the amendment and not subject to electoral shifts.

When I first conceived of SRGJs as a way to avoid creating an ongoing governmental bureaucracy, I worried that having thousands of such groups might seem overwhelming. But then I realized that we have tens of thousands of juries operating in the United States—and most of them get convened to judge crimes that have had an impact on only a very few people. We feel it perfectly reasonable to ask people to give their time to do this, because we want to ensure that these kinds of judgments are made by our peers and not just by an entrenched judicial bureaucracy. Large corporations have an impact on many people in our society, so it's certainly worth having their corporate behavior reviewed by a jury of ordinary Americans as well.

Sometimes we forget that corporations are a societal fiction. Created by state legislatures, they operate as "individuals" under the law, their "rights" protected in various ways that give them benefits we ordinary citizens don't have. So we have every good reason to want to ensure that these corporations are serving the common good—and this is one powerful way to do so.

All arrangements and treaties, like those with the World Trade Organization, would be declared null and void if they restrained the United States from implementing ecological and social responsibility demands on corporations. Fears that corporations might move out of the United States to avoid implementing the SRA are unfounded, because the SRA would apply to any corporation, no matter where it was based, that sought to do business in the United States. Few major corporations are prepared to abandon the most lucrative market in the world, and those that are would quickly be replaced by others that would gladly take their market share.

The SRA thus becomes an effective counterforce to the globalization of capital, requiring it to take a whole new set of "realities" besides the need to maximize profits seriously.

The SRA does not actually have to pass in order to have an important impact. The Equal Rights Amendment had an extraordinary impact in legitimating advances in the struggle for women's equality even though the amendment itself never passed. In the same way, the SRA might never pass and still have an immense impact in advancing one of the goals of Emancipatory Spirituality, namely institutionalizing a new bottom line.

If there is a serious campaign for the SRA or some close variant (and I expect there will be within the next fifty years), many of the most decent people in corporations will have a powerful internal argument for changes to the bottom line: "If we don't make these changes now and head off this SRA, we are likely to lose our entire ability to function. That would be so much worse for our investors that they would want us to take remedial steps right now." Of course, this argument will only work if passage of the SRA becomes plausible. Until then, a great deal of corporate money is likely to be dedicated to ridiculing the idea, portraying it as a spiritual conspiracy. But remember, the abolition of slavery was ridiculed less than two hundred years ago. Equal rights for women were ridiculed less than forty years ago. Spirituality itself is ridiculed today. But the desire to reign in corporate power is growing in our society. The SRA offers one powerful avenue to do so.

Watching the way corporate power was mobilized against extending health care to all Americans, it's not hard to imagine the distortions about this idea that would be promoted in corporate-dominated media. A spiritually centered movement would refocus the discussion on the core idea, but the struggle will be long and many decent and idealistic people will find themselves attacked or ridiculed as the campaign for SRA mobilizes support.

As I write this in the year 2000, the SRA seems very far from the practical realities of contemporary politics. But it will become a much more serious contender as more and more people begin to ask, "How are we ever going to save the environment and stop ethically and spiritually destructive corporate activities?" Or, "How can we create a new bottom line of love and caring and ethical/spiritual/ecological sensitivity when corporate executives are almost forced by the dynamics of the marketplace to make maximizing profits their singular bottom line?"

Some people imagine that the same kind of change in bottom line can be brought into existence by using market forces and consumer power. "Educate consumers about which companies are socially and environmentally responsible and then give them the power to vote with their pocketbooks, thus giving the corporations a market incentive to change their policies."

Well, they will have many years to test that strategy, because the SRA is not going to get passed in the next twenty years. Although I support their approach as an adjunct strategy, I believe that without the SRA it is unlikely to work very well for the following reasons:

Price considerations often drive people to buy the cheaper product because they can't afford to pay more. This creates the bizarre circumstance of upper-middle income people lecturing poorer people about their environmental irresponsibility, though the poorer people can't afford to buy the more environmentally or ethically sensitive products.

Some consumers will put short-term advantages over long-term well-being. For example, though information that cigarettes cause cancer is widespread, nicotine addiction is so hard to fight that tobacco companies make enough profits on sales to those who are already addicted. And clever marketing to emotionally vulnerable groups allows cigarette companies to override rational decision making and find markets for their products among people who will later regret their choices. Meanwhile, though the "leave it to the market" ideology seems to suggest that this is all just a problem for individuals who make their own choices, the consumption of cigarettes creates health problems that raise health costs for the entire society. The same is true with other such individual decisions—they often have systemic consequences (for example, the small group of people that wants to purchase ivory, a group powerful enough to threaten the elimination of the world's elephant population). In the case of cigarettes, it's the introduction of legal proceedings against the tobacco companies—not market pressures, not consumer information about health risks—that may be changing the story.

Many companies do not need the majority of the population to buy their products in order to stay in business and make huge profits. If 90 percent of the population realizes, for example, that handguns have the power to do irreversible harm, and that gun manufacturers are indirectly responsible for billions of deaths, but 10 percent of the population continues to purchase handguns, that 10 percent might be sufficient to ensure large corporate profits without any changes in corporate behavior.

Because the market operates on the principle of "one dollar, one vote" not "one person, one vote," market strategies always favor the power of the upper 20 percent of the population. Because that portion of the population has more disposable income, its judgments could easily outweigh the decisions of the majority of the population.

All of these are reasons to think that relying on our market power as consumers will not likely bring the changes we need.

Building a popular base for the SRA will require overcoming likely media hostility and derision, lack of interest from elected officials who must cater to the corporate elites in order to raise enough money to run for public office, people's fears of confronting corporate power, and the general sense of hopelessness and powerlessness that currently suffuses the population and leads many people to not even bother voting in elections.

We may also have to overcome opposition from the Left, which may argue that the SRA isn't really anticapitalist enough, because it doesn't dismantle the capitalist marketplace. Instead of recognizing that this could be an important transitional step to a new consciousness, they may oppose it for not explicitly building socialism.

In this last point they are right: Emancipatory Spirituality is not pro-socialism any more than it is pro-capitalism. Both of these systems are far too limited in their understanding of what really counts in human life. True, a spiritually centered society will need a new form of social organization in which all people democratically shape our economy and make the fundamental decisions about how to use the world's resources. But democratic decision making without spiritual vision can produce a democratically sanctioned monstrosity.

It is not that Leftists and socialists are too radical, it's that they're not radical enough. They don't really speak to the need to build a whole different kind of ethos based on love and caring on ethical, spiritual, and ecological consciousness, and on an orientation to the world that starts with awe, wonder, and radical amazement.

I've taken the trouble to lay out a detailed view of how to implement the SRA, but I *don't* mean to suggest that my details are absolutely the one right way to do this. For example, might there be a better and more morally sensitive way to evaluate the Ethical Impact Reports? Or might there be a better way to ensure that the relevant information is provided and assessed? Or might we add other elements to the Ethical Impact Report itself? Are there ways to get Congress and legislatures to pass processes like this without a constitutional amendment? (And could they do that without facing the problems of corporations threatening to move to communities where there was "a more favorable business climate"?)

I hope that others will take the concept of the SRA, modify and refine it, and make it even more appropriate for twenty-first-century American politics.

One objection seems wrongheaded: to claim that these kinds of changes are already taking place or will occur soon, so there's no point in advancing the SRA at this time. I'm very happy to encourage anyone who believes that global capital can be transformed internally through education and the enlightened attitude of new kinds of corporate managers who develop a deeper spiritual awareness, or that it can be changed through piecemeal legislation that supports ecological restraints, combats sweatshop conditions, and attempts to encourage responsible investment and advertising. In fact, I believe that the perceived "threat" of the SRA will make it more likely that corporations and legislators will be open to attempting these more partial steps.

I am confident that people will turn to the SRA only when it becomes clear that the internal changes in corporate life and the restrictions imposed by well-intentioned progressive legislation have failed to achieve a fundamental change in the bottom line of corporate decision making.

I personally hope that these other approaches succeed. Amending the Constitution is no easy task and the consequences are never fully predictable. In general, I am wary of social engineering, so I'd be truly delighted if the thousands of people who will be selling their services as spiritual consultants to corporations, or the many enlightened corporate executives, or the progressive reformers who seek public office, or the various movements for socially responsible investing and consuming manage to coordinate their efforts in ways that really change the bottom line of corporate life. I believe that we should be working on all those fronts at the same time as we also begin to develop a mass base of support for the SRA, so that we have already launched the campaign for this constitutional amendment in the (in my view unfortunate, but nevertheless likely) case that global capitalism manages to avoid or evade fundamental transformation. In short, multiple strategies can be tried, and they need not be in conflict, as long as those engaged in other reforms keep in mind the following question as they assess the impact of their strategies: "Are the changes we are seeing sufficient so that the net impact of global corporate power is no longer to undermine but to support the values of love and caring, ethical and ecological sensitivity, and awe and wonder?" I'll truly rejoice if we achieve this without the SRA!

Though I believe that we will need to advocate the SRA, I would not be part of a movement that advocated it but did not simultaneously focus on the full array of changes in consciousness and spiritual practice articulated in this chapter. The SRA makes sense only if it emerges from a spiritually balanced movement. Otherwise, we risk the possibility of thought police imposing the latest "politically correct" dogma on corporations and on society. One reason I've suggested the messy form of juries rather than a single governmental agency is that ordinary people are less likely to fall into the trap of imposing some distorted standards. I'm as wary of unrestricted governmental power as I am of unrestricted corporate power. So I encourage others to develop a "social responsibility" plan for government as well: one that would assess government bureaucracies with the same stringency the SRA imposes on corporations, so that government bureaucracies will be subject to the same kind of scrutiny and democratic control.

All of this testifies to the need for a balanced spiritual movement, one that avoids overzealous reformers but validates the central spiritual demand of building a world based on love and caring, ecological and spiritual sensitivity, and awe and wonder, no matter how "unrealistic" it seems given the current materialistic definition of productivity and efficiency. The SRA introduces a democratic dimension to economic life by involving ordinary citizens in assessing the social responsibility of corporations. But even democracy can get distorted as groups become impassioned by current media clichés and fads. That's why spiritual balance is the key—it's really the secret ingredient that can make democracy work. And that's why I caution against anyone seeking to compromise on the basic principles in order to "win," because there is no ultimate victory without a movement of people that actually embodies and lives the values it seeks to implement in the social world. Democracy depends on us, and hence it needs us to be balanced in the way that spiritual practice can facilitate.

The struggle generated by the SRA may be quite intense. All the more reason why those involved must be sure to incorporate a balanced spiritual practice in their lives and never lose sight of the humanity and fundamental worth of those with whom we may be engaged in debate or political struggle.

One reason the SRA is important is that it shows people that challenging the bottom line can really happen. The SRA provides a powerful way to get the discussion of corporate social responsibility into the center of American politics.

But I've also devised a far less visionary first step that might begin to create the framework for the SRA. This first step I call the Social Responsibility Initiative (SRI).

The SRI says the following: When this jurisdiction (city, county, state, or federal government) offers a contract of more than one million dollars for public bidding to fulfill some public purpose (whether that be to build a new school, to provide military hardware or scientific research, to build a highway, to reconstruct an airport, or whatever), competing contractors will be judged both on the basis of their ability to fill the contract and on their history of social responsibility, as measured by an Ethical Impact Report.

Among the four corporations that offer the lowers bids and can adequately fulfill the contract, the one that can demonstrate the best history of social responsibility will receive the contract.

The SRI is a far more modest proposal than the SRA. It can be won in cities, counties, state legislatures, and possibly even in the U.S. Congress in the next ten years. Local groups of citizens can put it on the ballot, providing there is a direct citizen referendum process, or demand that politicians seeking public office agree to back the SRI.

In popularizing the notion of an Ethical Impact Report, the SRI will become an important building block toward legitimization of the more transformative idea of the SRA. If people follow this route, within ten to twenty years we could make the notion of ethical impact reports a part of the vocabulary of our fellow citizens, an important step toward empowering each other to imagine a new bottom line of love and ethical and ecological responsibility.

The Sabbatical Year

The Bible unequivocally commands that every seven years all work cease, that the land lie fallow, and that all outstanding debt be canceled. Since this is a central part of Biblical economics, it deserves our attention as yet another strategy to put Spirit into the world of social institutions.

Imagine a society, or even a world, in which everyone were to have one year off out of every seven, and imagine if we decided that for about 85 percent of the population, it would be *the same year*.

One full year of no work out of every seven! A society-wide change of focus!

Anyone who wished to participate in the sabbatical year would commit themselves to using the time to:

•immerse themselves in some form of learning (which could include courses designed to provide you with the basic skills to start a whole different profession or life path in the next seven-year cycle or just be courses on topics that you had always wanted to pursue),

•participate in community discussions about how to restructure local communities and the larger society in the coming seven-year cycle, and

•participate in some community service activity (including child care, education, entertainment, elder care, massive global environmental repairs, building of housing and economic infrastructures, and sharing of cultural resources).

Time for these activities would be structured so that at least half of people's time was unstructured and allowed for play, artistic activity, relaxation, reading, meditating, resting, camping, picnics, and fun. Kids would not attend normal school but would have other child-oriented activities.

For the 15 percent who had to run essential services (food growing and distribution, energy services, communication services, and health services), there would be a rotating sabbatical over the other six years, plus a guarantee that they would could take the next sabbatical year (we would train personnel who could take their place).

There would be, of course, a dramatic slowdown in most people's lives. For at least one year, we would forego some of our frenetic production of goods and services. There would be a worldwide closure of stock markets and investment firms, of most government services and activities, and of most of the buying and selling in the society. We would have to live with the sad fact that we were not producing new computers or new scientific technologies, new automobiles or new cosmetics, many stores selling consumer goods would be closed, and we might not even have new TV shows or movies!

Life would slow down.

Implementing this biblical idea would be a powerful reminder that there's more to life than the frenetic accumulation of money and power. Slowed down in this way, the human race could catch its breath and begin to think seriously about what we have achieved, where we want to go, and what we really value. It would be a fabulous opportunity for a spiritual renewal of the entire society. And it would show us how much of what is done in this society could be done without—an important step toward reduction of the total amount of production as a way of saving the environment and eliminating needless work.

The effort to get this proposal considered and adopted would be fabulously exciting. On the one hand, people from a wide variety of spiritual approaches would immediately see the importance of the Biblical command for a sabbatical year (ecologists and evangelists joining hands?). On the other hand, cynics and technocratic pragmatists would argue that the barbarians are at the gate should we try for a moment to stop our furious-paced pursuit of more and more and more. And even many very idealistic people would raise reasonable worries: Could they go for a year without purchasing new clothes or new appliances? Would there be some way to get replacements on essentials (like refrigerators, stoves, pens, light bulbs, tires, computer printer cassettes, and copier toners)?

The debate itself will clarify the real values that people hold, and whether they are willing to begin a planning process (it might take five to ten years of planning after the initial proposal gets societal sanction) to take us in this very amazing direction.

Of course, we will be surrounded by people who think the very process of imagining such a possibility is inviting the sky to fall in and the earth to collapse beneath our feet. There will be plenty of hysteria. But I know many city planners, health-care professionals, technocrats of every sort, and pragmatic visionaries who believe that this could be made to work in ways that would not lead to a destruction of all the good things we get from contemporary technology (because to be spiritual is *not* to be a Luddite wishing to destroy all technology), and would not lead to crises in the availability of food, shelter, clothing, health care, energy, transportation, or education.

I believe this proposal could become a major focus on public debate sometime in the next hundred years as more people become open to the value of a world shaped by spiritual concerns.

It's not too early to begin imagining the details and to plan it out. But if you don't agree with this particular idea, that's also fine. There are many other ways to build a society that encourages rather than represses Spirit.

At the very least, the strategy I propose certainly counters those who say, "All this spiritual stuff has nothing to do with public policy." But I'm not stuck on the SRA or the Sabbatical Year as the only ways to move forward—I can easily imagine many people who believe in the framework in this book but who don't accept these two specific ideas. Please don't reduce all of Emancipatory Spirituality to the two proposals that seem most at variance with contemporary political reality.

In fact, my major reservation about the SRA and the SRI is that they may not embody enough of Emancipatory Spirituality, because they rely on economic incentives to get corporations to pay attention to something else besides the bottom line. There is something ultimately unsatisfying about this approach. So, too, the notion of having thousands of mini-grand juries reviewing the social responsibility record of corporations, while a plausible step to democratize review of corporate behavior without creating an ongoing bureaucracy with too much power, is still too bureaucratic and "external." (I believe that eventually we will have these concerns internalized in the consciousness of the society in such a way that whatever policing is needed will happen from within the corporate venture—but that may be still a century or two away.)

I'm serious when I say that the movement for Emancipatory Spirituality invites you to come up with other ideas. I hope you'll share your strategic ideas with me and others about how best to build a spiritually oriented society. It's that conversation that needs to start, and if the SRA and Sabbatical Year deflect you, forget about those ideas and come up with your own proposals instead. I'm sure I'll have much to learn from you once you accept the goal of building a society with the new bottom line we've been discussing. In fact, in TIKKUN magazine, you'll find a community of people who are regularly having this kind of discussion, and I hope you'll join that conversation.

I'm aware that I haven't even begun to address many important issues in this book, like the form of government we'd want as the globalization of spirit counters the globalization of capital. Neale Donald Walsch's *Conversations with God, Book Two,* describes a world government that might coordinate economic and political decisions. David Korten has argued in TIKKUN for a more decentralized vision of a future society. I am not going to try my hand at this in this book.

What I do want to say about government is this: I will only support a government that places subjective caring at the same level of centrality as objective caring. Whereas liberal and progressive movements have been great at fighting for objective caring (economic benefits and political rights), the government programs they set up rarely pay attention to the experience people have in dealing with government and its bureaucrats. Government needs to be reconceptualized as the public mechanism through which we all show that we care about everyone else, and government employees should be evaluated, rewarded, and promoted only to the extent they are able to make the public come away from those interactions with a renewed sense of hope and a deepened conviction that other people really do care, and have shown that by creating such a sensitive and caring government. That kind of feeling can only be generated if government does its best to recruit people whose biggest strength is their sensitivity to others and their commitment to serve—and then rewards those qualities in every aspect of government activity.

I'm aware that I have not detailed a vision of how a spiritually oriented economy might function on a local or an international scale—though if you put the suggestions in this and the past three chapters together, you get some ideas.

If ten or twenty major multinational corporations lost their corporate charters, it wouldn't be long before we saw major new sensitivity to environmental and ethical concerns throughout the world. But whether these kinds of changes could be accomplished within the framework of a capitalist market, whether they could be done on a regional basis or would require a global governmental structure, or how greater democratic control of the economy could be generated are issues I do not wish to address here. It may take many different kinds of experiments, both regionally and globally, before we can meet our spiritual criteria for a rational and productive society.

Let me say it again: You could be on board with me regarding the need for a new bottom line, yet have important arguments against the specific SRA and SRI strategies. What I feel certain of is this: the key to a spiritual transformation is to have criteria to evaluate productivity and efficiency according to love and caring, ethical, spiritual, and ecological sensitivity, and our capacity to respond to the universe with awe and wonder. I hope I've shown that this way of thinking has powerful and transformative implications. Perhaps you will be able to show me other ways in which these ideas can be applied. Frankly, I can't wait. Put those specifics together with a movement seriously involved in the spiritual practices outlined at the beginning of this chapter and we have the foundation for the only kind of social movement capable of succeeding in transforming and healing our world.

Timing

Sure, I'd love to see these changes well under way before I die. I think I'll be lucky if I see the beginnings of a movement that commits itself to these ideals.

We need to have a spiritually informed attitude toward building transformation. We might imagine ourselves to be midwives in the birth process of an Emancipatory Spirituality movement. The midwife must be carefully attentive to what is actually happening and what is possible at each moment. She must neither hold back the energy that allows for forward movement and birth, nor must she become so focused on the outcome that she tries to force the process beyond where it can go at the moment. Instead, she must stay in touch with the possibilities of the present.

Recognize how much there is to learn from the people around us who don't write books, don't articulate their ideas with ease, or don't have some obviously outstanding talents. We can learn from every person on this planet, because everyone is created in the image of God.

There is an old Kabbalistic notion that the world is sustained by thirty-six righteous human beings, and but for them the world would descend into total chaos. Those thirty-six don't know themselves to be such, and neither do the people around them. Any of the people you know might be one of them. Treat all people as though the future of the world depended on their well-being.

Act on your highest vision even when it doesn't seem realistic. The world is in distorted orbit precisely because so many wonderful people choose to act according to what others tell them is "realistic," rather than to act according to their own inner sense of what is right. For example, every four years people vote for candidates whom they don't believe really embody their own highest vision, because they "know" that it's "unrealistic" to vote for third-party candidates who are far closer to their own beliefs, or to create a party that really does embody what they believe. Yet the only thing that makes these choices unrealistic is our belief that they will be. The more people reject "the lesser evil," the more chance there is of a spiritual transformation. Not every area of our lives is as easy as voting for a third party—many times standing up for our own highest vision will be more costly to our short-term material well-being, the respect we get from others, our reputation, or even our jobs. But this is what it will take: people who stand up for the full vision of Emancipatory Spirituality, articulate that vision, and refuse to pretend that less than that is okay. Be impatient with what is, but compassionately so. That is the spiritual path to healing and transformation.

Conclusion

We are at the beginning of a wonderful period in human history in which we are reclaiming our deepest spiritual understanding. The human race is ready to move to a higher level of consciousness and spiritual fulfillment. But we are also at a moment in history when an older way of thinking and organizing our lives is leading to deep inner pain and paralysis and to the destruction of the life support systems of the planet.

There is no promise that Spirit will triumph before vast and irreparable damage is done to the environment and to our own souls. In fact, we live in a period in which the globalization of capital and the media's power to shape consciousness have reached new depths of perversion. We may well see a resurgence of confidence in the ability of our social system to provide material well-being for all, and a deepening commitment to the religion of money and material possessions. The talk of spiritual transformation will be dismissed as merely the momentary excitement that always accompanies *fin de siècle* and millennial periods.

Yet it is becoming ever clearer to ever larger numbers of people that the values around which our society is organized today are not really working. No matter how clever the manipulators of consciousness and the marketers of material reality may be, they face a fundamental contradiction: Spirit Matters. It matters to every human being because we all have essential spiritual needs that are being frustrated and repressed in this social order. Those needs may be ignored by the media and we ourselves may tell each other that they aren't "really" that important. But they are there. They don't go away. All that we've repressed will one day return to our daily lives. The timetable is uncertain, and at the moment I am writing the power of globalized capital seems invincible. But this too shall pass.

It will pass because people hunger for a deeper kind of recognition from each other than the current organization of society allows. It will change because people hunger for lives in which their spiritual needs are not relegated to the sidelines and to their weekends, but rather fully expressed and integrated into our daily lives. It will change because people need to live in a world based on love and on caring for each other. It will change because people are coming to recognize the intrinsic connection between the ecological crisis and the values of individualism and selfishness enshrined in the competitive market. It will change because people need a world whose social institutions are based on a joint sense of awe and wonder at the universe and on a collective understanding of our role as stewards and nurturers of Gaia. It will change because people will take their own spiritual understanding of the Unity of All Being seriously.

There are many other developments that still need to be played out. In the coming decades, liberal and progressive reformers may yet have a chance to try the reforms and social experiments they've been calling for over the past century. We may yet go through a period of social democracy and attempts at economic democracy. I certainly hope so, given the likely alternatives. But ultimately even these solutions will be understood as far too limited for the problems we face as a human race.

There may also be periods of political reaction—moments or even decades when fear becomes the dominant reality and people imagine they can deal with the problems caused by our society's spiritual vacuity through institutionalizing greater forms of repression. As the ecological crisis deepens, fear may lead to repression.

Or, we may just face many decades of "more of the same," a mindless drifting toward ecological insanity and emotional and spiritual depravity.

Nor will the path be easy. The first few thousands of people who "come out of the closet" as spiritual people committed to an Emancipatory Spirituality may face ridicule and antagonism, even from people who years later will themselves be involved in this movement. But this will change when we reach the point of a "critical mass" of people willing to publicly articulate their commitment to a transformative spiritual vision.

I do not have some Pollyannaish view that we are on a nonstop linear ascent to the good world or the messianic era. History hasn't worked that way so far.

Emancipatory Spirituality is on the rise, but how quickly the spiritual changes and the evolution of consciousness of the human race will take place is not some "fact" that will "reveal itself" or "unfold." That's one reason I resist developmental versions of spirituality that make it seem as if the next steps are an inevitable unfolding of what has happened already. As a basis for guiding social practice, it leaves out the centrality of our freedom, our choices, and our fallibility. It allows people to be spiritual cheerleaders when what we need at this moment are spiritual activists who take their spiritual understanding and bring it into the world of social change.

The central truth is this: we are embodiments of the Spirit of the universe and have the freedom and consciousness to make significant choices. The pace of change will depend in large part on the choices you and I and others make in the coming years and on how soon we are ready to act together toward achieving the kind of spiritual world described here.

How quickly Spirit manifests in the world depends in large part on what you and I and many others choose. The more we trust each other and the universe, the more we fully embrace Who We Really Are, the more we will make the world safe for Spirit. And the safer it feels, the more people will start to come out of their own closets and acknowledge their deep hunger for a spiritually grounded life.

This is a wonderful moment to be alive. We can already begin to see the outlines of a new consciousness that is spreading throughout the world. Nothing is more contagious than genuine love and genuine caring. Nothing is more exhilarating than authentic awe and wonder. Nothing is more hopeful than a genuine reorientation toward Nature. Nothing is more exciting than to witness people having the courage to fight for their highest vision. Nothing is more sustaining than a life filled with spiritual practices and joyful service to others.

Spirit Matters.

afterword

HOW YOU CAN BE INVOLVED

If you've read this book and found yourself wondering how to get involved, you are already involved! The way that transformation takes place is that more and more of us come to share these ideas.

So one thing you can do is to share copies of this book with others. Encourage them to read it. Meet with them to talk about these ideas and how you might implement them in your own lives. There is no one better suited to answer that question than you yourself. Deferring to experts, seeking someone who can map out your path, can easily become a way of avoiding our own responsibility for bringing about the very kinds of changes we all tell ourselves we want to see happen.

Here are some other things you can do:

• Create a study group to read and discuss this book with others. Friends, coworkers, colleagues, fellow students, students in a nearby college or university (or even high school), members of your religious or spiritual community, neighbors, or members of some organization with which you are affiliated (PTA, union, ecology organization, food cooperative, political party, social group)—any of these provide contexts where you'll find people who might be very grateful if you exposed them to the ideas in this book. Then go on to read the other books I've recommended throughout this book. In the list below there is a library of important spiritual thought, and you'll find it stimulating and enriching.

• Create a workplace group to do the kind of envisioning discussed in chapter six—about what your work could look like if it were based on a new bottom line.

• Start engaging in the spiritual practices outlined in chapter ten.

• Get a group of people together who wish to make Emancipatory Spirituality more central to our world. Give each other support as each of you discusses the details of what is happening in your lives, in your work, in the media, in the larger society. Discuss how you can work together to build a social movement in your own area that is committed to the vision articulated here. Then, challenge the media's antispiritual biases and insist that they present the perspective of an Emancipatory Spirituality as one of the options for news and social reality analysis.

• Engage in unprovoked and gratuitous acts of lovingkindness, generosity, and joyful abandonment to the glory of the universe.

• When other people tell you that "everyone is really selfish or cares only about themselves" tell them that it's not true of you and that you are not so sure it's true of them either.

• Let everyone in your life know that you think Spirit Matters and that you personally are committed to a new bottom line for our society. Come out of the closet as a spiritual person!

A Transformative Community

The Hebrew word *tikkun* means healing, transformation, and repair. And that is precisely what we set out to do when we created TIKKUN magazine.

TIKKUN features some of the most insightful spiritual thinkers of our day. In cities around the world, people in TIKKUN study groups help constitute a community dedicated to social and individual healing and transformation.

When we started, we realized that it made most sense for us to identify with a particular spiritual tradition. And since most of us were Jewish, we subtitled TIKKUN "a Jewish critique of politics, culture and society."

But TIKKUN is *not* just for Jews. At least half of our writers come from other traditions. While we tend to feature some articles having to do with Jewish spirituality or Israel, we also focus on American politics, culture, and society and try to bring a different perspective to them. At the same time, don't be surprised to find some articles in TIKKUN that reflect the very views critiqued in this book. As we build a transformative community, we must remain committed to ideological diversity. That means we print articles that I personally deeply disagree with, in order to create an arena in which many different voices get heard.

In TIKKUN you'll read people like Neale Donald Walsch, Jonathan Kozol, Peter Gabel, Ken Wilber, Elie Wiesel, Marge Piercy, Thomas Moore, Susannah Heschel, Andrew Weil, Yehuda Amichai, Susan Faludi, Cornel West, Naomi Wolf, Daniel Berrigan, Jean Bethke Elshtain, Letty Cottin Pogrebin, Matthew Fox, Zalman Schachter Shalomi, Jim Wallis, Riane Eisler, Thom Hartmann, Roger Gottlieb, Rev. Tony Campolo, Amitai Etzioni, Michael Bader, Jackson Lears, Fritjof Capra, Arthur Waskow, Paul Buhle, Martin Jay, Marcia Prager, Paul Wellstone, Marianne Williamson, Jack Miles, Joseph Skibell, Arthur Green, Svi Shapiro, Thane Rosenbaum, Andrew Ross, John Dominic Crossan, Zygmunt Bauman, Michael Sandel, Bernie Glassman, David Korten, Robin West, Charles Derber, Mordecai Gafni, Douglas Gwynn, Holly Near, Thandeka, and many more.

The TIKKUN community sponsors gatherings for TIKKUN readers, including study sessions, courses, weekend retreats and national conferences. To subscribe to TIKKUN, please send $29 to TIKKUN, P.O. Box 460926, Escondido, CA 92046. www.TIKKUN.org

Web Site for Spirit Matters

www.spiritmatters.net

That's the address to connect to when you are looking for more information about the community of people doing work around Emancipatory Spirituality.

Keeping in Touch

If you'd like to reach me directly, write to our TIKKUN office at 2107 Van Ness Avenue, Suite 302, San Francisco, CA 94109. Or you can e-mail me at rabbilerner@tikkun.org. You can also check our web sites at www.tikkun.org and, once it is activated,

www.spiritmatters.net

The best way to keep in touch is to subscribe to TIKKUN.

In the articles I select for TIKKUN, I'll let you know what is happening in the world that might contribute to Emancipatory Spirituality.

In order for me to know about you, send me an e-mail or letter telling me about how *Spirit Matters* has been useful to you, and what you are planning to do to be an embodiment of Emancipatory Spirituality (and send us a subscription to TIKKUN at the same time). If I get more than ten thousand responses, I'll start a newsletter to help connect people who have read *Spirit Matters*. And I will bring people together for a national gathering at least once every two years. So stay in touch—it's the only way I know you want to take the ideas you've found in this book a step further, and my only way to connect you with others who share your desire to be an ally in the development of Spirit.

The Spirit Matters Network

Many talented professionals, businesspeople, ministers, educators, community activists, corporate executives, philanthropists, lawyers, doctors, scientists, writers, poets, musicians, media people, high-tech workers, and people working for nonprofits see themselves as agents of the kind of spiritual transformation I've been discussing in this book—but few have a network in which they can meet other similarly talented people, share experiences, discuss their work in detail, and really get to know what other creative, spiritually alive people are doing. I know many people who get "turned off" at all the flakiness or free-floating neediness they encounter at spiritual gatherings, the spiritual emptiness they encounter at political and professional organizations, and the competitiveness they encounter with peers. They end up trying to make a difference in the world by themselves, keeping their spiritual values alive on their own and without much support. But alone it's hard to get feedback, or a safe context for meaningful reflection, on how what you are doing meets with your highest goals.

That's why I've decided to form a Network: to provide support to people who are doing top-notch work, but doing it on their own.

The Spirit Matters Network is not a mass movement, but a small group of people who really want to make Emancipatory Spirituality central to their lives in the period ahead.

If you are interested in learning more about the Spirit Matters Network, please write to me with a description of who you are, what your life has been about, the context of your work, the arenas in which you might already be doing Emancipatory Spirituality work (though you might not even have thought of it as "spiritual" until reading this book), what your special skills are, and what aspects of *Spirit Matters* spoke most deeply to you.

If you can't be actively involved, but wish to help us financially, make a tax-deductible contribution to the Spirit Matters Network.

Send your letter and/or contribution to TIKKUN, 2107 Van Ness Ave, San Francisco, CA 94109 or to rabbilerner@tikkun.org (it's far easier for me if you use the e-mail–you could even send credit card info for a donation, plus a TIKKUN subscription). Please don't be offended if I take an inordinately long time getting back to you. Until we get funding for the Spirit Matters Network there are going to be delays and screw ups.

Supportive Reading

Your own spiritual path can be enhanced by learning from others. I've found the following books to be particularly helpful. I strongly urge you to get hold of them and read them:

The Prophets, by Abraham Joshua Heschel (Harper Collins, 1975). This is a wonderful reintroduction to the ancient Biblical prophets. Reading them through the lens of this extraordinary theologian will give you a renewed sense of how the views articulated in *Spirit Matters* are not new, but fit into a long tradition that goes back thousands of years. Try also Heschel's *Who Is Man?*, (Stanford University Press, 1965); *The Sabbath*, (Farrar, Strauss, and Giroux, 1995); and *God in Search of Man*, (Noonday Press, CFSG, 1997).

A Brief History of Everything by Ken Wilber (Shambhala, 1996). A stunning and profound thinker examines the course of evolution as the unfolding of Spirit. If you want a detailed account of how Spirit has developed, Wilber is the person to read. Try also his *Integral Psychology: Consciousness, Spirit, Psychology, Therapy* (Shambhala, 2000).

Conversations with God, Book 1 by Neale Donald Walsch (Putnam, 1996) and *Conversations with God, Books 2 and 3* by Neale Donald Walsch (Hampton Roads, 1997, 1998). As an old-fashioned intellectual, I approached this work with a great deal of skepticism. But I found in Walsch's work some of the deepest truths about the realm of spirit, written in a very accessible style. Walsch hears God's voice in a way that regenerates hope. He deals with some of the most trouble-some issues facing a contemporary spiritual person—and what God tells him is something most of us already know yet don't allow ourselves to fully know. As if this gift were not enough, Walsch has created a newsletter called *Conversations*, and a community of people who are supporting his work (called ReCreation)—and I've been delighted to find that in almost every issue of his newsletter I learn new ways to think about the meaning of living a spiritual life. It's available through ReCreation at 3702 SW Troy Street, Portland, OR 97219.

The Bank Teller and Other Writings on the Politics of Meaning by Peter Gabel (Acada Books, 2000). Peter Gabel is one of the most creative intellectuals alive today, and his writing provides a deep and comprehensive foundation to many of the thoughts developed in this book. In *The Bank*

Teller, you'll find many of the articles Gabel wrote originally in TIKKUN magazine—and when read together, they constitute a powerful way to apply spiritual categories to the contemporary world.

The New American Spirituality: A Seeker's Guide by Elizabeth Lesser (Random House, 1999). Elizabeth Lesser provides an indispensable manual for how to make sense of the contemporary discourse on spirituality. Lesser is a cofounder of The Omega Institute, which offers weekend and week-long seminars in spiritual growth.

The Last Hours of Ancient Sunlight: Waking Up to Personal and Global Transformation by Thom Hartmann (Mythical Books, 1998). Thom Hartmann tells the story of our destruction of the planet—and what we can do about it. Simple in its presentation, profound in its insights, this is the first book to read if you want to understand how imminent the danger is to our planet.

State of the World edited by Lester R. Brown, Christopher Flavin, and Hilary French (WW Norton, 2000). Each year the Worldwatch Institute publishes a report on the progress we are making toward a sustainable planet. To keep in touch with their latest reports, write to them at 1776 Massachusetts Ave, NW, Washington D.C. 20036, or try their website at www.worldwatch.org.

A Spirituality of Resistance: Finding a Peaceful Heart and Protecting the Earth by Roger S. Gottlieb (Crossroad Publishing Co. 1999). An eloquent appeal to spiritual people to take seriously the challenge of healing the planet.

Faith Works: Lessons from the Life of an Activist Preacher by Jim Wallis (Random House, 2000). Wallis is the prophet of a new and powerful progressive movement among Christian Evangelicals called The Call to Renewal. This book is the engaging and compelling story of his own life experience and how it led him to the struggle for a spiritually grounded social justice.

From Age-ing to Sage-ing by Zalman Schachter-Shalomi (Warner Books, 1997). Reb Zalman is my spiritual master and guide, and in this creative approach to eldering, he presents the seeds of an approach that could dramatically transform the experience of the coming generations as they deal with inevitable aging.

A Heart as Wide as the World: Living with Mindfulness, Wisdom and Compassion by Sharon Salzberg, (Shambala, 1999), and, *It's Easier Than You Think* by Sylvia Boorstein, (HarperSanFrancisco, 1997). Two masterful teachers of Buddhist meditation share their wisdom in these little jewels.

A Year to Live: How to Live This Year As If It Were Your Last by Stephen Levine (Bell Tower, 1997). A spiritual thinker, who has spent over twenty-five years helping people face the approach of their own death. Also read his *Meetings at the Edge*.

Original Self: Living with Paradox and Originality by Thomas Moore (HarperCollins, 2000). Moore has many important insights and a sensitivity to spiritual nuance.

Sins of the Spirit, Blessings of the Flesh: Lessons for Transforming Evil in Soul and Society by Matthew Fox (Harmony Books, 1999). This book is a wonderful antidote for anyone who grew up in a religious community that demeaned the body or saw it as evil or fundamentally estranged from spirit.

Healing the Soul of America by Marianne Williamson, Touchstone Books, 2000). A gentle and wise spiritual teacher who manages to make deep teachings available to many who have been alienated from traditional religious communities applies her wisdom to the healing of American society. Williamson shows that the principles which apply to personal healing also apply to healing the world

A Final Word

Blessings to you for having read this book. Let us now work together to share this information with others. And as we do so, let's rejoice in the wonder of this universe and use to the fullest our capacities for love, generosity, and compassion.

bibliography

Abram, David. *The Spell of the Sensuous: Perception and Language in a More-than-Human World*. New York: Pantheon Books, 1996.

Armstrong, Karen. *A History of God: The 4000-Year Quest of Judaism, Christianity, and Islam*. New York: A.A. Knopf, 1993.

Barnet, Richard J., and John Cavanagh. *Global Dreams: Imperial Corporations and the New World Order*. New York: Simon & Schuster, 1994.

Bauman, Zygmunt. *Modernity and Ambivalence*. Ithaca, NY: Cornell University Press, 1991.

———. *Modernity and the Holocaust*. Ithaca, NY: Cornell University Press, 1989.

Becker, Ernest. *The Denial of Death*. New York: Free Press, 1973.

Bellah, Robert N., et al. *Habits of the Heart: Individualism and Commitment in American Life*. New York: Harper & Row, 1985.

Berman, Morris. *Coming to Our Senses: Body and Spirit in the Hidden History of the West*. New York: Simon & Schuster, 1989.

Berry, Wendell. *Sex, Economy, Freedom, and Community: Eight Essays*. New York: Pantheon Books, 1993.

Boff, Leonardo. *Ecology and Liberation: A New Paradigm*. Translated by John Cumming. Maryknoll, NY: Orbis Books, 1995.

Boorstein, Sylvia. *Don't Just Do Something, Sit There: A Mindfulness Retreat with Sylvia Boorstein*. San Francisco: HarperSanFrancisco, 1996.

———. *It's Easier than You Think: The Buddhist Way to Happiness*. San Francisco: HarperSanFrancisco, 1995.

Borg, Marcus J. *Meeting Jesus Again for the First Time: The Historical Jesus and the Heart of Contemporary Faith*. San Francisco: HarperSanFrancisco, 1994.

Borysenko, Joan, with Larry Rothstein. *Minding the Body, Mending the Mind*. Reading, MA: Addison-Wesley, 1987.

Brown, Lester, et al. *State of the World, 1996*. New York: W.W. Norton & Co., 1996.

———. *State of the World, 1999: The Millennium Edition*. New York: W.W. Norton & Co., 1999.

———. *State of the World, 2000 (State of the World Series)*. New York: W.W. Norton & Co., 2000.

Brueggemann, Walter. *The Prophetic Imagination*. Philadelphia: Fortress Press, 1978.

Buck, Susan J. *The Global Commons: An Introduction*. Washington, DC: Island Press, 1998.

Callenbach, Ernest. *Ecology: A Pocket Guide*. Berkeley, CA: The University of California Press, 1998.

Capra, Fritjof. *The Turning Point: Science, Society, and the Rising Culture*. New York: Simon & Schuster, 1982.

———. *The Web of Life: A New Scientific Understanding of Living Systems*. New York: Anchor Books, 1996.

Carnoy, Martin, et al, eds. *The New Global Economy in the Information Age: Reflections on Our Changing World*. University Park, PA: Pennsylvania State University Press, 1993.

Chodrön, Pema. *When Things Fall Apart: Heart Advice for Difficult Times*. Boston: Shambhala, 1997.

Coles, Robert. *The Spiritual Life of Children*. Boston: Houghton Mifflin, 1990.

Combs, Allan. *The Radiance of Being: Complexity, Chaos, and the Evolution of Consciousness*. St. Paul, MN: Paragon House, 1996.

Cooper, Rabbi David. *God Is a Verb: Kabbalah and the Practice of Mystical Judaism*. New York: Riverhead Books, 1997.

———. *A Heart of Stillness: A Complete Guide to Learning the Art of Meditation*. New York: Bell Tower, 1992.

———. *Renewing Your Soul: A Guided Retreat for the Sabbath and Other Days of Rest*. San Francisco: HarperSanFrancisco, 1995.

Cushamn, Philip. *Constructing the Self, Constructing America: A Cultural History of Psychotherapy*. Boston: Addison-Wesley, 1995.

Dalai Lama, and Howard Cutler. *The Art of Happiness: A Handbook for Living*. New York: Riverhead, 1998.

Das, Lama Surya. *Awakening the Buddha Within: Eight Steps to Enlightenment: Tibetan Wisdom for the Western World*. New York: Broadway Books, 1997.

Dass, Ram, and Mirabai Bush. *Compassion in Action: Setting Out on the Path of Service*. New York: Bell Tower, 1992.

Dickinson, Emily and Thomas H. Jacobs, eds. *The Letters of Emily Dickinson*. Cambridge, MA: Belknap Press of Harvard University Press, 1986.

Dossey, Larry. *Meaning and Medicine: Lessons from a Doctor's Tales of Breakthrough and Healing*. New York: Bantam, 1991.

———. *Prayer Is Good Medicine: How to Reap the Healing Benefits of Prayer*. San Francisco: HarperSanFrancisco, 1996.

———. *Reinventing Medicine: Beyond Mind-Body to a New Era of Healing*. San Francisco: HarperSanFrancisco, 1999.

Eisler, Riane. *The Chalice and the Blade: Our History, Our Future*. Cambridge, MA: Harper & Row, 1987.

———. *Tomorrow's Children: A Blueprint for Partnership Education in the 21st Century*. Boulder, CO: Westview Press, 2000.

Eisler, Riane, and David Loye. *The Partnership Way: New Tools for Living and Learning.* San Francisco: HarperSanFrancisco, 1990.

Elgin, Duane. *Awakening the Earth: Exploring the Evolution of Human Culture and Consciousness.* New York: William Morrow & Co., 1993.

———. *Voluntary Simplicity: Toward a Way of Life That Is Outwardly Simple, Inwardly Rich.* New York, William Morrow & Co., 1981.

Ernst, Carl W., trans. *Teachings of Sufism.* Boston: Shambhala, 1999.

Estes, Clarissa Pinkola. *Women Who Run with the Wolves: Myths and Stories of the Wild Woman Archetype.* New York: Ballantine Books, 1992.

Estes, Ralph. *Tyranny of the Bottom Line: Why Corporations Make Good People Do Bad Things.* San Francisco: Berrett-Koehler, 1996.

Etzioni, Amitai. *The Moral Dimension: Toward a New Economics.* New York, Free Press, 1988.

Faludi, Susan. *Stiffed: The Betrayal of the American Man.* New York: William Morrow & Co., 1999.

Finkielkraut, Alan. *In the Name of Humanity: Reflections on the Twentieth Century.* New York: Columbia University Press, 1999.

Fox, Matthew. *The Coming of the Cosmic Christ: The Healing of Mother Earth and the Birth of a Global Renaissance.* San Francisco: Harper & Row, 1988.

———. *Creation Spirituality: Liberating Gifts for the Peoples of the Earth.* San Francisco: HarperSanFrancisco, 1991.

———. *Original Blessing* Santa Fe, NM: Bear, 1983.

———. *The Reinvention of Work: A New Vision of Livelihood for Our Time.* San Francisco: HarperSanFrancisco, 1994.

———. *Sins of the Spirit, Blessings of the Flesh.* New York: Harmony Books, 1999.

Frankiel, Tamar, and Judy Greenfield. *Minding the Temple of the Soul: Balancing Body, Mind and Spirit through Traditional Jewish Prayer, Movement, and Meditation.* Woodstock, VT: Jewish Lights Publishing, 1997.

Frankl, Viktor E. *The Doctor and the Soul: From Psychotherapy to Logotherapy.* Translated by Richard Winston and Clara Winston. New York: Vintage Books, 1986.

Friedman, Thomas L. *The Lexus and the Olive Tree.* New York: Farrar, Strauss, & Giroux, 1999.

Friere, Paulo. *Pedagogy of the Oppressed.* Translated by Myra Bergman Ramos. New York: Continuum, 1993.

Gabel, Peter. *The Bank Teller and Other Writings on the Politics of Meaning.* San Francisco: Acada Press, 2000.

Giddens, Anthony. *The Consequences of Modernity.* Stanford, CA: Stanford University Press, 1990.

Gilligan, Carol. *In a Different Voice: Psychological Theory and Women's Development*. Cambridge, MA: Harvard University Press, 1993.

Giroux, Henry. *Stealing Innocence: Youth, Corporate Power, and Cultural Politics*. New York: St. Martin's Press, 2000.

Glazer, Steven. *The Heart of Learning: Spirituality in Education*. New York: J.P. Tarcher/Putnam, 1999.

Goldsmith, Edward. *The Way: An Ecological World-View*. Athens, GA: The University of Georgia Press, 1998.

Goldstein, Joseph. *The Experience of Insight: A Simple and Direct Guide to Buddhist Meditation*. Boulder, CO: Shambhala, 1983.

Goldstein, Joseph, and Jack Kornfield. *Seeking the Heart of Wisdom: The Path of Insight Meditation*. Boston: Shambhala, 1987.

Goleman, Daniel. *Emotional Intelligence*. New York: Bantam Books, 1997.

Gottleib, Roger S. *A Spirituality of Resistance: Finding a Peaceful Heart and Protecting the Earth*. New York: Crossroad, 1999.

Gorz, Andre. *Capitalism, Socialism, Ecology*. Translated by Chris Turner. London: Verso, 1994.

Green, Arthur. *Seek My Face, Speak My Name: A Contemporary Jewish Theology*. Northvale, NJ: Jason Aronson, 1992.

Grof, Stanislav, and Joan Halifax. *The Human Encounter with Death*. New York: E.P. Dutton, 1977.

Grosskopf, Barry. *Forgive Your Parents, Heal Yourself: How Understanding Your Painful Family Legacy Can Transform Your Life*. New York: Free Press, 1999.

Grossman, Richard L., and Frank T. Adams, . *Taking Care of Business: Citizenship and the Charter of Incorporation*. Cambridge, MA: Charter Ink, 1993.

Habermas, Jurgen. *The Theory of Communicative Action*. Translated by Thomas McCarthy. Boston: Beacon Press, 1984.

Habermas, Jurgen, and Jeremy J. Shapiro. *Knowledge and Human Interests*. Boston: Beacon Press, 1972.

Halifax, Joan. *Shaman: The Wounded Healer*. New York: Crossroad, 1982.

Hardt, Michael, and Antonio Negri. *Empire*. Cambridge, MA: Harvard University Press, 2000.

Hartmann, Thom. *The Last Hours of Ancient Sunlight: Waking up to Personal and Global Transformation*. New York: Harmony Books, 1999.

Harvey, Andrew. *The Direct Path*. New York: Broadway Books, 2000.

―――. *Son of Man: The Mystical Path to Christ*. New York: J.P. Tarcher/Putnam, 1999.

Hass, Robert. *Praise*. New York: Ecco Press, 1979.

Hawken, Paul. *The Ecology of Commerce: A Declaration of Sustainability*. New York: HarperBusiness, 1993.

Hayward, Jeremy. *Perceiving Ordinary Magic: Science and Intuitive Wisdom*. Boulder, CO: New Science Library, 1984.

Henderson, Hazel: *Beyond Globalization: Shaping a Sustainable Global Economy*. West Hartford, CT: Kumarian Press, 1999.

Heschel, Abraham Joshua. *God in Search of Man: A Philosophy of Judaism*. Northvale, NJ: Jason Aronson, 1987.

———. *The Prophets*. New York: Harper & Row, 1962.

———. *The Sabbath: Its Meaning for Modern Man*. New York: Farrar, Strauss, & Giroux, 1951.

———. *Who Is Man?* Stanford, CA: Stanford University Press, 1965.

Hillman, James. *The Soul's Code: In Search of Character and Calling*. New York: Warner Books, 1997.

Hooks, Bell. *Killing Rage: Ending Racism*. New York: H. Holt & Co., 1995.

———. *Yearning: Race, Gender, and Cultural Politics*. Boston: South End Press, 1990.

Hubbard, Barbara Marx. *Conscious Evolution: Awakening the Power of Our Social Potential*. Novato, CA: New World Library, 1998.

Jameson, Fredric, and Masao Miyoshi. *The Cultures of Globalization*. Durham, NC: Duke University Press, 1998.

———. *Postmodernism, or, the Cultural Logic of Late Capitalism*. Durham, NC: Duke University Press, 1991.

Kabat-Zinn, Jon. *Wherever You Go, There You Are: Mindfulness Meditation in Everyday Life*. New York: Hyperion, 1994.

Kapleau, Philip. *The Zen of Living and Dying: A Practical and Spiritual Guide*. Boston: Shambhala, 1998.

Karliner, Josh. *The Corporate Planet: Ecology and Politics in the Age of Globalization*. San Francisco: Sierra Club Books, 1997.

Keen, Sam. *Hymns to an Unknown God: Awakening the Spirit in Everyday Life*. New York: Bantam Books, 1994.

Keller, Evelyn Fox. *Reflections on Gender and Science*. New Haven, CT: Yale University Press, 1985.

———. *Secrets of Life, Secrets of Death: Essays on Language, Gender, and Science*. New York: Routledge, 1992.

Kinsler, Ross, and Gloria Kinsler. *The Biblical Jubilee and the Struggle for Life: An Invitation to Personal Ecclesial, and Social Transformation*. Maryknoll, NY: Orbis Books, 1999.

Kornfield, Jack. *After the Ecstasy, the Laundry: How the Heart Grows Wise on the Spiritual Path*. New York: Bantam Books, 2000.

———. *Living Dharma: Teachings of Twelve Buddhist Masters*. Boston: Shambhala, 1996.

Korten, David. *When Corporations Rule the World*. San Francisco: Berrett-Koehler, 1995.

Kotler, Arnold, ed. *The Engaged Buddhist Reader: Ten Years of Engaged Buddhist Publishing*. Berkeley, CA: Parallax Press, 1996.

Krishmamurti, Jiddu. *On Living and Dying*. San Francisco: HarperSanFrancisco, 1992.

Kushner, Lawrence. *Eyes Remade for Wonder: A Lawrence Kushner Reader*. Woodstock, VT: Jewish Lights Publishing, 1998.

———. *The River of Light: Spirituality, Judaism, Consciousness*. Woodstock, VT: Jewish Lights Publishing, 1990.

Langer, Ellen. *The Power of Mindful Learning*. Reading, MA: Addison-Wesley, 1997.

Lemann, Nicholas. *The Big Test: The Secret History of the American Meritocracy*. New York: Farrar, Strauss, & Giroux, 1999.

Lerner, Michael. *Jewish Renewal: A Path to Healing and Transformation*. New York: G.P. Putnam's Sons, 1994.

———. *The Politics of Meaning: Restoring Hope and Possibility in an Age of Cynicism*. Reading, MA: Addison-Wesley, 1997.

———. *The Socialism of Fools: Anti-Semitism on the Left*. San Diego, CA: Harcourt Brace College Publishers, 1992.

———. *Surplus Powerlessness: The Psychodynamics of Everyday Life and the Psychology of Individual and Social Transformation*. Atlantic Highlands, NJ: Humanities Press, 1991.

———. *Tikkun: To Heal, Repair, and Transform the World: An Anthology*. Oakland, CA: TIKKUN Books, 1992.

Lerner, Michael, and Cornel West. *Jews and Blacks: Let the Healing Begin*. New York: G.P. Putnam's Sons, 1995.

Lesser, Elizabeth. *The New American Spirituality: A Seeker's Guide*. New York: Random House, 1999.

Levine, Stephen. *Meetings at the Edge: Dialogues with the Grieving and the Dying, the Healing and the Healed*. Garden City, NY: Anchor, 1989.

———. *A Year to Live: How to Live This Year as if It Were Your Last*. New York: Bell Tower, 1997.

Levey, Joel, and Michelle Levey. *Living in Balance: A Dynamic Approach for Creating Harmony and Wholeness in a Chaotic World*. Berkeley, CA: Conari Press, 1998.

Lewis, Thomas, Amini Fari, and Richard Lannon. *General Theory of Love*. New York: Random House, 2000

Lovelock, James. *Gaia: The Practical Science of Planetary Medicine*. Pomfret, VT: Trafalgar Square, 1991.

Loye, David, ed. *The Evolutionary Outrider: The Impact of the Human Agent on Evolution: Essays Honouring Ervin Laszlo*. Westport, CT: Praeger Books, 1998.

Macy, Joanna. *World as Lover, World as Self.* Berkeley, CA: Parallax Press, 1991.

Maslow, Abraham Harold. *The Farther Reaches of Human Nature.* New York: Viking Press, 1971.

Matt, Daniel Chanan. *God and the Big Bang: Discovering Harmony between Science and Spirituality.* Woodstock, VT: Jewish Lights Publishing, 1996.

deMause, Lloyd, ed. *The History of Childhood: The Untold Story of Child Abuse.* New York: Psychohistory Press, 1974.

McLaughlin, Corinne, and Gordon Davidson. *Spiritual Politics: Changing the World from the Inside Out.* New York: Ballantine Books, 1994.

Merchant, Carolyn. *The Death of Nature: Women, Ecology, and the Scientific Revolution.* New York: Harper & Row, 1980.

Miller, Alice. *Thou Shalt Not Be Aware: Society's Betrayal of the Child.* Translated by Hildegarde Hannum and Hunter Hannum. New York: Farrar, Strauss, & Giroux, 1984.

Mitchell, Stephen, ed. *The Enlightened Heart: An Anthology of Sacred Poetry.* New York: Harper & Row, 1989.

Molino, Anthony, ed. *The Couch and the Tree: Dialogues in Psychoanalysis and Buddhism.* New York: North Point Press, 1998.

Moore, Thomas. *Care of the Soul: A Guide for Cultivating Depth and Sacredness in Everyday Life.* New York: HarperCollins, 1992.

———. *Original Self: Living with Paradox and Originality.* New York: HarperCollins, 2000.

Muller, Wayne. *Sabbath: Restoring the Sacred Rhythm of Rest.* New York: Bantam Books, 1999.

Murphy, Michael. *Golf in the Kingdom.* New York: Dell, 1972.

———. *The Future of the Body: Explorations into the Further Evolution of Human Nature.* Los Angeles: J.P. Tarcher, 1992.

Orr, David W. *Earth in Mind: On Education, Environment, and the Human Prospect.* Washington, DC: Island Press, 1994.

Palmer, Parker J. *The Company of Strangers: Christians and the Renewal of America's Public Life.* New York: Crossroad, 1981.

———. *The Courage to Teach: Exploring the Inner Landscape of a Teacher's Life.* San Francisco: Jossey-Bass, 1998.

Rankin, Robert, ed. *The Recovery of Spirit in Higher Education: Christian and Jewish Ministries in Campus Life.* New York: Seabury Press, 1980.

Rappaport, Roy A. *Ritual and Religion in the Making of Humanity.* New York: Cambridge University Press, 1999.

Remen, Rachel Naomi. *Kitchen Table Wisdom: Stories That Heal.* New York: Riverhead Books, 1996.

Rifkin, Jeremy. *The End of Work: The Decline of the Global Labor Force and the Dawn of the Post-Market Era.* New York: G P. Putnam's Sons, 1995.

Roche, Lorin. *Meditation Made Easy*. San Francisco: HarperSanFrancisco, 1998.

Rosenberg, Larry. *Breath by Breath: The Liberating Practice of Insight Liberation*. Boston: Shambhala, 1998.

———. *Living in the Light of Death: On the Art of Being Truly Alive*. Boston: Shambhala, 2000.

Ruether, Rosemary Radford. *Gaia and God: An Ecofeminist Theology of Earth Healing*. San Francisco: HarperSanFrancisco, 1992.

Russell, Peter. *The Global Brain Awakens: Our Next Evolutionary Leap*. Palo Alto, CA: Global Brain, 1995.

Sacks, Peter: *Standardized Minds: The High Price of America's Testing Culture and What We Can Do to Change It*. Cambridge, MA: Perseus Books, 2000.

Salzberg, Sharon. *A Heart as Wide as the World: Living with Mindfulness, Wisdom, and Compassion*. Boston: Shambhala, 1997.

———. *Lovingkindness: The Revolutionary Art of Happiness*. Boston: Shambhala, 1995.

Sandel, Michael. *Democracy's Discontent: America in Search of a Public Philosophy*. Cambridge, MA: Belknap Press of Harvard University Press, 1996.

Sassen, Saskia. *Losing Control?: Sovereignty in an Age of Globalization*. New York: Columbia University Press, 1996.

Schachter-Shalomi, Zalman. *From Age-ing to Sage-ing: A Profound New Vision of Growing Older*. New York: Warner Books, 1995.

———. *Spiritual Intimacy: A Study of Counseling in Hasidism*. Northvale, NJ: Jason Aronson, 1991.

Schachter-Shalomi, Zalman, with Donald Gropman. *The First Step: A Guide for the New Jewish Spirit*. Toronto; New York: Bantam Books, 1983.

Schachter-Shalomi, Zalman, and Ellen Singer, ed. *Paradigm Shift: From the Jewish Renewal Teachings of Reb Zalman Schachter-Shalomi*. Northvale, NJ: Jason Aronson, 1993.

Schiller, Herbert I. *Information Inequality: The Deepening Social Crisis in America*. New York: Routledge, 1996.

Segal, Jerome M. *Graceful Simplicity: Toward a Philosophy and Politics of Simple Living*. New York: H. Holt & Co., 1999.

Shapiro, Rami M. *Minyan: Ten Principles for Living a Life of Integrity*. New York: Bell Tower, 1997.

Shapiro, Svi. *Between Capitalism and Democracy*. Westport, CT: Bergin & Garvey, 1990.

Shiva, Vandana, ed. *Close to Home: Women Reconnect Ecology, Health, and Development*. Philadelphia: New Society Publishers, 1994.

———. *Staying Alive: Women, Ecology, and Survival in India*. New Delhi: Kali for Women, 1988.

Shor, Ira. *Empowering Education: Critical Teaching for Social Change.* Chicago: University of Chicago Press, 1992.

Shuman, Michael. *Going Local: Creating Self-Reliant Communities in a Global Age.* New York: Free Press, 1998.

Smith, Huston. *Beyond the Post-Modern Mind.* New York: Crossroad, 1982.

————. *The Religions of Man.* New York: Harper, 1958.

Spretnak, Charlene. *The Resurgence of the Real: Body, Nature, and Place in a Hypermodern World.* Reading, MA: Addison-Wesley, 1997.

Steiner, Rudolf. *The Child's Changing Consciousness and Waldorf Education.* Translated by Roland Everett and edited by Rhona Everett. Hudson, NY: Anthroposophic Press, 1988.

————. *Intuitive Thinking as a Spiritual Path.* Translated by Michael Lipson. Hudson, NY: Anthroposophic Press, 1995.

Suzuki, Shunryu. *Zen Mind, Beginner's Mind.* Edited by Trudy Dixon. New York: Walker/Weatherhill, 1970.

Swimme, Brian, and Thomas Berry. *The Universe Story: From the Primordial Flaring Forth to the Ecozoic Era—A Celebration of the Unfolding of the Cosmos.* San Francisco: HarperSanFrancisco, 1992.

Tarnas, Richard. *The Passion of the Western Mind: Understanding the Ideas That Have Shaped Our Worldview.* New York: Harmony Books, 1991.

Taylor, Charles. *Sources of the Self: The Making of the Modern Identity.* Cambridge, MA: Harvard University Press, 1989.

Teasdale, Wayne, and the Dalai Lama. *The Mystic Heart: Discovering a Universal Spirituality in the World's Religions.* Novato, CA: New World Library, 1999.

Teilhard de Chardin, Pierre. *The Future of Man.* Translated by Norman Denny. New York: Harper & Row, 1959.

Theobold, Robert. *The Rapids of Change: Social Entrepreneurship in Turbulent Times.* Indianapolis, IN: Knowledge Systems, 1987.

Thurman, Howard. *The Creative Encounter: An Interpretation of Religion and the Social Witness.* New York: Harper, 1954.

Thurow, Lester. *The Future of Capitalism: How Today's Economic Forces Shape Tomorrow's World.* New York: William Morrow & Co., 1996.

Tich Nhat Hanh. *Living Buddha, Living Christ.* New York: Riverhead Books, 1996.

————. *The Miracle of Mindfulness: A Manual on Meditation.* Translated by Mobi Warren. Boston: Beacon, 1976.

Toulmin, Stephen. *Cosmopolis: The Hidden Agenda of Modernity.* New York: Free Press, 1990.

————. *The Return to Cosmology: Postmodern Science and the Theology of Nature.* Berkeley, CA: The University of California Press, 1982.

Trungpa, Chogyam. *Crazy Wisdom.* Edited by Sherab Chödzin. Boston: Shambhala, 1991.

————. *Shambhala: The Sacred Path of the Warrior*. Boulder, CO: Shambhala, 1984.

Wallerstein, Immanuel. *After Liberalism*. New York: W.W. Norton & Co., 1995.

Wallis, Jim. *Faith Works: Lessons from the Life of an Activist Preacher*. New York: Random House, 2000.

Walsch, Neale Donald. *Conversations with God: An Uncommon Dialogue (Book One)*. New York: G.P. Putnam's Sons, 1996.

————. *Conversations with God: An Uncommon Dialogue (Book Two)*. Charlottesville, VA: Hampton Roads, 1997.

————. *Conversations with God: An Uncommon Dialogue (Book Three)*. Charlottesville, VA: Hampton Roads, 1998.

Waskow, Arthur Ocean. *Godwrestling*. New York: Schocken Books, 1978.

————. *Godwrestling—Round 2: Ancient Wisdom, Future Paths*. Woodstock, VT: Jewish Lights Publishing, 1996.

Weil, Andrew. *Spontaneous Healing: How to Discover and Enhance Your Body's Natural Ability to Maintain and Heal Itself*. New York: Knopf, 1995.

Weiss, Joseph. *Psychotherapy Works: Process and Technique*. New York: Guilford Press, 1993.

Welch, Sharon. *Sweet Dreams in America: Making Ethics and Spirituality Work*. New York: Routledge, 1999.

West, Cornel. *Race Matters*. Boston: Beacon Press, 1993.

Whitehead, Alfred North. *Science and the Modern World*. New York: The Macmillan Company, 1925.

Wilber, Ken. *Boomeritis*. Boston: Shambhala, 2000.

————. *A Brief History of Everything*. Boston: Shambhala, 1996.

————. *Integral Psychology: Consciousness, Spirit, Psychology, Therapy*. Boston: Shambhala, 2000.

————. *The Marriage of Sense and Soul: Integrating Science and Religion*. New York: Broadway Books, 1999.

————. *Sex, Ecology, Spirituality: The Spirit of Evolution*. Boston: Shambhala, 1995.

Wink, Walter. *Naming the Powers: The Language of Power in the New Testament*. Philadelphia: Fortress Press, 1984.

Wise, Stephen M. *Rattling the Cage: Toward Legal Rights for Animals*. Cambridge, MA: Perseus Books, 2000.

Wolpe, David. *Making Loss Matter: Creating Meaning in Difficult Times*. New York: Riverhead Books, 1999.

index

a

Abraham, 284
abundance, human beings sharing equally in, 5
"achievement society," 190
adversary system of law, ending, 223-225, 232
aesthetic creativity, encouraging, 170
AIDS health, 215
alcohol abuse, signs of spiritual crisis, 87-89
Aleynu, 183
alienation, 23, 26, 135
All Being, Unity of, 5, 28, 31, 34, 46, 55, 95, 98, 101, 122, 161,164, 173, 274-275
altruism, natural in children, 106
American society, spiritual crisis in, 26
Amini, Fari, 137
anger, 26-27, 292, 295-296
in children, 108
anxiety, inherited, 101-102
archaic individual, stage of spiritual development, 189-190
argument, as spiritual practice, 295-296
Aristotle, 33, 231, 257
atonement, 296-298
reconciliation and, 225-228
Awakening the Buddha Within, 278
Axis Powers, alliance to defeat, 178

b

balance
getting in, 278-279
keeping in, 42-43, 296
losing, 44, 262
The Bank Teller and Other Writings on the Politics of Meaning, 336-337
beauty, inner, 14

Becker, Ernest, 298
becoming involved, 331-339
being. *See also* spiritual beings; Unity of All Being
the fullest beings we can be, 36
goodness of, 103
beliefs, pathogenic, 17-20, 85, 94, 99
Beyond Globalization, 163
Beyt Tikkun synagogue, 131
Bhutan, King of, 162
Bible, Christian, 47
Big Bang, 32-33, 42
The Big Test, 239
Bill of Rights, 221, 225, 245
birth and death, teaching students about, 265-266
Black Muslim movement, 177
blame. *See* self-blame
body
dancing, 275
teaching students about miracle of, 264
treasuring, 287-289
boomer consciousness, 191-193
Boorstein, Sylvia, 276
Breath by Breath, 278
Breyer, Morty, 45
A Brief History of Everything, 336
Brown, Lester R., 140, 307, 337
Brunberg, Isabelle, 162
brutality, 186-189
Bush, Mirabai, 278

c

cancer
analogy for loss of balance, 44
and choice, 60
Cantor, Jennifer, story of, 130-136

About the Author

Michael Lerner is editor of *TIKKUN* magazine, rabbi of Beyt Tikkun Synagogue in San Francisco, and author of *The Politics of Meaning* and *Jewish Renewal: A Path to Healing and Transformation*. He holds Ph.D.s in philosophy and in psychology. Described by some as America's preeminent Jewish intellectual, and by others as one of the most significant spiritual innovators of our time, Lerner was honored by *Utne Reader* as one of America's 100 most visionary thinkers. He is currently working on a spiritual commentary on Torah and creating a network of spiritually oriented professionals from all walks of life to implement the vision articulated in this book.

WALSCH BOOKS is an imprint of Hampton Roads Publishing Company, edited by Neale Donald Walsch and Nancy Fleming-Walsch. Our shared vision is to publish quality books that enhance and further the central messages of the *Conversations with God* series, in both fiction and non-fiction genres, and to provide another avenue through which the healing truths of the great wisdom traditions may be expressed in clear and accessible terms.

Hampton Roads Publishing Company
. . . for the evolving human spirit

Hampton Roads Publishing Company
publishes books on a variety of subjects including
metaphysics, health, complementary medicine,
visionary fiction, and other related topics.

For a copy of our latest catalog,
call toll-free, 800-766-8009,
or send your name and address to:

Hampton Roads Publishing Company, Inc.
1125 Stoney Ridge Road
Charlottesville, VA 22902
e-mail: hrpc@hrpub.com
www.hrpub.com